I'm Back for More Cash

I'm Back for More Cash

A TONY KORNHEISER COLLECTION

(Because You Can't Take
Two Hundred Newspapers
into the Bathroom)

Tony Kornheiser

VILLARD
NEW YORK

Library of Congress Cataloging-in-Publication Data

Kornheiser, Tony.
I'm back for more cash: a Tony Kornheiser collection
(because you can't take two hundred newspapers
into the bathroom) / Tony Kornheiser.
p.   cm.
Contents: It must be me—Love in the time of Viagra—You get
what you vote for—Bill, Monica, and a shooting Starr—Waiting
for a snowstorm and a 38-inch waist—My peeps.
ISBN 0-8129-6853-0
I. Title.
PN4874.K67 A25 2001
814'.54—dc21   2001046921

Villard Books website address: www.villard.com
Printed in the United States of America

24689753

Book design by Jennifer Ann Daddio

For my uncle Arnie Allison,
a saint,

and

my aunt Shirley Allison,
who saw the best in everyone

An Introduction by General George Washington

Although I've been dead for a long time, this Kornheiser guy cracks me up. If you see him, tell him he's really a hoot. Well, that's it. Gotta go.

Acknowledgments

My great thanks to Don Graham and Len Downie for their generosity; David Von Drehle and Gene Robinson for their supervision; Tom Shroder and Richard Leiby for their editing; Kathy Orton for pulling this book together; Tracee Hamilton for her cheerful contributions; and most of all to Jeanne McManus and George Solomon for their enduring friendship and unlimited patience.

Contents

It Must Be Me   1

Love in the Time of Viagra   71

You Get What You Vote For   143

Bill, Monica, and a Shooting Starr   179

Waiting for a Snowstorm and a
Thirty-eight-inch Waist   235

My Peeps   315

It Must Be Me

Disney on Fear

I recently got back from a family vacation at Disney World. Family vacations are great. I got to spend quality time with two teenage children, who love and respect me. (I rented them. My own kids wouldn't be caught dead anywhere near me. At the Animal Kingdom I overheard them plotting to push me out of the halftrack in the hopes I would be trampled by a gnu.)

Obviously, I have decided to write about my vacation at Disney World—at great personal risk, since the radio show I do on ESPN is part of the Disney empire. So in a way I am biting the hand that feeds me.

And in the case of the "character breakfasts" at Disney World—where people dressed up as lovable Disney characters, like Chip and Dale, come up to your table and paw you incessantly while you eat—I considered literally doing that.

In fact, at one breakfast when Goofy began sucking on my head as I was eating my scrambled eggs, I flirted with the idea of whipping out a Zippo and setting him on fire.

How many years on a psychiatrist's couch do you think the average five-year-old would have needed after seeing a Goofy flambé?

(Hey, I'm joking. I wouldn't actually set Goofy on fire. The Little Mermaid, maybe.)

I've got nothing against Disney characters, but what explains their powerful attraction for me? Do I look like such a dork that I'd want to have a photo taken with a grown adult wearing a Styrofoam chipmunk head? Plus, the breakfast is crawling with kids, whose idea of a buffet is to grab anything with sugar and glaze on top—and drown it in syrup. These kids are stickier than Monica Lewinsky's closet. And then they run to Chip and Dale, and rub their gooey hands and faces on them. And I'm supposed to snuggle up to these oozing fur balls? I'd rather be locked in a room with Roberto Benigni.

After breakfast we headed for the theme parks and the rides. At the entrance to each ride there's a sign that tells you how long a wait you have before you ride. You get on a line and walk through a complex, serpentine system of ropes until you either: (1) reach the ride, or (2) your bladder is the size of the *Hindenburg*.

I probably picked a bad week to go to Disney World, it being spring break. I don't want to say the place was crowded, but as we walked out the door of the hotel I saw this sign: FROM THIS POINT YOU ARE 8 HOURS FROM ANY RIDE. IN THIS HEAT AND HUMIDITY, BY THE TIME YOU GET THERE YOU'LL BE SPROUTING MOSS LIKE A CHIA PET.

I should confess that I am not an "action ride" guy.

Tower of Terror, for example, isn't for me. You're sitting in a bucket, it's pitch-black dark, and suddenly you drop thirteen stories in less time than it takes to say Slovakian Milosavitch, er, Slobodan Rostopovich, er, Jackie Chan. I would rather be trampled by gnus.

I don't like anything that moves fast or goes upside down or scares me in any way. And I'm easily scared—seeing Madeleine Albright early Sunday mornings on *Meet the Press* terrifies me.

I like gentle rides. I want to go to an "assisted living" amusement park.

I love the Pirates of the Caribbean ride because it moves slowly and it's underground, so it's cool. There is nothing even vaguely exciting about this ride, which may account for why there was no waiting line. I rode in a boat with three women just slightly older than the Inca mummies.

Somehow, I let my daughter prevail upon me to join her on the Extra-Terrestrial ride, in which you are strapped into a chair in pitch-black darkness, and cautioned that something has gone terribly wrong in a scientific experiment, and a carnivore that has been transported through time and space is about to rip out your pancreas. At this point your seat drops with a thud, everyone around you shrieks—like they've just seen Linda Tripp nude—and something wet and cold (that you hope is water) sprays the back of your neck.

I don't remember much after that because I passed out. But I must have done okay, because my daughter said that now we had to go to the Star Wars ride. So we walked over, and by then I was feeling pretty good about myself, so I didn't pay as much attention to the warning sign in front of the Star Wars ride as I should have.

The sign advised that because the ride had "dramatic visual effects simulating changes in altitudes," and had "sudden movements" and made "rocking motions," that certain persons should not ride. As I recall, these included "pregnant women," "people who suffer motion sickness," "people with heart problems," "people, people who need people," and "Pat Buchanan supporters." Inexplicably, I missed the line that said "fifty-year-old bald, white men who are afraid of airplanes and scared of the dark should not ride. This means you, Tony Kornheiser."

So I followed my daughter on. I strapped in. The room went pitch-black. (What is with this pitch-black darkness on every ride? Who designs these things, an opossum?)

And then, suddenly, a field of stars came up on a cyber screen, the seat felt like it was whooshing forward—and we hurtled into deep space, bucking around like that cow in *Twister.*

I was terrified. I tried to sing a familiar tune to calm myself down. Sadly, all I could think of was "Tell Laura I Love Her." Every pore opened and leaked enough water to float the Sixth Fleet. By the time the ride ended I was sitting in a pool of sweat. I looked like I had come from the log flume ride. People stared at me, wondering how come I was so wet and they weren't. They felt cheated.

My daughter did what teenage girls do when their fathers embarrass them: She pointed at me and laughed.

I stood up, soaked, thinking: *Where the heck are Chip and Dale when you need them?*

Experiments in Terror

Each of us has a certain phrase that makes us cringe the moment we hear it. For many folks, it's "Oh, look, Al Gore is doing the macarena!"

For me, it's "science fair."

I can still see the smug smiles on my classmates' faces as they brought in their fussy science fair projects—which their NASA scientist fathers spent weeks working on in the basement. (God, how I hated the kids who rolled their projects in on *dollies*!) I came in carrying pathetic scraps of colored paper in a cigar box. And my teacher snickered, "What's your project supposed to prove, Tony?"

"Um, that I should consider a career in the lucrative field of pizza delivery?"

I know nothing about science. I don't *associate* with people who know anything about science. My friend Andy, for example, once did a science fair project on erosion. Talk about sophisticated: Andy fastened sod on one side of a poster board and plopped dirt on the other side. He ran a hose on the thing. The dirt turned to mud and spilled on the floor.

When his teacher asked the point of his project, Andy chirped, "We need grass to prevent erosion." I'm surprised MIT didn't send a limo for him. Rest easy, America, our agricultural system is safe. Andy is now a sports-radio announcer.

Regrettably, my son Michael's eighth-grade class wasn't permitted to make mud at their science fair last weekend. They were assigned a Rube Goldberg project: Build an elaborate contraption with pulleys, levers, fulcrums, slides, and weights that eventually causes toothpaste to be squished from a tube and fall onto a toothbrush. (And you wonder how America keeps its edge in the new technology.)

Do you want to know why life is unfair? Because schools always have a science fair and not a newspaper column fair or a comedy fair. If every kid had to do a five-minute stand-up, I'd be a gold mine. My kid would crush! "Hey, teach, is that your real nose, or did a boa constrictor get loose from the National Zoo?"

Anyway, Michael and his partner, Maria, spent the previous two weeks building their project in our den. No parental help. (Usually losers yelp, "His father built it!" I went to high school with the nephew of J. Robert Oppenheimer, the scientific genius behind the building of the A-bomb. The teachers lived in terror of him coming in with a thing in a briefcase and announcing, "My uncle built it.")

When Michael and Maria were done, their project was the size of a Toyota 4Runner and had more moving parts than Jennifer Lopez. Your teeth could *rot* by the time the toothpaste got squeezed.

They tested it five times. It worked once, possibly by accident. I got nervous. What if it didn't work in front of the judges?

"Don't worry, Dad," Michael said. "Maria can cry on demand."

Maria smiled.

I like that kid. Cute as a button and plays to win.

I wandered around the science fair looking at projects. About half actually worked. There was one stunner. At the last second, the toothbrush *slid* under the toothpaste just as it began to flow! The execution was so professional that I was tempted to scream, "His dentist did it!"

I was crestfallen when I turned back to Michael and Maria. (*Crest*-fallen, get it?)

By luck, the science teacher and the judges converged on Michael and Maria simultaneously—meaning their project had to work only this one time.

Theoretically, a toy VW Beetle went down a ramp into a basket that caused a button to be pushed, that set a golf ball in motion, that resulted in toothpaste liftoff. Michael and Maria had practiced enough times that a long strand of stale toothpaste was already dangling out of the tube.

Mr. Peterson, their science teacher, asked Maria, "Do you want to wipe that off?"

"Why? That's how it always looks in our house."

Okay. Show time!

Michael sent the Beetle down the ramp.

It went left and wedged into the side of the ramp.

He tried again.

Same result. Wedged.

Two more times. Wedged. Wedged.

Freakin' *fahrvergnugen*!

The kids were mortified. We parents were, um, laughing. But in a good way. Really.

"Michael, use the Porsche," Maria said.

(The secret to life, I thought.)

Their backup car was a Porsche. Alas, since it was smaller and lighter than the Beetle, it overshot the basket. Oops.

With the teacher and judges watching, Maria took matters into her own hands. She hit the button herself.

And things proceeded as smoothly as the Bradley campaign. The button failed. The golf ball didn't move. The toothpaste stayed in the tube.

The judges smiled politely and said they'd be back later.

Yeah, sure. When, Y3K?

Trying to lighten the mood, I said to Maria's parents, "This is good because now we can scratch off all the colleges with engineering programs. Don't worry about us. Michael intends to be a superstar professional golfer. He'll be so rich, he'll hire people to squeeze his toothpaste for him."

I consoled the kids, saying, "You did great. And remember,

utter failure is actually a blessing. It gives you a better story to tell when you get older—or if they ever have a humor fair." Then I got out of Dodge.

Michael came home a few hours later and excitedly told me that Mr. Peterson had given them one more chance. And this time, the project worked! The car worked. The button worked. The toothpaste was squeezed—and a big glob hung on the end of the tube like a stalactite and wouldn't budge.

Mr. Peterson looked at his watch. Two full minutes went by.

Classmates gathered and began chanting, "Drop! Drop!"

"I'll give it another minute," Mr. Peterson said.

"Drop! Drop!"

Finally, it dropped. *Splat!* A perfect landing on the toothbrush. We're now considering dental schools.

Playing with Opossum

The following is a true story. (It may not be funny, but if you want I could send it over to Stephen Glass and Patricia Smith, and they could punch it up.)

The other night my kids ran into the house, screeching, "Daddy, Daddy, come quick! Maggie has killed something."

Why couldn't it have been the other way around, I sighed.

My dog, Maggie, eats my money and clothing. She can't grasp the simplest obedience training, she gets sideswiped by a bus, she gets munched by a pit bull—this dog belongs on *The Jerry Springer Show*. "Brittany Spaniels: Loving Pets or Satan's Spawn?"

Anyway, I wasn't overly concerned, as Maggie routinely stalks and kills birds in the yard, then rolls around in their guts to soak herself in the scent of the kill—and ends up smelling like she's done the backstroke in a septic tank.

When I walked outside I found Maggie hovering over something large and furry that at one time might have made a nice collar for Greta Garbo's coat.

"It appears that Maggie has killed an aardvark," I informed the children.

My daughter, Elizabeth, rolled her eyes. "Dad, you're such a loser," she said. "Aardvarks don't live anywhere near here. That's an opossum."

"Yes, it's an opossum," I said, sounding like Clark W. Griswold. "The tail threw me off. It looked like an aardvark's tail." (Like I could pick an aardvark out of a lineup with the Spice Girls.)

Thinking we were playing "snatch the bacon," Maggie grabbed the opossum by the neck, took a victory lap around the yard, and then deposited it back at our feet. She was so happy.

I knew I had to get rid of the critter before Maggie rolled in it. I told my son Michael to get the shovel. I scooped the animal onto the shovel and then did what any sensitive father would do to provide learning experiences for his children—I stuck the carcass in my daughter's face!

Hey, I'm a boy, I had a dead animal on a stick, and there was a girl around. I was simply obeying my genes.

Obeying hers, Elizabeth shrieked and ran into the house.

I slid a plastic grocery bag over the blade of the shovel and neatly deposited the opossum inside. Then I tied the bag shut.

Burying the opossum on my property was out of the question. Maggie would get it. I'd have to bury it deeper than Susan Molinari's TV career.

(Speaking of opossums: Why does a chicken cross the road? To show a opossum it can be done. Hahaha.)

I decided to dump it in a garbage can in the alley. But not ours, of course. Our garbage gets picked up only once a week, and with two kids and just one Supercan I wasn't about to waste valuable garbage space on a dead opossum. We're overflowing every week. I routinely send Michael into the alley to scout out a half-empty can to handle our overage.

One family near us has two cans, and Michael regularly used them. Once, though, they caught him and scolded him. So I decided to leave Mr. Opossum with them. I felt pretty good about it. And then I went to sleep.

At 3 A.M. I bolted upright—one and only one thought blazing through my head:

Playing possum!

But of course!

Like some malevolent monster in an Edgar Allan Poe short story, I had tied a helpless fur ball in a bag and sealed him alive in a garbage can for all eternity. I was a callous murderer. The PETA people would put my picture on every pet store in town.

I had to undo my horrible deed. But not at 3 A.M., when God only knows what was happening in that can. By dawn I was out there sneaking through the alley, opening my neighbor's garbage can. I peered in and saw the opossum curled up in the same fetal position he had assumed on my lawn. Except for one small detail—he was out of the plastic bag!

Aha! He *had* been playing possum.

Now I felt worse, because I figured he had crawled out of the bag and then had been asphyxiated in the can. I imagined him gasping to death. I wondered if there was some gesture I could make to honor opossums everywhere. Perhaps I could hang upside down in a tree thirty minutes a day for a month?

Then it occurred to me that perhaps the little kidder was playing possum again. I mean, what do I know about opossums? I thought it was an aardvark, for heaven's sake. And my second choice was "armadillo." Figuring that even if the critter was alive, it couldn't climb out of a four-foot-tall Supercan, I laid the can on its side to give him a chance to escape.

I studied the opossum for ten minutes. Its eyes never blinked. Its tail never moved. It didn't seem to draw breath.

I wrote it off as dead and walked away to prepare to draft a letter of confession and send copies to Ricki Lake and Naomi Campbell . . . and maybe head over to Denny's for one of those Grand Slam breakfasts.

Ten minutes later I anxiously wandered back to the alley and peered into the garbage can. To my delight the opossum was gone. Then I was overcome by a sense of dread. What if some dog had carried it off? What if, instead of playing possum, it was now breakfast?

Maggie?

The Bar Mitzvah Boy Blues

Yesterday was my son, Michael's, bar mitzvah. According to Jewish tradition, this ceremony marks the day a thirteen-year-old boy becomes a man. This tradition obviously began in the old days—before "middle school." As soon as a kid turned thirteen, he was out in the fields picking dates and herding sheep (or *dating* sheep in the remote regions). By fifteen, he was married. By eighteen, he was having a midlife crisis and shopping for a faster donkey.

If only it still worked that way. Then I wouldn't have to keep socking away money for college, and I could spend it on something worthwhile—like hair plugs and a set of Callaway Steelhead Woods.

Still, bar mitzvahs are great entertainment, although they do create a certain unease for gentiles who are unfamiliar with the event. My friend Nancy, a *shiksa* if there ever was one, asked, "Do I have to eat gefilte fish, or could I say a few Hail Marys instead?"

Sometimes you can have fun with the fact that the rituals of bar mitzvahs are mysterious to gentiles. For example, I told Michael Wilbon that at some point during the luncheon he would be circumcised. (I understand the anxiety. If I was invited to Easter dinner at a Catholic's home, I'd want to know, "Is someone going to ask me if I killed their Lord?")

I remember going to bar mitzvahs when I was my son's age. It's a great thing being a thirteen-year-old boy at a bar mitzvah. First of all, the thirteen-year-old girls are there, and they're fantastic! You've never seen them like this before. They're dressed up, their hair is done, they've got perfume on—and for the first time in your life you actually *want* to dance with them.

Something wonderful happens when you hold them in your arms. I recall coming home breathless, with some girl's perfume on my cheek, and my knees literally knocking. Which, in retrospect, qualified me to be president.

(Speaking of girls like you've never seen them before, last Wednesday, seventy-two hours before the bar mitzvah, my daughter showed me what she intended to wear. She claimed it was a skirt. I called it a napkin. "You are not wearing that to a house of worship," I told her. "The House of Blues, maybe, but not a house of worship." I'd seen more material on an oven mitt. I went right out and bought her a dress the Amish would be proud of. After she wore it, she used it as a pool cover.)

The bar mitzvah boy may not actually be a man that day, but at these parties you see what it's like to be a man. You see adult men smoking and drinking and eating and dancing dirty, and you think to yourself: *What a putz. I've been worrying about spelling homework. Where can I get me some of* this?

As father of the bar mitzvah boy, I have a limited role. During the service, I get to say a small prayer. I was encouraged to keep it brief, as parents tend to gush on and on, extolling their children as brilliant students, tireless workers for world peace, and humble, caring angels who would never, ever set off a stink bomb in the Willow Wood Manor Assisted Living Wellness Center, despite what you may have read.

The speeches often last so long that, by the end, the bar mitzvah boy has outgrown his suit. I went to a bar mitzvah in Boca Raton where the mother got up to speak, and after dabbing at her eyes with both hands so everyone could see her jewelry, her first words were, "Can we dim the lights now so I can start the slide show?"

I remember when my daughter, Elizabeth, was bat mitzvahed three years ago, and I was called to meet with the rabbi. I told him what I'd thought about saying during the service, including some A-list jokes, like the one about a rabbi, a priest, and a minister who go golfing together.

It seems they're stuck behind an unbelievably slow group. The front nine holes take them four full hours to play, and they seek out the course's golf pro to complain.

"Oh, but the people in front of you are blind," the pro explains.

"Blind!" the minister says. "It's a miracle. I'm so moved I'm going to compose a sermon on how inspirational these men are."

"Blind!" the priest says. "I'm so impressed I'm going to tell this to the Vatican and urge them to make a charitable contribution in these men's names."

"Blind, huh?" the rabbi says. "So why can't they play at night?"

The rabbi said that a temple was an inappropriate setting to do shtick, and that whatever I said had to be very brief and somber. I ended up offering this small, somber prayer: "Thank you, God, for enabling me to find a good parking space."

And I sat down while the rabbi went into his sermon. Which consisted of, one after another, every line I'd given him. The duck joke. The O'Malley twins. The whole Sol and Sadie catalog, including the best one: Sol and Sadie have just gotten married. Sol is eighty-six, and Sadie is eighty-three. Sadie says, "Sol, it's our wedding night. Come up the stairs and make love to me." And Sol says, "I can only do one or the other."

And he *crushed*! He closed by saying, "I'll be here all week. Don't forget to tip your waitress, and drive home safely."

My agent had come down from New York for the bat mitzvah. She loved him. He's on Comedy Central now with his own show, *The Jolly Jew*.

So I vowed not to make that mistake again. This time I was ready. I tailored the jokes to the crowd: Sol is driving down the highway to Miami Beach when he gets a worried call from Sadie on the car phone. "Sol, I just heard on the news there's a car going the wrong way on I-95. Please be careful." And Sol says, "It's not just one car, Sadie, it's hundreds of them!"

"But aren't you concerned that you humiliated your son?" I was asked.

My very *existence* humiliates my children. So what the heck.

"A rabbi, a priest, and Boutrous Boutros-Ghali are in a canoe . . ."

Now Playing:
Waiting for Gazdluzky

Here is my life, in two acts.

ACT I. THE TELEPHONE MESSAGES

"Hi, I'm home. Did anybody call?" I ask my daughter, who is lying on the couch, watching MTV with her face so close to the set that if Britney Spears's new augmented breasts explode, she will be toweling off silicone.

"Yeah. One call. I took a message," she says.

I see scribble on a piece of paper.

It looks like "Bleev Gazdluzky."

"Sweetheart," I say, "this looks like 'Bleev Gazdluzky.' "

"Yeah."

"Bleev?"

"Yeah."

"What kind of a name is Bleev?" I ask.

There is no answer from my daughter. She is entranced by some rap group on TV. I think they are exhorting her to commit first-degree felonies.

"Elizabeth? Elizabeth?"

"What do you want?" she says in exasperation. "You've been in the house for two minutes, and you've already asked me a million questions."

"Who is Bleev Gazdluzky?"

She throws her hands in the air. "How should I know? They called for *you,*" she says.

"They?"

I ponder this for a second, and seek to ask a follow-up question, but my daughter has stormed out of the room and into the den, where she immediately throws herself on another couch and turns on MTV. She is done with this conversation. I have driven her from the room. It must have been something I said—perhaps "Hi, I'm home."

The fact is I am lucky to get the message that "Bleev Gazdluzky" called, whoever they are. Most of the time neither of my teenage children writes down any message at all. Not that they don't care about phone messages. They care avidly about phone messages. The first thing they do coming in the door is replay the message tape, deleting all the nuisance messages—the ones that aren't for them.

What do your kids care if someone from the IRS called. The IRS—is that, like, the surviving members of INXS?

My aunt called three times in one day last week with news about my father, who had broken his hip, then called me at work to find out why I hadn't responded.

"Don't you care that your father is in the hospital?" she scolded me.

What???

"Did Aunt Shirley call yesterday?" I asked the kids.

My son, Michael, shrugged. "Yesterday" is a tough concept for him. He has the attention span of goat cheese; sometimes at breakfast he'll ask, "What meal is this?" Anything that happened more than ten minutes ago is prehistoric, like the Fonz.

"Yeah. She did," my daughter said. "She called a few times, actually."

"Why didn't you *tell* me?" I demanded.

Her response was classic sixteen: "Why are you always picking on me?"

Sometimes, they'll manage to relay an actual name, "Mark," then half a phone number: "96685."

"Mark who? Was Mark a first name or a last name?" I'll ask.

"I don't know."

"And what is this number? A phone number has more digits

than this. This is a *Zip code*. There's no way I can call this Mark back."

"That's too bad," the kids say. "He said it was urgent."

ACT II. THE DOG

Have you noticed that it gets light now at 5:03 A.M.? Of course you haven't. You're sound asleep at 5:03, like you should be. That's because you don't have a satanic dog who wakes you at the first sign of light by sitting at the edge of your bed, her wet nose a mere three inches from yours, whimpering and whining in a pitch only you can hear. Not your spouse. Not your kids. Not anyone in the world but you. She's like a cell phone vibrating in your pocket—only you can't throw her against the wall. (And that new legislation makes it a little late to sell her to the Burlington Coat Factory.)

That's amazing, isn't it, how a dog can home in on one person's frequency, and the rest of the people in your house wouldn't hear the Mir space station if it crashed through the upstairs bathroom?

In her Tony-whistle whine she is saying to me: "Take me out now, stupid. Take me out so early, they're still serving drinks downtown. Take me out now so that when we come home I can fall asleep on the cool tile floor, because I'm a dog and I can sleep anywhere, whenever I want—and you're totally screwed for the rest of the day. You're up at 5:03 A.M. You're meat. I *own* you."

It's not enough for me to simply open the door and let the dog go outside by herself, like every other dog in America. Oh, no, not Ms. Maggie the Queen Mum. She won't go! She stands by the door whimpering for me to leash her up and take her on a walk—so she can do ABSOLUTELY NOTHING! Nothing comes out of her body but dog laughter.

Why?

Because it's too early!

It's barely dawn. Why would she have to tinkle now? It's not like she's a sixty-year-old with a prostate problem. She's a dog!

She walks briskly for a few blocks, barely deigning to sniff the ground, then she sashays home. Now it is 5:12 A.M., and the little rodent bounds up the stairs, jumps on *my* bed, lays her head on *my* pillow, and falls blissfully asleep, laughing to herself about the tale she can tell the other dogs when they play poker, like in the velvet paintings.

"You know Tony? That fat bald dope I live with? I gave him such shpilkes when I yanked his chain this morning . . ."[sounds of slobbering dog guffaws]

And hopelessly wide awake, I stare at the ceiling, obsessed with a single thought. *Who the heck is Bleev?*

Unhappy Campers

My birthday was the other day, and my sweet baboo Elizabeth, who is at summer camp, sent me a card. Here is what my loving, sentimental daughter wrote:

"Happy B-day! Kate said her parents are sending 200 extra dollars for her to use at the mall. Getting any ideas? No, but really $100 isn't enough for our trip to the mall. I would really appreciate it if you would send up more money. I'm sorry to bother you about this in your B-day card, but I had to talk to you before it was too late. P.S. Please show this letter to Mom."

Parents of fifteen-year-old girls will recognize the basic structure:

There is an introductory thought about you. Now, here is the urgency of my need. And make sure you show it to Mom, who is even more of a sucker than you are.

Of course, I did what any parent would do upon receipt of such a letter. I laughed.

"There's no way Kate's parents are sending her two hundred dollars to go to some mall in West Virginia," I said. "You can buy the entire state for a hundred thirty-five. Half the homes there are on wheels!"

So I called Kate's parents.

"Elizabeth says you're sending Kate two hundred dollars for a trip to the mall?" I asked.

"No, we sent twenty dollars," they said.

Hmmm.

"Maybe she just forgot to write in the decimal point," my son offered.

"Excuse me, Mr. Dershowitz, but was I talking to you?"

Again, parents of fifteen-year-olds will recognize the pattern.

Write "200." If you're confronted with "20," say something like: "Oops, my pen slipped." (Politicians under investigation by independent counsels might recognize this defense as plausible deniability.)

Time and again my daughter and I butt heads about "freedom issues," including money, curfew, and what types of movies she is allowed to see. I think I can fairly state both our positions. Her position is, "Come on, I'm fifteen." My position is, "Come on, you're fifteen."

Recognize this conversation?

"Hi, Dad. My friends were going to the movies tonight, and I'd like to go, too."

"What will you be seeing?"

"Um, I don't know, something educational."

"Oh? Recommended by Dr. Stephen Hawking, I'm sure. Can you tell me the name of it?"

"*I'm Going to Slash Your Throat and Mutilate Your Mama*. But it's not nearly as bad as it sounds," she'll say perkily. "One of the girls from *Friends* is in it."

"Great. And what might it be rated?"

"Um, PG?"

"Come on, honey, it's a slasher movie. It's a hard R. They won't even sell you a ticket."

"Carla's mother is buying the tickets."

"Carla's mother thinks it's okay for kids to see this crap? What's Carla's number? I'm going to call her mother right now."

Suddenly there is a gasp from my daughter. Followed by tears.

"You do this all the time, Dad. You are the strictest parent in the whole world. If it was up to you, all I would see is *The Sound of Music* with those stupid kids, in their stupid Swiss cheese outfits, singing, 'Do, a deer, a female deer.' Agggghh. I hate you. And don't you dare call Carla's mother and embarrass me. You treat me like I'm still fourteen!"

So of course, I let her go to the movie, which starts at 7:15—provided she calls me as soon as it's over, which I tell her will be 9 P.M.

See if you recognize this one:

"Hi, Dad, it's Liz."

"Where have you been? I told you to call at nine," I'll say.

"No, you told me to call at ten."

"Well, it's eleven-fifteen."

"It is?"

"Sweetheart," I'll say. "You have a watch on, don't you?"

"Yes."

"WELL, WHAT TIME IS IT ON YOUR WATCH?"

"Um, my watch is broken." (A variation of "Oops, my pen slipped.")

"Okay, where are you? Are you still at the movie theater?" I'll ask.

"We didn't actually go to the movie. We, um, went to Georgetown instead."

"You did WHAT???"

"Yes, but I thought you would be happy because I didn't go to an R-rated movie."

I give my daughter ten dollars a week allowance. She tells me *all* her friends get twenty-five dollars—*everybody* in the school. I'm always the only one who's so strict. In all of history there's John Calvin and me. I passed Hitler.

I offered her five dollars more for emptying the dishwasher twice a week. Easy money, right? She did it for two weeks, then started complaining about the number of plates and utensils that her brother used.

"Everything in here is his," she said. "I'm tired of putting away his stuff. He's doing it deliberately. It's not fair to me. I think he should eat with his hands."

The new battleground is her ears.

See if this is familiar. She wants a second earring hole. And another in her upper ear cartilage.

All her friends have them. ("And don't you dare call their parents.")

She has changed her tactic on getting new holes lately. Now, before asking, she gives me a hug, and tells me how much she loves me. She actually purrs. I can only assume she saw this behavior in a Cameron Diaz movie. Sadly, I'm not Ben Stiller. I'm old enough to be Jerry Stiller.

"You're too young," I say. "Wait until you get to college."

The truth is, I don't care about a second earring. I'm trying to draw the line at her ears so I don't have to hear about tongue studs and bellybutton rings. I live in fear of going into my daughter's room to kiss her good-night and discovering she has driven a ten-penny nail through her upper lip, or has stapled her fingers together in the name of fashion.

So my standard answer to everything she asks for is "Wait until you get to college."

I went to college. I know how it works. Like my parents before me, I figure what I don't see can't hurt me.

On her first trip home she'll probably have a huge tattoo across her stomach that says, YOU HAPPY? I WAITED UNTIL I GOT TO COLLEGE.

Dad, Can I Have
the Keys to the Edsel?

Last week I faced the moment the father of a teenage girl dreads most.

Oh, God no, not THAT moment.

No, my daughter got her *driver's license*!

She had little help from me. I only took her out once, to the local high school parking lot, where I had her drive backward around the lot repeatedly—as my father had done with me almost thirty-five years ago. I never questioned my father's purpose in doing this. I accepted it as the fundamental building block of driver education: One needed to learn how to drive backward in order to truly understand how to drive forward. So around and around my daughter and I went, until I begged her to pull over so I could get out and throw up.

"Dad, you're so pathetic," she told me. "This is nuts. I'm never going to have to drive backward. When I get out of college, do you think I'm going to find a rewarding career in valet parking?"

That night I called my father in Florida and asked him why he made me drive around backward. He said, "Oh, that. I wanted to make you nauseated so you'd stop pestering me about teaching you how to drive."

So I left my daughter to the rigors of the District of Columbia driving test, which she described as follows: "Go around the block once and don't kill the mayor."

I asked her how she did, and she said, "I had enough points to pass."

So I think she may have *hit* the mayor, but not killed him.

Now she wants a car.

The other morning we went out for breakfast to talk about

cars. I wanted to explain to her, for example, that I didn't get my first car until I was a sophomore in college, and that she's a junior in high school, and that she ought to go out and work and save money for a car like I did, and that things were a lot tougher when I was her age, and we only had one car for the entire family . . .

She yawned. "Wake me when you get to the part about walking to school in the snow. I love that part."

We began to talk about what she felt was important in a motor vehicle, and her conversation revealed a surprisingly high level of sophistication.

"I don't want a white car," she said. "And the main reason is, it says: 'Hi, I'm a white car, and I'm ugly and stuff.'"

"And I don't want a big Buick. It reminds me of Grandma."

(What she doesn't know is that Grandma used to drive muscle cars, until that unfortunate incident in the GTO when she stood that bad boy up at 120, and the wind resistance pushed her upper bridge straight down her throat.)

I asked her if there was anything she particularly wanted in a car.

"Automatic lights, because I don't really know how to turn the lights on myself yet."

(And doesn't *that* fill all you commuters with confidence?)

I felt euphoric, because my daughter and I had spoken for about seven minutes—the longest conversation we'd had in five years that did not include the sentence "Dad, you're so pathetic."

But I still had a problem: I think she's too young to have her own car. But now that she's got her license, she's going to want to borrow my car. And I don't want her to borrow my car, because:

a. It's *my* car.

b. I remember what we did every time we borrowed our parents' cars. First, we drove into ditches to see if the wheels would come off. Then we drove at high speeds and slammed on the brakes to see if the guys in the backseat would catapult through the windshield. And if we were lucky enough to borrow our parents' cars during an ice storm, we deliberately fishtailed into a wild 360, hoping to smash into something. And we did all this even when we *weren't* on acid.

This, of course, is boy behavior. I needed to know about girl behavior. So I consulted my friend Nancy, who told me: "We always said, 'Can I have the car to go to the library and do homework?' 'Homework' is the magic word. Then we'd pile as many girls into the car as possible and just drive wantonly around the city, trying to attract as many boys as possible. Which, as it turned out, wasn't all that difficult."

Inevitably, I'm going to get my daughter a car. But what kind of car? Something small and fast, with a spoiler and a bumper sticker that says I BRAKE FOR UNPROTECTED SEX? Oh, hahaha, I don't think so.

I intend to say to the car dealer: "Give me something that won't operate over forty miles per hour, won't enter the Beltway, and at eleven P.M. will automatically start heading for home."

A first car ought to be a hideous, indestructible bomb. Your friends should be the only people on Earth who would consider sitting in it. It should have springs sticking out of the backseat. It should smell like someone is decomposing in the trunk. My friend Tom's first car was so horrible to look at that the first thing he did with it was to paint an American flag on the roof, with *house paint*! Which actually made it look much better.

"How old is Lizzie now?" Nancy asked.

"She's sixteen," I said.

"I crashed a boy's car the night of my sixteenth birthday," Nancy mused.

Hmmmm.

"He let me get behind the wheel," Nancy said. "I believe there may have been some beer involved. I remember I was driving just fine going straight. But then the road curved, and I drove the car into a tree. I couldn't consider myself an expert on such things, but from the steam hissing from the radiator and the smoke and the crumpled hood, I sensed there was something wrong with the car."

I know exactly the kind of car I want for my daughter. Something large and slow, with only one seat and no radio, like a fork-lift, or one of those things that tow the space shuttle to the launching pad. Something so solid and formidable that my sweet baboo will not be injured when she plows into her first tree, or house, or police car—which will probably happen the first time she grabs for something she thinks will turn on the lights.

A Knock at the Dork

This is not about my daughter. I don't have a daughter. And her name is not Elizabeth Lauren Kornheiser, and she is not fourteen. But if I *did* have a daughter, and if she were in ninth grade, and if she did play junior varsity soccer, then she would not want me anywhere near her games. She would not want me to walk the street within fifteen feet of her, because someone might think us related. She would most emphatically not want me to mention her in a column, because then people would *know* I am her father. That would be humiliating for her, because I am a dork.

I was not a dork when she was eight.

When she was eleven, I became an apprentice dork. At twelve, I made the varsity, with full dork privileges. Now that she's fourteen I am the sheriff of Dorkingham. I am the Dork in Chief. I am Pope Dork II.

We'll be in the car, and I'll ask something innocent, like, "Do you have any tests today?"

There'll be no response, so I'll say again, "Do you have any tests today?"

She'll say with some disgust, "That's the second time you've asked that question."

"I want to know if you have any tests today!"

And she'll say, "You're boring me. Can we just drop this conversation?"

Conversation? This was conversation?

My sins are too numerous to list. They include that I "wear my hat wrong." Just the other day my daughter insisted she couldn't do her homework because, and I quote, I "eat too loudly."

I was eating a cheese sandwich. How much noise could I have been making?

"Wait until she's twenty-five," I have been told. "Then she will come around."

Great. By then she can come around to the nursing home.

This has been a breakthrough year for me and my daughter, however, in that I am finally actually allowed to attend her soccer games. But there are certain rules I have to follow:

I have to sit quietly with the other parents, who have been similarly warned.

I cannot stand up. I cannot wave. I cannot shout. I cannot do anything to indicate whose parent I am or that I have any interest in any particular player's performance. I cannot criticize the ref.

"Can I clap?" I asked.

"Um, okay, but not loudly," my daughter said. "Don't embarrass me."

"I'll clap inwardly," I promised. "My spleen will rejoice at your good fortune."

When I got to the first game, I saw a crowd of about fifty people, and I immediately knew precisely where I was supposed to sit: Tucked in a corner of the stands with a group of ten or so chastened-looking adults who all appeared to be on Thorazine—obviously, the parents. I did pretty well for the first half, and then disaster struck. My daughter made a nice kick, and I leaped up and shouted proudly, "Elizabeth!"

Oops.

So I'm standing there, having broken the cardinal rule. The word is barely out of my mouth when I realize that all the other parents are staring at me.

The "Elizabeth!" is still echoing in the air, and I stammer, ". . . um, Elizabeth, yes, the Queen of England. Elizabeth II. A jolly good queen. So sorry about Diana," my voice getting softer all the time, as I slink back in my seat.

Anyway, people tell me not to worry, because all fourteen-year-old girls are like this—they all think their parents have cooties. My friend Gino warns me that it will get worse before it gets better. When his daughter was fourteen she thought he was a dork, too, but at least he saw her every once in a while for as many as ten minutes at a time, in the car, while ferrying her to and from social engagements. A few months ago his daughter turned sixteen and got her driver's license. Now Gino sees her only at 6:08 every morning when she bursts into his bedroom, turns on the light, and bellows to no one in particular something like: "Where the heck are my clean bras?"

As a parent of a girl and a boy, I can tell you there is a big difference between the two. Let's use the example of each child saying, "Dad, take me to the mall."

What a boy means is, "Dad, take me to the mall."

What a girl means is, "Dad, drop me off outside. Don't let any of my friends see you. If you go inside the mall and you see me, pretend you don't. And don't ask me the names of any of the boys. And please put on some clothes that match. And if you go into a record store, don't move your head along with the music. It's terribly dorky. Oh, and can I have twenty dollars for earrings?"

And speaking of earrings, did you see that President Clinton is being fitted for hearing aids? I guess he sat too close to the loudspeakers all those nights he didn't inhale. Supposedly, Clinton is deaf to sounds of certain pitches, and news reports stated that this means there are particular words he cannot make out. They did not specify what those words were, but I have secretly obtained the official list. Here they are:

"No"

"Mister"

"President"

"I"

"Don't"

"Want"

"You"
"To"
"Remove"
"Your"
"Pants."

The Comb-over That Came in from the Cold

My sweet baboo Elizabeth, a high school senior now, has finally given me permission to attend her softball games. This was a long time coming. The last time she said it was okay for me to be anywhere near her was 1992—but that's because I was driving her to the mall. She insisted on sitting in the backseat, and made me promise not to speak to her or play the radio. "Omigod, what if we drove past one of my friends, and you were bobbing your head to the music the way you do? I'd have to, like, transfer schools!"

I remember when she first expressed horror that I was alive. She was eleven, and I had committed the unpardonable sin of "chewing too loud." She looked at me with revulsion and pushed away from the table. "You're disgusting," she said. "You make me ashamed to be in this family."

"Wait!" I called out. "Give me another chance. I'll gum my meat."

I called a friend who had grown daughters. She assured me this was "just a stage they pass through."

"When will it end?" I asked.

"Probably by the time she's twenty-five, thirty at the latest."

For the last eight years I haven't been allowed at any of her games—soccer when she was in middle school, softball in high school. She'd say something like: "NO! YOU ALWAYS EMBARRASS ME. YOU SIT AND TALK TO THE OTHER PARENTS, AND ASK THEM STUPID RANDOM QUESTIONS, LIKE ABOUT CELL PHONE USE. YOU'RE ALWAYS SPYING ON ME. YOU THINK YOU CAN DO IT BECAUSE YOU WRITE A COLUMN IN THE NEWSPAPER. IT'S VERY STRESSFUL

TO ME. YOU CANNOT COME SEE ME PLAY. NO! NO! PLUS, YOUR COMB-OVER IS AWFUL."

It started at a soccer game when she was ten. I used to cheer for her unobtrusively. Like: "Great play, Elizabeth." Or: "Good kick, Elizabeth." Or: "Hey, ref, I don't know which game *you're* watching, but my daughter just got knocked down by a girl so large she ought to have running lights. Seriously, I want chromosome testing on that girl. I don't want to say she's over age, but she *drove* here!" Somehow, comments like this embarrassed my daughter.

Then once, I happened to make a mild remark to the referee: "How about calling them *both* ways?" The ref immediately stopped the game and attempted to eject me because in the country of his youth, fans weren't permitted to say anything to soccer referees. I said, "Oh, please. I've seen videotapes of soccer matches in your country. I've seen fans chase the refs out of the stadium and try to kill them. You're lucky to be here, pal, where you've got twenty-four-hour Safeways. If you were back there, you'd be on a stick."

From then on I was parenta non grata at her games.

"If I see you anywhere near my games," she'd tell me, "I'll poke out my own eyeballs with a melon scooper."

Once when Elizabeth was a sophomore I tried to sneak to see her play softball. Her school, Maret, was playing at Sidwell Friends, and there was a toolshed down the right field line, about 150 feet from Maret's bench. I hid behind the toolshed. Every so often I peeked out to get a glimpse of Elizabeth batting. I was confident she never saw me. But when the game ended she strode over to me, tears in her eyes, and said, "I can't believe you did this. Everyone on my team asked me, 'Who is that psycho behind the shed?' I had to explain that psycho was my father. And *look* at you. You don't even match! You're wearing green pants with a brown sports jacket. You look like someone they let out of a home!"

I tried once more when she was a junior. She was playing at a field in Virginia that sat way down in a valley. I stood on the bank of the hill way out past left field, so far away I literally couldn't pick out my daughter. For all I knew I could have been cheering for

Camilla Parker-Bowles. (Not that I would cheer out loud. It would get back to my child that I was there. If anyone approached me I was prepared to say, "Please to help me seek asylum in your country of bountiful fruits and vegetables. God bless Dave Thomas for Biggie fries.") I stood so far away I'm not sure I was in the same area code as the game. And the moment it was over she was running up the hill and shouting, "How could you embarrass me like this? All I could do the whole game was watch you standing up here twitching, making a fool out of yourself."

And I said, "Really? What did you use to see me, the Hubble telescope?"

So you can imagine how thrilled I am now to be able to watch my daughter play softball without having to lie or wear a disguise or worry that my physical presence will cause her to throw herself on a hay thresher.

I have no such problem with my son. He likes me to watch him play sports. Though I didn't know that until earlier this week when I watched him in a golf match. I picked him up on the back nine, and because of my experiences with Elizabeth, I hid behind a bush on the tenth tee so he wouldn't see me.

Of course, crouching behind the bush I couldn't see him tee off. I listened through four drives, then waited for Michael to walk down the fairway to his ball, so I could emerge and look for where he'd hit his drive.

I listened for the telltale sound of golfers moving away from the tee. But the sound I heard was: "It's okay to come out, Dad. I hit it down the middle."

"How did you know I was here?" I asked.

"When we were coming up the ninth fairway one of the guys asked, 'Who's that psycho with a horrible comb-over hiding behind the bush up on the tenth tee?' And I knew it had to be you."

A Chip Shot
Off the Old Block

I am resting now, having recently returned from the two-week Elizabeth Lauren Kornheiser College Tour.

Do you have any idea what it's like to travel in the same car (and stay in the same hotel) with two teenage children for two weeks?

It makes quintuple-bypass surgery seem like a pedicure.

It's not that by the end of two weeks everybody in the family hates each other—because by the end of two *days,* everybody hates each other. By the end of two *weeks,* the violent energy in the car is such that you could go from 0 to 90 without touching the gas pedal. After the first week, I would get up each morning and pray that the car would turn into the set of *Survivor* and I would be the lucky one kicked off the island, even if that meant being devoured by sharks. Or worse, having to tell my story to Sally Jessy Raphaël.

Not that there aren't funny moments. We were cruising through Pennsylvania to Upstate New York when Michael, awakening from a nap, blurted out, "Where are we?"

We're in Pennsylvania, he was told, driving north on Route 81.

"Can we stop at the Rawlings outlet?" he inquired.

"Where is it?" I asked.

"Somewhere in Pennsylvania," he said.

It's a big state, I told him. You think you can pin it down a little? You have an address?

"No, but it's got to be on one of the main roads."

Oh.

Anyway, with Elizabeth entering her senior year in high school, we went off in search of a college she might like. As the high school guidance counselors tell you: "There are thousands of colleges in the country, and one of them is bound to be right for your child."

This is meant to make parents feel better when their kid winds up in some unaccredited two-year school, majoring in badminton or plumbing supplies. But who's kidding who? Have you noticed the top of the political tickets? George Bush, Yale; Al Gore, Harvard; Joe Lieberman, Yale; Dick Cheney, Yale. Thank God for diversity.

But you'd have to be a dope to miss the message. Recruiters from Dartmouth, Amherst, and Stanford can go on for hours about the superb quality of education at their joints, but, hey, if you can't provide a shot at a national ticket, what good are you? If I were a high school senior and I saw I couldn't get into Harvard or Yale, I wouldn't crack open up another book until I got a job as a cashier at Barnes & Noble. I'd withdraw all my applications, find me a party school, and let the *bons temps rouler.*

We divided the labor on our trip. Elizabeth visited the schools. And Michael and I played golf. That's how I hoped she'd pick a college—by the quality of golf courses nearby. If they were top-notch, I might be inclined to visit her. I assured her that since I was going to pay her tuition regardless of what she decided, there was no point in me actually seeing each school. I told her the only thing that mattered about college was ingratiating yourself with the rich kids.

"Is there anything in particular you want me to look for in a college?" she asked.

"Wide-open fairways and not too much water," I said.

While Lizzie toured Cornell, we played golf at a Robert Trent Jones course on the Cornell campus. (The famous golf course architect was an undergraduate there.) While she toured Colgate, we played at a Trent Jones course on the Colgate campus. While Lizzie toured Trinity College in Hartford, we played the tour course where the pros play the Greater Hartford Open. And while she toured Connecticut College in New London, Michael and I played a Donald Ross course in Waterbury. I was so inspired, I suggested she consider going to the University of California at Pebble Beach.

All in all, it was a very successful trip. Elizabeth found that in general she liked small colleges a lot more than she thought she would. And I learned to hit a flop shot with a lob wedge.

I'm not quite sure how Lizzie felt about each individual college, since our conversations were somewhat limited. For example, I would ask her, "Did you like the school today?" And she would say something that sounded like, "Unnnnuuuhh." And I'd be left standing there wondering if she'd actually answered my question or simply belched.

"Do you think you could go into some more detail?" I'd ask.

"Your questions are so annoying, Dad. Do you spend hours thinking them up?"

I would then point out that I was simply asking if she liked the school—something I felt I had a right to know, since room, board, and tuition for just one year were going to cost me more than I had paid for the first house I bought. And at least that had resale value. What's a non-Harvard or Yale diploma worth these days? You'll be lucky to wind up with one of those dopey jobs nobody cares about, like secretary of commerce.

But by then, of course, she had tuned me out completely. I may as well have been Al Gore.

I expect to have a much better rapport with Michael when he takes his college tour three years from now. On Michael's college tour, there won't be any point in me asking him anything about the schools we visit, because he won't even see them. We can agree right now on where he's going to college: somewhere on a main road, like I-95 in Florida, at the University of Miami, Doral Campus.

Hey, They're Already Experimenting, Bub

My sweet baboo Elizabeth is going away to college next fall, and her high school recently held a meeting for seniors and their parents. Its purpose was to smooth out the kids' transition from living at home with Mom and Dad to living at college. I went to college in the '60s, and looking back I wish someone had given me advice on critical college issues, such as how to take care of money, how to budget my time, and how to keep a hash pipe lit while having sex with the dorm proctor's girlfriend. (Whoa! Some demon must be inhabiting my body. Nothing like that *ever* happened to me. I spent all my time in the library. If you're reading this, Lizzie, I was in the library.)

The meeting featured a psychologist, who told parents: Give your kids freedom in their senior year. That way, if they make mistakes, you can help them through the rough spots—because next year you won't be around to help. (That is, until spring semester, after your kid flunks out, comes home, and lies on the couch all day watching MTV and eating cheese fries.)

I couldn't attend the meeting myself. I was in the library. But my peeps were there. They brought back the psychologist's specific recommendations:

1. Stop waking your child up in the morning.
2. Give your child a credit card.
3. Don't give them a curfew.
4. Stop paying their parking tickets and library fines. ("Library fines"? Oh, please. Like my child has been in a library since seventh grade. The only way she'd walk into a library is if it advertised "Free body piercing.")

So let's review:

I should stop waking my child up in the morning?

I tried that the next day. Here's what happened: She slept until 5 P.M. She missed school altogether. I asked her why she bothered to get up at five. Why not sleep through? She said she didn't want to miss dinner. I said, "What do you think this is, the night flight to Paris?"

I have two teenagers at home. They are capable of sleeping through nuclear war. What do you mean, don't wake them up? If I don't wake her up, she will sleep through *college*.

And I shouldn't give her a curfew? If she can't wake up in the morning now, what'll it be like if she can straggle in at dawn? Besides, we're not open all night. I'm not running Mel's Diner.

I don't care if there's no curfew in college next year. Next year I won't be waiting up for her, pacing, wondering what sort of deadbeat she's out with. The curfew isn't for her. It's for *me*. I want to get some sleep.

And, come on, "give her a credit card"? This psychologist got his diploma where, Visa University? For her to get a credit card, I have to co-sign for it. I'm obliged to pay off her charges. Do you have any idea what kind of bill an eighteen-year-old girl can run up? Her hair products alone weigh over sixty pounds and cost more than a pardon for a millionaire fugitive. And let me tell you about her shoes. It's like I'm living with Imelda Marcos. I open up my kid's closet, I'm surprised Cole *and* Haan don't fall out.

The psychologist says: Your kids are going to be independent next fall anyway, so let them start experimenting now.

By that logic, why not let the kid sitting in 22B fly the plane? I mean, he wants to be a pilot someday. Let's give him a chance to make some mistakes now, with *you* in 22C.

Does it ever occur to psychologists that the reason we are paying through the nose to send our kids to some distant campus is so that when they do "keg stand"—where you place your lips over the nozzle of a keg of beer, and a few of your pals lift you up and hold you upside down by your ankles, then open the tap, *ka-blooey!*—it won't be *our* carpets they barf on?

When I was eighteen I was a sophomore in college. There are three words for what would've happened to me if all the stuff I did in college I'd done in high school instead. Those words are: "Massanutten Military Academy."

Finally, everyone was asked to write down the best and worst aspects about kids going to college. Parents expressed sadness at setting one less plate at dinner. (My reaction: Some families have dinner together? With their own kids, or kids they rent? I'd have more success getting Barbra Streisand to perform another last-ever concert at my dinner table—then wash the dishes before she left.) On the plus side, parents look forward to having sex after their kids leave for college. (My reaction: Sex? Like with *another* person? I'll be happy just to have my own bathroom.)

The kids' main anxiety was drawing a loser roommate; you know, someone who might study. But they were overjoyed at the prospect of having sex, drugs, and alcohol whenever they wanted. (Obviously I was thrilled to hear that. Who wouldn't want to cough up $30,000 a year in tuition so their child could go to *Temptation Island*?)

Parents and children were also asked what their farewell words would be. The parents revealed deep emotion: "We love you." "We'll miss you." "We'll keep your room just as it is." "We have faith in you." The sentiments were very caring. Even the parent who wrote, "Don't flunk out, dear; that's what your brother did, and now he's working at Jiffy Lube" clearly meant it with great affection.

The kids saw the farewell as an opportunity to get something off their chests, then disappear for four months. My favorites were: "That money you had stashed in a shoe box in the closet? I hope you weren't saving it for like a kidney operation or something." "Um, the dog didn't exactly run away." "In retrospect, I may not have told the complete truth about her parents being home." "I don't trust you, so I've padlocked my room."

And then there was this one: "Don't worry, Dad, I won't get a tattoo. At least not first semester."

Ah, I'd recognize my child anywhere.

The Commencement Redress

Because my sweet baboo is graduating from high school this week I thought I might be asked to deliver the commencement address.

I did it once before, and I was a rousing success—especially when I offered congratulations to "the graduates of St. Michael's," and the school was actually named St. Matthew's. Okay, I made a mistake. But as I told them, "There's a lesson in this for all of us. The lesson is: This is what happens when you don't pay your graduation speaker."

It turns out I won't be making graduation remarks this year. In a foolish moment, one they'll regret during the fall fund drive for years to come, Maret School got some nobody to take my place. I don't even know why I'm mentioning his name. Ted Kennedy.

Not that I'm bitter. But let me say I won't be at all shocked if he steers clear of a real meaty topic like "Is Maret's Mystery Burger made from mad cow?" ("Steers" clear, "meaty," get it? God, I'm funny! Those people don't know what they're missing.), and he concentrates on something a little less controversial, like "Contour Plowing in the Next Century."

Actually, a graduation address is a perfect place for that Kennedy fellow to show off his wide-ranging grasp of important issues that face us as a nation. With his decades of distinguished public service, he could really send these young people off with purpose, dedication, and direction. But isn't that overrated? I mean, really, who cares? My advice to the graduates would have been, "Who do I look like? Ted Kennedy? Hey, figure it out yourselves."

I wasn't going to make a speech, per se. But if I did, I'd have sprinkled it with a huge wad o' cultured foreign phrases like "per se" and "up the ying-yang." And I'd have thrown in some of them brilliant insights I'm famous for, such as, "I know graduation can be a frightening time. But remember, boys and goils, the word 'commencement' does not mean ending. Rather, it has its origin in an Old French word meaning "to cough up something bluish green.' "

I intended to confine my remarks to practical advice gleaned from my hard-won experience. Like: "On job applications, when it asks you to list 'personal achievements,' do not write 'got my tongue and nipples pierced.' "

Stuff like that.

Ah, what the heck. I might as well let you hear the rest.

"Graduates, faculty, parents, and honored guests:

"As the proud father of a graduate myself, I know I speak for all the parents here when I say to each and every graduate: 'Clean up your room. It's a pig sty. And believe me, the day you leave for college I'm going in there with a shovel.'

"I have been asked to say a few words about what I've learned in my life. Here it is: Don't make the same mistake I did. I waited too long to buy a gas grill. Other than that my life's been pretty good.

"Except for my senior prom. If I had it to do over again, this time I'd take a hooker. I hear hookers are terrific dancers.

"My senior prom was a disaster. Carrie had a better time than I did. Carrie's *classmates* had a better time than I did.

"The girl I wanted to ask didn't think of me in 'that' way; she thought of me in 'this' way: a cross between the most annoying person she actually knew—and Jerry Springer.

"There was one girl who liked me a lot, and who I probably could have gotten to third base with (and remember, this was in the pre-expansion era, before the pitching was so depleted). I don't want to say she was homely, but she was sponsored by Ryland. Not that I was some sort of prize. At my twenty-year high school reunion, everybody who recognized me said the same thing: 'Wow, your face cleared up.'

"I ended up taking Cathy, a girl I didn't particularly like and who didn't particularly like me. And by 'didn't particularly like me,' I mean, when I picked her up at her house, she suggested we take separate cars. Wait, there's more: She introduced me to her mother, who smiled and said, 'I disagree, dear. This might not be worse than no date at all.'

"During dinner I had an allergic reaction to the shrimp cocktail, and I started sweating profusely—right through my powder blue dinner jacket. It looked like I'd eaten dinner under a garden hose. I tried to be nonchalant, but it may have embarrassed my date when her friends wondered why she had agreed to go to the prom with Flipper.

"The couple we double-dated with wanted to drive to the beach and stay out all night. But Cathy said, 'I have to be home by ten. My father is performing elective gallbladder surgery on me in the morning.'

" 'Wait a second,' I said, thinking perhaps she was making that up. 'I thought your father was a veterinarian.'

"Her response reassured me. 'He's both,' she said. 'He operates on people *and* animals. He grew up in a very small town. It didn't pay to specialize.'

"Years later I ran into her and I told her the experience was traumatic for me. I said, 'I never went to another prom, never put on another powder blue dinner jacket, never ate another shrimp, I never even drove to the beach. After that night I didn't date another woman for four years! I wallowed in a black pit of self-loathing and . . . Hey, will you look at me monopolizing the conversation, going on and on about traumatic dates and how they change the course of your life forever. But I guess I don't have to tell *you* that, Sister Catherine.' "

Remembering Ricky

Please forgive me if I don't feel funny today. My cousin Ricky died last week.

He was only forty-four. It seemed like he'd barely even lived.

It happens all the time, in every family. He didn't feel right. So he went to the doctors. The doctors said it was one thing. But it turned out to be something much worse. Colon cancer.

They operated. They thought they got it all.

They didn't.

I can't say that we were particularly close. I don't think I'd seen Ricky three times in the last fifteen years. So I've been wondering why his death affected me so—why a couple of days ago I found myself sitting alone in my house, at the dining room table, crying.

Maybe it's because Ricky was younger than I am. It's a stunner, the first time somebody in the family younger than you dies. You feel your breath catch in your chest. Half of you grieves for him, the other half for you, because you might be next.

It's funny, but when I close my eyes, I don't see Ricky as an adult. I see him as a child. I see him at ten or eleven, with a Yankees cap on, tossing a baseball back and forth with his older brother, Mike. One was Mantle. One was Berra.

The two things they loved most were music and baseball, particularly the New York Yankees. Mike played guitar and did some folksinging back in the days when you could do that without being laughed at. Ricky played drums, and later piano. For twenty years he was in a band that did weddings and bar mitzvahs on weekends. He did it all the way into last year, when he got too sick to play anymore.

We all went to camp together. A couple of summers I was

Ricky's counselor. I'm going back a lot of years now, but I remember one time when he got hit in the head in a baseball game, and I had to carry him up to the camp infirmary. I can see it so clearly, me carrying him in my arms. He had the softest skin. It felt like one of those chamois cloths you use to wipe an expensive car.

The rest of the kids trailed after us to make sure Ricky was all right, and he was. All the kids liked Ricky—the wild ones, the troubled ones, the spoiled ones, even the mean one. Ricky was a nice kid. That's the first word, and the best word, that comes to mind: nice. The others felt better about themselves just being close to him.

My cousin Ricky was an ordinary man who lived an ordinary life. He lived in the same town on Long Island his whole life. In fact, when his parents moved to Florida, Ricky bought their place, so he actually ended up living in the same house his whole life.

He married his high school girlfriend, Linda. He worked for a florist during the week and played music on the weekends. Flowers and music. So you see, everything Ricky did made people happy.

A couple of weeks ago I found out Ricky was quite ill, that he might have just a short time left.

I called his brother Mike and asked if Ricky was taking calls.

"Not many, but he'd love to hear from you," Mike said.

I called that afternoon. Ricky was resting. His wife said she'd wake him up. She was sure he'd be excited to talk to me.

I cursed myself for not calling earlier.

"Hey, Ricky," I said, trying to sound chipper. "I'm coming up for the bar mitzvah in a few weeks. I was hoping to see you."

Mike's twin sons are to be bar mitzvahed in mid-May. I was holding the invitation in my hand. One of the reasons I'd made up my mind to go was to see Ricky, thinking it might be the last time.

"I'm not gonna make it," Ricky said.

"Well, I guess that whole thing might be a bit strenuous," I said. "Going to the service, and then to the luncheon. But maybe I could come over to your house?"

"I don't think I'm gonna make it, Tony."

This time I understood what he meant.

"It's okay, really," he said. "I know I'm going to die. I've made peace with that. I'm not afraid."

I make my living with words, but at that moment I didn't know which ones to use.

"You playing any piano?" I asked.

"I can't. It's real hard to sit up and play."

"Well, at least spring's here, right?" I said. "And baseball's starting."

"Yeah, the Yankees look pretty good this year."

"You watching them on TV?"

"Yeah. And you know what I miss, Tony?" Ricky said, his voice thinner than I remembered. "I miss having a catch. I miss standing outside on the front lawn throwing a baseball around. You remember when we were kids, and you used to come over here, and we'd have a catch?"

"I do, Ricky. You were always a terrific baseball player."

"I'd give anything to have a catch again," he said.

Ricky didn't stay on the phone long after that. I asked to talk to Linda, who'd been so strong through all this. I could hear music in the background. Linda told me it was Ricky playing. He had come out of the bedroom and sat down at the piano. She was thrilled.

I went home earlier than usual that day. I took my old baseball glove down from the shelf in my closet. I went outside on the lawn with my kids, and we had a catch.

Bald Out by Dad

Here's how my day started: I called my father in Florida to say hi, and we had our usual conversation—which is to say he informed me that the high temperature in Washington, D.C., on Tuesday was 89 degrees, the low was 68, the high on Wednesday was 91, the low was 71, and a large frontal system passed through accompanied by thunder showers, dropping as much as two inches of rain on Baltimore, and the outlook for Thursday called for a high of 92, with winds gusting up to 20 miles an hour in the outlying suburbs.

This was a typical conversation between my father and me. They go like this: How are you? How are the kids? Do you know the barometric pressure in Washington is dropping? There might be monsoon winds and hail the size of eggplants. You better go out and buy milk and toilet paper.

"Thanks, Willard," I say.

See, I accept this as one of my father's idiosyncrasies.

He has lost much of his eyesight—by that I mean that on the street my dad frequently stops to chat with large shrubbery. When he watches TV all he can see are shapes and colors shifting around. This depresses him if he is trying to watch, say, *Suddenly Susan*. But the Weather Channel is all Doppler radar, which is just shapes and colors shifting around; this pleases him. He feels it levels the playing field. So the Weather Channel is all he watches.

Whenever my dad sees (by the bright, pulsating reds and oranges chugging across the TV screen) that some killer thunderstorm is bearing down on Washington, he calls me to inquire, "Do you still have power?"

And if I didn't, what good could he do about it? He's fifteen hundred miles away. He can't drive. He can barely walk. It's not like he's gonna rush over and nail up storm shutters.

Apparently my dad isn't the only person who calls during storms. My friend Nancy and her mother do the same thing. Do you have power? Do you have flashlights? Do you have whiskey? (Nancy is Irish.) Nancy knows of one older parent who doesn't call her children during storms because she believes that if lightning strikes during the phone conversation, it will come straight down the telephone pole, into the receiver, and *explode everyone's heads*!

Speaking of heads, it was after his weather update that my father said to me, and I am quoting him verbatim: "Have you ever thought about getting a hair transplant?"

This is a sensitive issue for me. My dad is almost eighty-seven years old, and he has a head of hair like Einstein. He has the same hairline now that he had when he was thirty. When we walk down the street together, if you just looked at the tops of our heads you might think *he* was the son, and I was the old man—if it were not for the fact that he has shrunk to the size of a hedgehog, and he walks stooped over, and he's always bumping into walls, and I keep calling him "Dad" in a voice loud enough to wake a hibernating bear because let's face it, his hearing isn't what it used to be, either.

I was stunned that my father brought up my baldness. I didn't think he cared that I was bald. Actually, I didn't even think he could see that I was bald.

Note to geriatric readers: Please do not be concerned that this column is insensitive to my dad. It is all in good fun. I had him read this column and approve it before it went to press. Of course, for all he knew, he was reading *The Brothers Karamazov*.

But I digress. My dad was on the phone, asking me about my hair in that subtle, diplomatic way dads can broach a sensitive subject.

"So, Tony," he said, "you think maybe you wouldn't look like such a schlemiel if you just had a little something on top? Your head looks like somebody's thumb. Don't you have a friend in the transplant business?"

It was so quaint the way he said "the transplant business," like the guy was a furrier.

"I know someone who does hair weaves," I said. "They take someone else's hair and weave it into your hair."

"Nah, not someone else's hair—you'll never be sure where it came from. I'm talking about growing your own hair. How long would that take?"

"About two or three years," I said.

"Even for just a few strands?" my dad asked.

"Dad, it's a human head, not a pot holder."

I felt bad.

"Just out of curiosity, Dad, why do you think I should get new hair?"

"I think it might help your career," he said. He has seen me on TV.

"My career? My career? Dad, this may come as a shock to you, but I'm almost fifty years old. I'm not up for those Brad Pitt parts anymore. I don't think a few strands of hair is standing between me and international stardom. . . . What made you think of this now?"

"The announcers on the Weather Channel all have hair."

Oh.

Blue Face Special

I have just returned from visiting my eighty-seven-year-old father in Florida, and I am pleased to report that he is still blind, deaf, and short.

How short is he, Tony?

Amazingly, my dad is now the same size sitting down as he is standing up. He reminds me of a footstool. It is quite convenient for us to travel together because he can be stowed neatly in the overhead.

Now, you all know I love my dad. So don't send me nasty letters about how cruel and heartless I am, and how glad you are that I'm not your son. (By the way, your son is a cross-dresser.) The fact is, my dad loves that I write about him. I tell him he's in the column almost every week. He thinks he's my friend Nancy.

Anyway, I called him about a month ago to let him know when I was coming down. And he said, "Hold on, let me check my schedule."

And I said, "Please do that, because I wouldn't want my visit to conflict with your arrival in Oslo to pick up the Nobel prize for peace."

At this point my father's schedule consists mainly of breathing. He can't drive. He can barely walk. It takes him so long to go from his apartment to the mailbox that he has to bring lunch.

A few days later he called to inform me that he cleared his calendar, just for me.

"But we're eating all our meals out," he said. "I don't intend to cook."

I was greatly relieved. I don't want this man going anywhere near a gas range.

You all know about dinners in Florida, namely the "early bird specials," which people begin dressing for around dawn. At about 4 P.M., every schlock restaurant in the state offers fixed-price, multi-course dinners, featuring some of the best iceberg lettuce for blocks! The conversation is very congenial: "Hey, I get dessert with that! And coffee. Whaddya mean coffee is eighty-five cents extra? Okay, gimme water then." And after a pleasant meal you're done by 4:45. You've eaten your last meal of the day, it's blinding daylight outside, and you have nothing to look forward to but death and Tom Brokaw.

My first day in Florida, we went to this chain steak house that looks like a bad Tudor castle and offers a wide variety of eight-ounce prime rib. My aunt and uncle joined us, bringing discount coupons. The highlight of the meal was the check. With the coupons, the dinner for four ended up costing $28.95. Being a sport, my dad threw $30 on the table.

"That's sufficient, isn't it?" my dad asked me.

"Sure," I said, "if the waitress goes home and eats dog food."

"How much should I leave her?"

"I'd give her five more dollars, and ask Uncle Arnie to throw in a car wash coupon."

The next night Dad wanted Chinese food, and we ended up at a place with a buffet for the extravagant price of $3.95. (If Uncle Arnie were here, he'd have a coupon where they would pay *us* to eat.) The food was set up in a giant steam table—maybe thirty different dishes, twenty-eight of which looked like sesame chicken in brown sauce.

"What's that?" he'd ask.

I'd read the label, and he'd say, "That sounds good, give me some of that."

When we got to the tenth dish I realized that it could be Dog's Intestine in Custard Sauce with Dead Flies, and my dad would say, "Yeah, give me some of that."

So I got him a little of everything. By the time I was done I'd filled six plates. A waiter came over and asked if I was expecting anyone else at the table.

"The Taiwan Little League team," I said.

My dad had been coughing all day, and his coughing suddenly got worse. He was hacking and hocking. Loudly. The sound he made suggested what would happen if you crossed a moose with a rabbinical student.

"I've got something in my windpipe," my dad said.

"What, the *Hindenburg*?"

He coughed furiously and began to spit stuff into napkins.

"Give me another napkin," he'd say.

I went from table to table, picking up napkins. Meanwhile, the terrible guttural noises had driven away the other three couples sitting near us.

"Are you okay?" I asked.

"I'm fine," my dad said. "I think I just need to give myself the Heimlich maneuver."

Pardon me?

I'm no Nervous Nellie, but I think it's reasonable to be concerned about the health of an eighty-seven-year-old who is pounding himself in the chest, trying to cough up something the size of a hedgehog.

"There's a hospital a quarter mile from here," I said. "Let's go there and fix you up."

"No," he said. "Just give me another napkin."

I could feel the cold sweat on my face. "I'm really beginning to worry," I said.

"You're just like your mother," he said. "You worry too much."

I noticed the owner of the restaurant looking nervously our way. "How about if we just go home?"

I could see this was a difficult decision for my dad, because three full plates of food remained untouched. "Let me have some of that egg foo yong," he said.

Finally, he agreed to let me drive him home. In the apartment he told me sternly, "I'm going into the bathroom now. No matter what you hear coming from in there for the next fifteen minutes, do not come in."

I felt like I was trapped in a Sigourney Weaver movie.

Actually, the sounds weren't so bad. I could barely hear them over the beating of my own heart.

True to his word, my dad came out in fifteen minutes with a big smile on his face.

"So where do you want to eat tomorrow night?" he asked.

They Took
the Wrong Geezer!

My dad is steamed at NASA. "How come they sent a young punk like John Glenn into space?" he groused the other day. "He's only seventy-seven. If they really wanted a geezer, they should have sent me. I'm eighty-eight."

So what if my dad has shrunk so much he can't see over the dashboard on the space shuttle? It's not like anybody's going to ask him to drive.

No. 1. He'd ride the brake and keep the turn signal on the whole way.

No. 2. He'd back into the Hubble telescope by mistake.

If my dad got on the shuttle, he'd be thrilled just staring out the window for the whole ride, like my dog Maggie. It would play right into his obsession about weather. Every phone conversation I have with him is the same. I call him in Florida. He asks about the kids, and after a brief pause he inquires about Washington's weather. "Is it cold up there yet? I saw on the Weather Channel it was twenty-four degrees in Cleveland, and it was headed your way. Bundle up. Take the plants in." It's like talking to Willard.

But if my dad were in space, he wouldn't need to ask about the weather in Washington, because he'd be able to *see* it. And even if he had short-term memory loss, because of how fast the shuttle orbits Earth, every ninety minutes he'd see it again.

I'm sure it's smarter to send John Glenn. And to people who say that John Glenn going up in space is just a publicity gimmick, I say John Glenn is an American hero. If he wants this ride, he has earned it. If for some inexplicable reason Johnny Carson decided that he wanted to return to TV to host *World's Most Dangerous*

Aardvark Awards, you might question his judgment. But you'd have to let him do it.

I have a few questions about Glenn's trip, though:

Is *Discovery* spending nine days in space because it's cheaper when you stay over a Saturday night?

Will Glenn wear a bathrobe? All guys his age pad around in bathrobes.

Under weightless conditions, how do you keep your false teeth in a glass of water?

And at seventy-seven, what, exactly is the Right Stuff? Polident or Ensure?

Normally, I'd make a joke about how old somebody like Glenn is in dog years. But the fact is if we sent a dog into space who was the equivalent of Glenn in *human* years, that dog would be eleven! A dog that old can't even sniff. That dog would need his own Seeing Eye dog!

When he announced his retirement from the U.S. Senate last year, he said he was too old for the job. Now here he is romping in space. Talk about your Viagra fantasy: a seventy-seven-year-old man strapped into a gigantic cigar-shaped rocket ship, thrusting into the heavens. If that isn't symbolism, I don't know what is. And don't think that symbol was lost on Bill Clinton, interim president of the United States, who was in attendance at the launch.

Ostensibly, Glenn is up there having experiments conducted on him about aging. Scientists already know that prolonged time in space causes the body to age. One of the theories Glenn is testing is that an older person might not show as much aging as a younger person. But if that theory proves wrong, and aging is accelerated, next week Glenn could come back looking like Gabby Hayes.

There's a series of experiments tailored to see how an older person can function in space. One involves Glenn taking Metamucil; scientists want to find out—and trust me, so does Glenn—if geezers can successfully, um, have a movement in space. (What, you were expecting something more esoteric? Hey, intergalactic trips are long; you can't just say: Let me out at the next gas station.) Glenn was, however, left out of the sleep experiment for obvious reasons: At his age, who can sleep? You have to get up every twenty minutes to go tinkle.

NASA assures us that the senator's duties and responsibilities are the same as all the other astronauts, even though they are thirty-five and forty years younger than he is. There is one concession to Glenn's age, though: For an hour a day all experiments will cease while Glenn gathers everyone around to watch *Matlock*.

When the hero returns to Earth, people will suggest new tasks for him to take on, to demonstrate how an aging man can do anything a younger man can do.

I'm inclined to put him on the Redskins' defensive line.

The greater question, though, is: We're not actually thinking of sending eighty-year-olds into space, are we? Because if we are, then let's move them out of Florida and resettle them in condos on the moon. I can picture my dad now, in his white shoes, out in front of the Man in the Moon Deli, a couple of blocks from the Sea of Tranquillity, at three in the afternoon, in line for the early bird special.

Like Father, Like . . . I Forget

I just got back from Florida, where I spent some time with my father, who is eighty-eight years old.

I know what you're thinking: *Here comes another of Tony's cruel columns about his aging father. He'll string together a series of superficial, stereotypical anecdotes about how his father can't see and can't hear—what's next, that his father has no teeth? I'd like to see Tony try to wring a laugh out of that. How can he profess to love his father and write such nasty things about him? What does Tony's father say when he reads these terrible things?*

Oh, please.

My father can't see well enough to *read*.

But somehow, incredibly, he can maneuver in total darkness like one of those cave-dwelling fish.

"Tony, are you up?"

Am I up? Nobody is up. Conan O'Brien is asleep. My father is the only person in the whole world who's up. And of course the first thing he does is turn the radio on loud enough to liquefy every Miracle Ear in the condo.

"Mmmmfff."

"You're going to have to move your car," my dad said. "The roofers are coming."

"What time is it now, Dad?"

"It's five fifty-two."

5:52? I happened to know that roofers don't usually show up in the same geologic epoch as the day they promised, much less when it's still high noon in Okinawa.

"Okay, Dad. Let me know when you see them on the roof, and then I'll move my car."

I drifted back to sleep. What seemed like just six minutes later, I heard pounding on my door again.

"Tony, you'd better go move your car."

"Are the roofers here yet?"

"No, but they're coming soon."

"What time is it now?"

"Five fifty-eight."

Why fight it? He gave me life, right? I moved my car at 6:02 A.M. Now we're even.

By the time I shuffled back into the house, I could see well enough to notice my father's feet. He was wearing a pair of slippers I'd bought him a year ago—but they had large strips of bright yellow tape around them.

"Why do you have tape on your slippers?" I asked.

"The soles fell apart, and I taped them together."

"Dad, this isn't Valley Forge. Let's get you a new pair."

"They're perfectly good this way," he insisted.

"It's bright yellow tape, Dad. You look like a police crime scene. The slippers cost eight dollars at Wal-Mart. We'll drive down there. I'll buy you a new pair."

"I don't want you wasting your money on me," he said.

"Dad, at your age wasting my money would be if I bought you a Jet Ski or a hooker. A pair of slippers is life-sustaining."

That evening we went to dinner at Steak & Ale (a chain specializing in warm food), where I was not only the youngest diner, I was also the only one who could see well enough to go to the salad bar without a guide dog.

"Take me around the salad bar. They have a very good salad bar here," my dad said, meaning the foods are in various shapes and colors. The more different shapes and colors he can pick out, the happier he is. I could park my father in front of a Lava lamp for weeks.

"What do you want?" I asked.

"Cauliflower."

"There is no cauliflower," I said.

"What's that?" he asked, pointing to something on his left. "That looks like cauliflower."

"That's potato salad."

He moved around the salad bar slowly, like we were circling some wily prey.

Now he pointed to something on his right.

"Is that cauliflower?" he asked.

"No, Dad, that's the potato salad again. It's on your right this time."

"Are you sure it's not cauliflower? It looks like cauliflower."

"You can't see, Dad. To you, I probably look like Harrison Ford."

He put his hands on my face and smiled. "I may not see well anymore, but I see well enough to know you look a lot more like Henry Ford."

I see myself in him more and more these days. As he shrinks, as he steadies himself after each step, as he uses a magnifying glass to clip out the "25 cents off" coupons for macaroni and cheese from the Sunday newspaper, I see the man I will become and am becoming.

His wife—my mom—died twenty years ago. He has been alone for so long, he has become used to the silence in the halls (which is why he turns the radio up so loud), and the indentation on the side where he sleeps on the big bed, and the familiar smells of himself in the rooms. There is no one for him to dress for anymore. He takes for granted the face that looks back at him in the mirror.

I looked up from the tape-wrapped slippers.

"What happened to your teeth, Dad?" I asked softly. There were gaps. Rose Mary Woods gaps.

"My upper plate keeps falling out. And last month I broke a tooth on the bottom."

"Last *month*? When are you going to see the dentist?"

"I have an appointment in three weeks. But I don't know if he can fix them."

"Of course he can fix them," I said. "You're going to a dentist, not an accountant."

"It's very tricky, working with teeth."

"That's why he went to dental school, Dad, not bartenders' academy. . . . You can't walk around without teeth, Dad. I love you. But you need teeth."

"I'm fine without them. I can eat anything. Let's go to the rib joint now and see."

"I'd love to, Dad. But I forgot where I moved the car."

This Home Was Made for Walkers

Many of you have been kind enough over the years to say you've enjoyed the columns I've written about my father and the idiosyncratic things he's done: like collecting Styrofoam trays in case of a worldwide Styrofoam shortage, or driving thirty miles out of his way to pick up a tin of spice for four cents less than he could have bought it one block from his house.

That was in the old days when he was still driving, before they took away his license. I knew he was done as a driver when he stopped at what he thought was a stop sign—and it was a mailbox.

The last time my father renewed his Florida driver's license, they flunked him because he couldn't identify the gigantic **E** at the top of the eye chart. Of course, he brought that on himself by facing the wrong wall. My dad was stunned that they wouldn't renew his license at eighty-five for three more years. He insisted that the people at the DMV were anti-Semitic.

I just came back from visiting my dad, and he's not as mobile as he once was. In the past year, he's broken both of his hips, so he has to use a walker. He's in a retirement home, with a caring live-in nurse named Barbara who cooks bacon and eggs for him every morning. He's so happy, he's gained twenty pounds.

When my dad lived alone, he scrimped on food. His pantry was stocked with boxes of macaroni and cheese. (It looked like a child in East Asia had adopted *him*.) He made a two-pound chicken last five days. He'd strip the bird like a '57 Chevy; he did everything but make the carcass into a party hat. Now he eats like a Rockefeller.

"How come you're eating so high on the hog now?" I asked him.

"Because you're paying for it," he said.

My dad watches *Jeopardy!* and *Who Wants to Be a Millionaire* every night. He tries to answer every question, but it's hard to keep pace because he can't see the questions on the TV screen. Sometimes the question will be: "Which of the following is not a mushroom? A. portobello. B. shiitake. C. Steve Forbes. D. porcini." And my dad will blurt out, "Give the Dog a Bone," clearly the answer to a previous question—perhaps from yesterday's *Wheel of Fortune.*

Anyway, I was pleased to see my dad still has his sense of humor. We were walking down the hall on the way to the elevator, and he looked at me and said, "I think you've grown."

"I haven't grown, Dad. I stopped growing thirty-five years ago."

"Maybe. But you definitely look taller to me."

I smiled at him and pointed out, "Dad, you're hunched over a walker, you're legally blind, and you've shrunk to about four feet. The bathroom sink looks taller to you."

I don't understand why people get angry when I point out that my father has shrunk. Of course he's shrunk. He's eighty-nine years old. Whaddaya think Wilt Chamberlain would have looked like at eighty-nine? Like my dad—only darker.

People decried how insensitive I was the last time I did a column about him because I wrote: "I could fit my dad in the overhead baggage rack of the plane." I apologize for making that offensive statement. I would never say that again. It would be wrong. Now I could stow him under the seat.

The retirement home is quite nice. My only complaint is with the elevator. Because of the common use of walkers, the elevator doors are timed to accommodate a slow pace. They tend to stay open for, um, ever.

My dad lives on the second floor. I got into the elevator on the ground floor, pressed "2," and waited for the door to close. I was in there for a while, and the door remained open. I pressed "Close

Door." Nothing happened. I waited a while longer. Still nothing. I pressed "2" again, harder this time. Still nothing.

Now I figure I've been standing in this elevator as long as it took to film *Titanic*—or worse, as long as it took to *watch* it. It's not just that I could have gotten to the second floor faster by walking. I could have gotten there faster by going outside and shinnying up a drainpipe.

My visit with my dad was great. I was there four days, bunking in his old apartment not far from the retirement home. So I was able to sit by the pool and plug in to all the old, familiar conversations about the Holy Trinity of retirement—food, money, and major medical.

Here is a typical conversation at the Sands Point condominium:

"Did you see where an egg omelet costs $8.99 now? It used to cost $2.99. It's just three eggs. Chickens have a union now?"

"I can't eat eggs. Too much cholesterol. My stocks should only be as high as my cholesterol. I can eat Egg Beaters. But for what Egg Beaters cost, I can buy a new car."

"My sonny just bought a Lexus. I wouldn't tell you what it costs—fifty-one thou with the heated seats. I remember when all we got from Japan fell apart in our hands."

"Is something wrong with your hands? Mine are killing me. These pills I get from the Medicare, they don't help at all. They're so big. They're like horseshoes. Who can eat pills like this?"

"Okay, you convinced me. Let's eat."

All the while, Muzak is blaring around the pool—vaguely familiar tunes. And then I realize what it is. It's "Love Her Madly" by the Doors. Only there's no Jim Morrison. No words, even. It's actual Muzak of the Doors! The next song is "Honky Cat" by Elton John, then "More Than a Feeling" by Boston.

These are the very songs—rock songs from the '60s and '70s—that these people loathed. And here they are, forced to listen to them in their old age. At a volume you could hear on the moon!

Imagine me being eighty and sitting around a pool in Florida listening to Coolio.

Classic rap.

I think I want an omelet.

Fire in the Sky

This is the column I never wanted to write.

My father, Ira James Kornheiser, died on July 4, a few weeks shy of his ninetieth birthday.

People ask me if it was sudden and unexpected. I tell them it is always sudden. One minute you're on the phone with him, talking about how your air conditioner conked out, and the next time the phone rings it's your aunt calling from Florida, saying, "He's gone."

That's what she said: "Tony, he's gone." It was 6:15. I was getting ready to drive to the Mall for the fireworks. My dad had been in the hospital for a few days because he had fluid built up in his lungs. I hadn't liked the tinny sound of his voice when I'd called the day before, and I'd asked my aunt—who lived near my dad in Florida and visited him every day—if I should hurry down.

She said the doctors assured her this sort of thing was episodic; there was no immediate danger.

"Come down in August, around his birthday, like you'd planned," she told me.

The day he died, I'd phoned my aunt and left this message: "I didn't call my dad today because I stupidly left the number of the hospital at work. Tell him I'll call him tomorrow. I figure he's okay, because you'd have called me if there was anything terribly wrong."

I was walking out the door when she called to tell me he was gone.

She had been there. They'd been chatting. My father mentioned I hadn't called him yet—I called every day. "He's probably playing golf," Dad said. "He'll call me tomorrow."

Excuse me, Tony, but are you going to be funny in this column?

Sorry. Not this one.

My father was born in 1910, before radio stations, before frozen foods, before Babe Ruth played major league baseball. He lived so long, he saw Halley's comet twice!

He wasn't cheated like my mother was. He was healthy, and his mind was still sharp. He got more answers right on *Who Wants to Be a Millionaire* than most of the contestants.

My dad's problem was his eyes. Macular degeneration hit him in his mid-eighties and left him legally blind. He had to give up driving. (This, as I've written, was a godsend for other Floridians, because he couldn't tell the red lights from the green lights; once, he stopped his car for what he thought was a stop sign, and I said, "Dad, you've just stopped for a mailbox!") Then, walking became problematic because his eyesight was unsure.

Last year he fell and broke his hips on two separate occasions. But he was still hale and walking reasonably well with a walker. Surely there is a technical medical explanation for what my dad died of. But I say it was from old age. His body just wore out.

After he moved into a retirement home sixteen months ago, I kept up his condominium in the event he ever wanted to come back—but I told him point blank: "I've thrown out all the Styrofoam trays. I'm sorry because I know you thought if there was a worldwide shortage of Styrofoam, you had the market cornered."

I tried cleaning out the apartment last winter, and I found collections of things that only someone from the Depression would value: nails, rubber bands, pencil lead, old combs. He had a comb that said VOTE FOR ABE BEAME. Abe Beame first ran for mayor of New York in 1965! (My dad had combs everywhere. Have I mentioned how much I hated him for living to almost ninety with a FULL HEAD OF HAIR?)

Life at the home obviously agreed with him. In the past year, Dad had gained fifteen pounds. He was shrinking vertically and expanding horizontally. In five years, he'd have looked like a Brunswick bowling ball.

"You should see how he eats, Tony," his nurse, Barbara, an angel, would tell me. Bacon and eggs every morning. Big hunks of red meat for dinner.

"What happened to macaroni and cheese?" I would ask him. "I remember when you bought four of them for a buck and ate them every night. You ate like a pensioner."

It made me laugh because I knew why he was suddenly eating like a truck driver: because he thought *I* was paying for it!

Another few decades, and maybe I could begin to pay him back for what he gave me.

Years ago I'd made my peace with my dad about how this would end. I had brought him up to Washington to look at an apartment in a Rockville high-rise. "I don't want to live in cold weather," he'd told me. "And I don't want to live in a high-rise. I want to stay where I am."

"Okay, but it means you're going to die in Florida, and I may not be there when you go," I said.

"I love you," he said. "And I know you love me. Now let me live where I want."

I called him every day. I made sure to say "I love you" during every call. I don't regret a second of our relationship—other than being one thousand miles apart.

The last time I saw him was in late spring. The family was down in Florida for a week, and every night my son, Michael, and I went to see my dad. We'd watch TV with him, and then, when he got tired, we'd leave. I kissed him every night, never knowing if I'd get the chance again.

The day he died, I was up early, walking my dog, and in the still of the predawn morning I could hear myself saying out loud, "It's not really important if he makes it to ninety. Because his tombstone will read '1910–2000.' Which is quite a run. And if he died today, on July 4, then every year there'd be fireworks in his honor."

It was a premonition, I guess.

When my aunt told me he was gone, I stood there holding the phone for a second, remembering the day twenty-two years ago when my dad called to say my mother had passed away.

I never had any brothers or sisters. Now I had no parents.

"I don't know what to do," I said. "We were just going to the fireworks."

"Go," my aunt said. "He'd have wanted you to go."

Actually, he'd have wanted to go with me. (Which would've been fine, as long as he didn't make me drive twenty-five miles out of my way to get nutmeg on sale for forty-nine cents instead of the usual fifty-nine cents.)

I wrote about my dad often and told funny stories about the quirks he had. I used to tell him not to read them, but he did anyway. And he'd call and say, "You're exaggerating terribly about me. I didn't drive twenty-five miles out of my way to save ten cents on nutmeg. First of all, it was paprika—and it was a big tin, and I saved a dollar."

I went to the Mall to watch the fireworks. I sat back, listened to the great, booming noises, and watched the colors explode all around me, rising and falling in giant plumes, and I thought: *This is how I'm going to remember him every year.*

I am still in shock, I think. At least once a day I pick up the phone to call him, then I gently put it down. I want to tell him about Elizabeth's summer job as a baker and how Michael is doing at camp. I never did anything major in my life without consulting my dad and seeking his advice and his approval. I want to ask him about buying a new car, or how often to clean the gutters, or how much I should tip the plumber. And I'll never be able to do that again.

Love in the
Time of
Viagra

Good-bye AAA

What separates man from the lower animals?
Concierge service.

(*Concierge* is from the French and, loosely translated, means "For a good time, call Babette.")

Concierge service, baby. They have it in hotels. They have it in law firms. They have it in office buildings. They have it in high-end health clubs.

And now it's in my *car*.

I recently bought a car that came with a year of OnStar service. That's one of those global-positioning deals that direct you when you're lost, or you have an emergency—like you'd *kill* for a tall skim decaf latte with extra foam and a shot of vanilla.

To activate the service, all I have to do is press a button on the console attached to my rearview mirror. Though with my astonishingly low level of technical skill, this is easier said than done, as you'll see:

There are three buttons. The one on the left has a plain white dot. The one in the middle says "OnStar." The other one has a red cross. To activate OnStar, I pressed . . . the one with the white dot! Sometimes it's like I have the IQ of a ficus tree.

Nothing happened. Duh. (God knows what I was waiting for, someone to shout "Whasssup?" As it turns out, the white button is the "off" button. Who knew?) So I pressed the "OnStar" button. The next thing I heard was a voice saying, "What can I do for you, Mr. Kornheiser?"

This was an actual person calling me *in my car!*

You press, your fairy godmother answers.

"It's like somebody up in Heaven watching out for Mr. Tony," my friend Nancy said the other day when I pressed the magic button.

What can I do for you, Mr. Kornheiser?

The voice identified herself as Tamara.

"And where are you today, Tamara?" I asked.

"In the Carolinas."

"Do I have to guess which of the Carolinas?" I asked.

"The North," she said.

The North?

Before I could pursue this, Tamara was gone. Her signal faded. Most likely she was whacked by the geography police.

I pressed the button again.

"You've reached OnStar. All available advisers are assisting other callers. Please remain on the line."

At least nobody said, "Your call is very important to us. In the meantime, please continue to enjoy selections from *The Very Best of Yanni.*" But I must say it was disturbing to be on hold with an emergency road service. What if I'd been in an accident and my car was on fire? By the time they actually got to me I'd be . . .

"Toast," Nancy offered.

Fortunately, Debbie came to my rescue.

"Can you pinpoint where I am?" I asked. (And don't be a wiseguy and say, "In your car.")

"I'm showing you in Washington, D.C.," Debbie said.

"That's easy, Debbie. You could have gleaned that from my OnStar ID card."

"Let me zoom in," she said. "I see you on . . . Fifteenth Street Northwest?"

Wow. She was right on the money. I should have asked, "Where do you see me in five years?" But I was a little off balance. I felt like I was onstage and the Amazing Kreskin had just told the crowd what kind of underwear I had on. (And thank God it wasn't the Victoria's Secret stuff.)

"Can you see that there's a woman in the car with me?" I asked Debbie.

"No, but I'll bet she's quite good-looking."

Yeah, right. Like they can pinpoint your car from five hundred miles away, but they can't see who's in there with you. Like they can't see every move you make. Like they don't sit around in *The Carolinas* watching you and whoever you're in the car with, doing whatever you're doing in there. Like this isn't the Voyeur Channel.

I asked Debbie what level of service I had, since I feared a Doomsday Concierge Scenario: Like, let's say I'd packed up the whole family to go visit more colleges for Elizabeth, and by the time we hit Franklin & Marshall College I realized—God, I forgot my son, Michael! If I called OnStar and asked them to pick him up in a limo, would they say to me, "I'm terribly sorry, Mr. Kornheiser, but you have 'Economy' OnStar. That option comes with DeVille, not Catera."

Here's what I've got: OnStar will make hotel and restaurant reservations for me while I'm driving. It'll get me tickets to plays, concerts, and sporting events. Debbie said she could get me World Series tickets.

Tony, do you think she could get you . . .

No. Forget about Heidi Fleiss. It's over!

I have an emergency button (the one with the red cross, stupid) to press in case something catastrophic happens—like my hair plugs get caught in the moon roof.

I have "air bag notification": If my air bag deploys, Debbie will know in The Carolinas. (I asked if I had "old bag notification" as well. Would a buzzer sound if I started making out with some fifty-year-old floozy in the backseat?) I have "remote diagnostic": If the "check engine" light comes on, they can tell me from The Carolinas if it's a real emergency or if it's okay to drive nine thousand more miles the way cabdrivers in New York do. "Look, 'brake' light is on. Hahaha. Is big joke. Not to worry, boss! We go to Bronx now, yes?"

They can even unlock my door by remote control. What's more unbelievable than that—I mean, besides icky Paula Jones getting naked and saying, "I'm just doing this to feed my kids"?

Most of all, though, I can't tell you how great it is to hear somebody say, "What can I do for you, Mr. Kornheiser?" At home I never hear that. At home I hear, "Dad, tell the little freak to give me the clicker, or I'll beat his fat butt."

Dumb to a Turn

I feel so ashamed.

Last night, I was innocently watching a quality movie on TV, *Bikini Biker Babes from the Beyond* (I thought I was on PBS, but in hindsight, I guess I wasn't), when an infomercial came on. I should have looked away, but it was too late. The next thing I knew, the phone was in my hand, and I was ordering kitchen cookware.

God help me. I bought the Ronco Showtime Rotisserie & BBQ.

What a piece of hardware! You could roast a Doberman in there!

I felt gleeful. I felt liberated.

Pray for me. Maybe next I'll have the urge to see *Cats*.

"You bought something from *Ron Popeil*?" my friend Nancy said. The way she said "Ron Popeil" made me uneasy. It was the same way a theater critic might say "Pauly Shore" if he were reviewing *Pauly Shore's Hamlet*.

"You're kidding, right?" Nancy said.

"I'm not kidding," I said. "I'm fifty years old. I've missed out on Mister Microphone and the Pocket Fisherman, and, dammit, I'm not going to miss out on *this*. It can cook four chickens at once!"

(I told this to Man About Town Chip Muldoon, and he said, "Do you have a need to cook four chickens at once? Are you opening up a carryout? I think you've crossed a line here. Soon you're going to wake up in a motel next to Tonya Harding. Did you get the Ginzu knives, too?")

"You bought this item on impulse, right?" Nancy said knowingly. "How big is it? How hot does it get? Can you regulate the temperature? Does it have a timer? You don't know the answer to any of these questions, do you?"

Details!

I didn't expect her to understand. Ronco is a guy thing.

Take another Ronco classic, the Inside the Shell Egg Scrambler. A woman would ask: How hard is it to scramble an egg by yourself?

Of course it's not hard to scramble an egg. The point is this baby scrambles an egg *inside* the shell! How cool is that? (Plus, while the egg scrambles itself, a man has his hands free for more important things, like scratching himself.)

Here's the deal with cooking: There's something about *watching* food cook that turns a guy on. It's the same impulse that drives guys to gather around the dryers in a Laundromat and watch their clothes tumble around. Men like looking through glass and seeing some action. That's why there are Peeping Toms, not Peeping Tinas. (Also, that explains the Super Bowl.)

I looked at that rotisserie on TV. I saw prime rib turning around, cooking before my eyes, sizzling, glistening, dripping—and I said, "I'VE GOT TO HAVE IT!"

"Of course you did," Nancy said. "It's boar on a spit. It's the caveman in you. You're encoded. This gizmo is the perfect confluence of a man's interest: large slabs of meat cooking in something that looks like a TV."

I couldn't have said it better myself. I'd watch anything cook on a spit, including George F. Will.

"You'll use it once and never again," Nancy warned.

"Once is fine. I've always wanted to make restaurant-quality prime rib at home," I said.

"Restaurants don't cook prime rib in a rotisserie, Tony. They use an oven. There are no Ronco products in restaurants."

What?! Not even the Electric Food Dehydrator and Yogurt Maker that "makes great beef jerky" and is "ideal for camping and hikers?" (Hiker-jerky?) Or the Popeil Automatic 5-Minute Pasta and Sausage Maker, where "one load feeds four?" (Gosh, I wish they wouldn't use the word "load.")

I told my friend Tom about my purchase. He was ecstatic.

"You know what's beautiful about a rotisserie?" he said. "You just rig it, turn it on, and stand back. It satisfies a man's most pressing culinary need—you can drink beer while you cook."

Tom learned his kitchen licks from his dad, who every now and then began bragging about the fabulous omelet he made. Everybody had to stand back in awe while he went to work. "When he was done, there were eighteen pots in the sink, which he left for my mom while we went to watch football."

I showed Tom the picture of my Ronco.

He looked at it reverently. "Of course you know there's no way in a million years this is actually going to work," he said. "Have you seen it in a store?"

"It's not available in stores," I said.

"Of course not. It's probably made out of tinfoil."

Oh, ye of little faith. You can scoff all you want. But when you have a Super Bowl party, and your life will be ruined if you can't rotisserie four chickens at once, you'll be calling and begging to use my quality Ronco product.

I could have bought more, you know. When I ordered the rotisserie, the operator didn't want me to stop at just one. She read from a prepared text of Ronco offers, and began each new item with the words "Ron wants you to have . . ." like we were buds, and he was in a generous mood.

I was offered marinades, rubs, meat racks, vegetable trays, thermometers, discounts for CDs, movie rentals, nasal hair remover, live iguanas, answers for the law boards; I'm pretty sure I heard the words "time share." In the end she told me I could get $30,000 worth of stuff for $29.95.

"Wouldn't you like Ron to send this to you?" she asked.

"No," I said. "But give Ron my best, and tell him we should do lunch some time. Rotisserie chicken, maybe?"

Scratched by the Cat

I recently bought a new car. I arrived at work the next day puffed with pride, because I finally owned a vehicle of class and dignity, a car that complements my personality.

One of the first people I ran into was my boss's boss's boss, a man of immense power and prestige, renowned for his judgment. I told him what I had purchased. He regarded me with a curious look, a look I had not seen before. I took it to be respect.

Then he started to laugh.

"What a dope," he said.

See, I bought a Cadillac.

When you are hurting in your soul, you seek solace from friends. I went to my friend Gino and explained what had happened with The B-B-Boss.

"You bought a Cadillac?" he said.

Uh, right.

"You're a jerk. I can understand someone of your age, pushing fifty, buying a Jaguar or a Lamborghini or even a lovingly restored 1972 powder blue Karmann Ghia. But a Cadillac? What can you possibly say in defense of a Cadillac—that it's the top of the line of General Motors? That's like ordering the best bottle of Yoo-hoo money can buy."

My car is the Catera, the new pint-size Caddy. I love it. Unfortunately, owning a Catera means you are stigmatized by driving a Cadillac without the attendant advantage of having a car so large and swinish it says to the world: "Hey, world, bite me, okay?"

That's what Cadillacs used to be like. My friend Mit has an old Cadillac, a Fudgsicle-brown 1976 Eldorado drop top. My Catera can fit comfortably in his trunk, which, by the way, has a power device that closes it automatically, on the assumption that the average 1976 Eldorado owner no longer possesses the upper-body strength to slam it shut, what with his walker and all.

Mit's car is eighteen and a half feet long, seven feet wide, and weighs just under three tons. I asked him, "Are you gonna drive it or christen it?"

Mit says: "It came with an eight-track tape player. So if you've got any Mantovani tapes . . ."

It's got a five-hundred-cubic-inch V-8 engine and a thirty-gallon tank, which gives Mit the opportunity to have the following conversation with a gas station attendant:

"Fill 'er up, sir?"

"Nah, just stop at forty dollars."

Unfortunately, the car gets six miles a gallon. There is no vehicle anywhere that gets worse gas mileage than Mit's Cadillac. Mir is more economical.

("I bought it on Earth Day," Mit said. "Everybody celebrates his own way.")

Mit's Caddy cuts a wide swath. "It uses a lot of lane, if you know what I mean," he said. "You pull behind a Miata—all they see in their rearview mirror is grille. They get reeeeall peppy when the light turns green."

That was the heyday of the Cadillac, of course. 1976. What depresses me about my new car is a recent article I read about how Cateras aren't selling. Worse, the people they are selling to are ancient.

Half of Catera's owners are at least sixty-five!

It must be the official pace car of Leisure World.

I had the same feeling a couple of years ago when I bought a Buick . . .

Of course! I remember now. You bought a Buick. You have a Buick and a Cadillac now. You and Bob Dole, right? Ladies and gentlemen, there is no reason to continue with this column. The man has a Buick and a Cadillac. That is ludicrous. Let us just buy him a pair of white shoes and a white belt, send him on a cruise and be done with him.

. . . and every time I'd see another Buick on the road, it was being driven by someone whose head didn't reach above the steering wheel. The people who bought Buicks were so old that one of the options on my LeSabre was a dashboard denture holder.

When people hear that I have a Cadillac, they naturally assume it is filled with ridiculous power options. This is a slander of me and my car. Sure, it has power steering and power brakes and power door locks and power windows and a power sun roof and power seat controls and power backrest positioning devices and power mirrors. But it's not like it has electrically heated seats for the wintertime warming of one's big soft American behind.

But Tony, it DOES have tush warmers.

Shhhhh.

They marketed the car as "the Caddy that zigs." But when you look at who's buying it, it's more like the Caddy that shuffles and kvetches. I may be the youngest person in America to buy a Catera.

Here's a true story: The other day I went through the carwash, and the guy in front of me looked at my car admiringly and said, "That's a Catera, right?"

He was my age, and he was driving a Mercedes C220, which goes for about the same price as the Catera.

"I'm thinking of buying a Catera," he said.

"You'll like it," I told him.

"Oh, not for me," he said. "For my father."

Bee All You Can Bee

My vacation is over. I devoted it to playing golf. I played golf every day. I played golf in Washington, Maryland, Virginia, West Virginia, New York, New Jersey, Pennsylvania, and Connecticut. I teed it up in every state there was a drought—hoping to get more roll on the fairway.

My goal was to get better at golf, and I am pleased to report two results:

1. I got better.
2. I still stink.

I still struggle to break 100. The ultimate goal among senior golfers is to shoot their age. I'm lucky to shoot my body temperature.

It's pathetic to shoot 100 when you've been playing golf as long as I have, fifteen years. My thirteen-year-old son, who started playing golf a couple of months ago, is already in the 80s. I expect my dog to break 90 by Wednesday.

"Maybe you ought to play tennis," my daughter said sweetly.

"If I can't hit a golf ball that's sitting still, what chance would I have with a moving tennis ball?" I asked her.

I don't get it. I bought the best equipment. I bought the best shoes. You oughta see my golf shirts.

So it's gotta be me, right?

I am my own handicap, hahaha.

(That's a golf joke. So is this: Two guys are on the fourteenth tee one afternoon when they notice a funeral procession going by the golf course. One of the men takes off his hat and bows his head. Moved by this unusual display of respect, his playing partner inquires politely, "You knew the deceased?" The man nods, then hits his tee shot and says, "We would have been married thirty years today." *Bada-bing*.)

Anyway, my golf story concerns the time a few weeks ago that I played golf in Gettysburg, Pennsylvania. There were four of us: Me, my friends Johnny and Fred, and Johnny's friend Jack. Jack was the biggest hitter of the bunch, and he'd just hit a huge drive on the sixth hole when disaster struck: Taking a big gulp from a can of soda, Jack swallowed a bee, which stung him in the throat on the way down!

Jack immediately began coughing violently, trying to expel the bee. But it was too late. The bee was already on its way to his stomach.

"What should I do?" Jack asked all of us.

"Are you allergic to bee stings?" Johnny asked.

"I don't know," Jack said.

"Well, are you swelling up?" Johnny asked.

"No. Not yet anyway," Jack said.

Jack looked at us. We looked at Jack.

I didn't know Jack well at all. But he looked okay to me. And we'd driven over an hour to play at this course, which was really nice. And it was such a lovely day. And we were only on the sixth hole. And we had paid nearly one hundred dollars for the round. And me, personally, I was hitting my five-wood great. So I said, "Let's keep playing."

I mean, what's the worst that could have happened? Jack dies, right? Then we'd have had to drag him hole to hole until we finished the round. But as my friend Denis says, "That's why there are two seats in a golf cart."

So we played on, and finished all eighteen holes.

Jack was still hitting big drives, but by the end of the round, he was having trouble breathing. Jack's left side began to swell up on No. 16. He said he could feel himself expanding, like a balloon. A couple of times he wondered if he should stop playing, in case he risked having a heart seizure. But Jack was a real trouper. He even made a few pars on the back nine, after he stopped coughing.

Which I really appreciated, because Jack and I were partners, and I couldn't putt for squat.

After the round, we stopped at the grill and ordered lunch, but in consideration of Jack's medical condition, we told them to wrap it "to go" then took Jack to the emergency room in Gettysburg.

I told this story to my friends Nancy and Susan, and they were aghast that we finished the round—and ordered lunch.

"Guys are unbelievable," Susan said. "If these had been women playing, we would have driven her to the emergency room immediately. The only thing that could have stopped us was a good sale."

"How could you not go straight to the hospital as soon as your friend got that bee sting?" Nancy asked.

"Because there was no hospital between Number 6 and Number 7," I said.

Women! I mean, it's not like Jack got his foot caught in a fairway mower.

(Did I mention how well I was hitting my five-wood?)

So we took Jack to the hospital, and they kept him under observation in the emergency room for three hours to make sure he wasn't suffering toxicity. Jack phoned his wife to explain he'd swallowed a bee, and he wouldn't be home for a while. Twice he had to ask her to stop laughing.

Jack didn't want us to wait for him; he said he'd take a cab home, which I thought was a real nice gesture on his part, because if we left then, we'd have been back in Washington by 3:30, and we could have gotten in another eighteen before dark. But a cab from Gettysburg to Washington would've probably cost a hundred dollars. So we waited for him.

"That's the least you could do," Nancy said. "Was there anything good to read in the waiting room?"

"How should I know?" I said. "We had three hours to kill. We went into town and toured the battlefields and had some ice cream."

"You left him alone in the emergency room?" Nancy asked in horror.

"Sure," I said.

"Are you crazy? You *never* leave somebody alone in an emergency room. You never, ever leave the waiting room. Because when you come back, they're gone! And nobody knows where they are."

I know where I'd be. In the rough.

And Come out Swinging

I can talk about it now. Now that I haven't killed anyone.

That was my great fear as I stepped to the first tee—killing somebody on the course. There's got to be like, what, a two-stroke penalty for that?

Last week I played in a nine-hole charity match with three professional golfers at the Kemper Open.

Three pros.

And me.

Grant Waite, Billy Andrade, and Tommy Armour III, the grandson of the legendary golfer Tommy Armour, the "Silver Scot," who died in 1968—and could *still* beat me. Among them, they have more than $9.5 million in career winnings.

I once won a $2 Nassau from a one-legged man, and I had to sink a ten-footer on 18 to do it.

I have a 22 handicap. I am not Tiger Woods. I am *in* the woods.

Oh, did I mention the *gallery*?

Yes, two hundred people lining the fairways to watch us play. It's one thing to trust a pro's accuracy. But the only way spectators could guarantee safety around me would be to stand in the *middle* of the fairway.

There I was on the first tee, my legs shaking. There was a pool of water at the base of my spine that could fill the Grand Coulee Dam. The sole reason I wore long pants was so nobody could see the *drip-drip-drip* down my leg. I chose a pewter shirt, to coordinate with my ashen complexion.

"Is there anything you need?" a tournament official asked me.

"I need a catheter," I said.

It's not like I hadn't been warned against doing this. My friend Mike Lupica, the big-shot New York sports columnist, had called and said, "I did this last year, and I was shivering in my shoes. And I'm a good golfer. I've played with you, Tony. You're rancid. You'll make a fool of yourself. Get out of it now. Tell them you're having a liver transplant."

If that wasn't enough, I'd talked to Joe Jacoby, the Redskins' great lineman. Joe is six feet seven and 325 pounds. Week after week, year after year, he was in hand-to-hand combat with the biggest, strongest men in the NFL. He is fearless. He said to me, "I did this once. On the first tee, I was so frightened I thought I was gonna heave."

Yet there I was on the first tee for all the world to see, shaking like Tina Turner—only looking less appealing.

My friend Monty was caddying for me. He told me to take a deep breath and "think positive swing thoughts."

"Okay. I think I can. I think I can . . . avoid killing anyone. With luck, I'll just maim them."

So the pros have already hit from the back tees, which are located in the general vicinity of Nebraska. Three towering drives down the middle. I'm teeing off a cab ride in front of them. I call out to the crowd, "I'm a twenty-two, boys and girls. Get ready to scatter."

They laughed. Nervously.

"Slow backswing, and keep your head down. You'll do fine," Monty told me.

Instead, all the failures of my life flashed before my eyes—all the way back to seventh grade, when Denise Levine refused to play Seven Minutes in Heaven with me. (The tart was holding out for Lloyd Glauberman.)

I did everything wrong. I swung way too fast, and I jerked my head up like someone had just hollered, "Look, there goes Anna Kournikova!"

The ball squirted dead left into grass that hadn't been mowed since disco was king.

"Mulligan!" I shouted, and the people echoed, "Mulligan!"

The second ball I hit solidly, though way off line, somewhere to the right of Tom DeLay. I don't want to say the rough where I landed was deep, but I found Amelia Earhart in there. By the time I got the ball back near the fairway, the pros had already finished No. 1 and were on the tee at No. 2.

I didn't hit a single shot onto the fairway in the first three holes! I crisscrossed the terrain so many times I felt like Lewis and Clark.

Grant Waite, who's Australian, went wading calf-deep in the rough looking for my ball and said with a big grin, "Where I come from, they call this the outback."

Just what I needed, Crocodile Nicklaus.

I was so frustrated and embarrassed, I went into the crowd to get my son Michael to hit a shot for me. But apparently I had embarrassed him, too. As I approached, he said, "Get away from me. Who *are* you? Somebody call the cops!"

Finally, on the fourth hole, I hit a drive straight.

"What happened?" Andrade asked me.

"I think the drugs kicked in," I said.

I got to the green in four shots. Andrade was there in two, looking over a twelve-foot putt. "Can you give me a good read?" he asked.

"Tuesdays with Morrie," I said.

The fifth hole was my shining moment. I hit a good drive, with a 9-iron shot left to the green. Then with Monty lining me up—I had initially aimed myself into a guy's backyard—I hit a shot as pure as Heaven. It landed four feet from the flag and stuck there like a dart. I walked to the green on a cloud. The gallery cheered. I thought: This is what the Anti-Hillary, Rick Lazio, must have felt like just before he fell on his face in the Memorial Day parade and split open his lip.

I begged the pros for a "gimme."

It was a charity match. (All I wanted was a little charity!) Whoever won each hole got one thousand dollars for his favorite nonprofit.

"I'll split the money with you if this is a 'gimme,' " I said.

They said no.

"I'll *give* you the money," I said.

They made me putt.

I tried to force good swing thoughts into my head, but all I could think of was the Pamela Anderson–Tommy Lee tape. Which caused me to perspire even more.

I stood over the ball longer than *Battlefield Earth* was in the theaters. Finally, I swung my putter. The ball went left but caught the hole in time, rolled around and down. I'd made a birdie and won the hole from three pros in front of two hundred people.

I was the happiest journalist in the world. Well, maybe just behind that guy who married Sharon Stone.

Someone in the gallery called out, "What's the secret of your success?"

"I wear women's clothing," I said.

Scuffed Links

Once again I was invited to play in a nine-hole Celebrity Skins match with three pro golfers a couple of days before the start of the Kemper Open. The reason I got chosen as the "celebrity" was because Jim "What's in It for Me?" Jeffords's Labrador retriever, Strom, turned them down.

I got to the driving range early. I hoped that hitting a few buckets of balls would calm me down. I don't want to say that I was nervous, but when I asked why my drives weren't going very far, my caddie pointed out, "You didn't take the head cover off, Einstein."

There were about twenty-five golf pros hitting, and I wanted to get as far away from them as possible. I'm a 20 handicap, which means if you're standing anywhere near me when I swing, you've got a fifty-fifty shot of needing CPR. Unfortunately, the only open spot was next to two-time U.S. Open champion Lee Janzen, who had no clue that they'd let civilians onto the range. I nodded to him and started spraying four-irons. No two of them went in the same direction. My shot pattern looked like the walls in Linda Blair's bedroom.

When I finished, Lee was gone. Later a marshal told me this story: "Lee Janzen came up to me and said, 'I need security.' When I asked him what he needed security for, he said, 'There's a guy next to me on the range, and he must be a twenty!' "

Lee Janzen was afraid of *me*! He takes one look at my swing and he calls security. Maybe he was scared it was catching, like foot fungus. But give him credit for knowing a 20 when he sees one, boys and girls. That's why he's a professional.

I wasn't going to be humiliated. I boldly took a few more swings, unearthing a couple of divots the size of dinner plates, then walked to the first tee to meet the pros I'd be playing with. (By the way, the range balls—which are usually so beat up they look like they tried to hold out on Paulie Walnuts—were brand-new Titleist Pro V1s. Pro V1s *rule*! They go about twenty yards farther than most balls. The guys where I play refer to them as "Viagra balls." They cost at least six dollars apiece. I stuffed three in my pocket. Had I thought I could get away with it, I'd have poured a whole bucket down my pants and walked around like Marty Feldman in *Young Frankenstein*.)

I made some changes to my game this year. Most important, I wore darker clothing so it was harder to see the stains from my flop sweat. And believe me, I was sweating—especially when I found out one of the pros I was playing with was John Daly, who is so long even Clarence Thomas won't play with him. So much water collected at the base of my spine you could have held the three-meter springboard competition on my behind.

My son, Michael, couldn't believe it. "You're playing with John Daly!" I almost had to revive him. Later he told me: "I was scared for you. I was afraid he'd get a bogey and you'd say something ruthlessly sarcastic, and he'd spear you with the flagstick. I'd be fatherless. Then I couldn't go to the country club anymore—because *you're* the member."

It turned out Daly was great fun. When he found out a gathering thunderstorm would reduce the match to six holes, Daly said, "Let's just play one and go eat."

The other pros with me were Bradley Hughes and my partner from last year, Grant Waite, whom I really like. Grant saw me top a shot, maybe twenty-five feet, and remarked to the gallery, "I recognize that shot. Then again, I played with Tony last year." Grant remembered my travails on No. 2: "We lost him for a while. He went into the woods and didn't come out. He showed up on No. 3 tee, and we welcomed him back with a fruit basket."

A lot of people wished me well. They said they'd followed me around last year. Which explains why they were wearing helmets. *Bada-boom.*

My proudest moment was when I teed off on the first hole and hit it in the fairway. I thought I actually heard somebody yell, "You da man!" Though looking at my legs it's possible he said, "Get a tan!" Last year I yanked my tee shot sixty yards dead left into rough so thick you could lose your Senate majority in it. My son was walking behind two guys who were amazed at my improvement. "At least he got off the tee," they said. "Last year he was so terrible we thought they'd send a ranger out and pull him off the course."

Sadly, I hit my second shot into sand, and I couldn't get out. The same thing happened to me on the next hole, too. I spent more time in the sand than the Kuwaiti National Guard. But let me tell you about Daly. The pros play No. 2 at 615 yards, the longest hole on the course. Without even taking a practice swing, Daly blasted his tee shot 310. The ball could be heard yelping in pain. If Mir had a trajectory like this, it'd still be up there.

Meanwhile, I'm in the sand. I ask Daly what I should do. Daly has now seen me swing maybe five times. He pulls out his cell phone and calls, "Security!"

I top a five-wood and barely get out of the trap. I hit it again. And again. I'm laying 4 and I haven't even *seen* Daly's ball yet.

I ask Daly, "How far am I?"

Daly laughs. "You don't have that club. It hasn't been invented yet."

We finally get to Daly's ball. He didn't even set his feet—he just hit it three hundred yards while he was *moving*! Like he was playing polo. Next time maybe he'll hit it from a horse. The course was wet, so Daly got no roll, and he was five yards from the green in two. Then, approaching his ball like he was hurrying to take advantage of the Rudy Giuliani *Three's Company* Memorial Day Weekend Package, Daly nonchalantly chipped to within a foot of the hole.

If the rain hadn't come then, I have no doubt he'd have birdied No. 3 while walking on his hands and eating a meatloaf sandwich.

I felt so cowed and insignificant beside him. But then I thought, *Sure, but can he write quality airline poop jokes?*

My Berlin Call

The world needs a new Isaiah Berlin. Let it be me.

Berlin, the noted Oxford scholar, died recently. He was very famous. Well, okay, I never heard of him—I thought maybe *Irving* Berlin died again—but he must have been a huge deal because *The New York Times* front-paged his obit and filled up a whole inside page with praise: "Sir Isaiah defied classification . . . a bon vivant, a sought-after conversationalist. Sir Isaiah seemed to know almost everyone worth knowing in the twentieth century. Freud, Nehru, Stravinsky, Boris Pasternak, T. S. Eliot, W. H. Auden, Chaim Weizmann, Virginia Woolf, Aldous Huxley, Bertrand Russell, and Felix Frankfurter."

(Yeah, but was he ever on *Larry King Live,* like Kato Kaelin?)

I want an obit like that. Of course, I don't know that I can measure up to Sir Isaiah. He *knew* Nehru and Frankfurter. I've worn one, eaten the other.

He defied classification. In the '60s I simply tried to *avoid* classification.

What a life Sir Isaiah led. Eating. Drinking. Partying. Schmoozing. He was like Sammy Davis Jr., but with two good eyes.

I need to change my life. The way it's going now, my obit will run just below the one that said: "J. W. Tinklepaugh, fifty-one, died recently while attempting to give himself a colonoscopy. Mr. Tinklepaugh was employed in the fast-growing amusement field as a coin changer. He spent much of his spare time at a Laundromat. He once bowled a 194. Funeral arrangements are pending, as no one has claimed his body yet."

Sadly, I have no bona fides as a bon vivant. Last week *People* came out with its list of the world's sexiest men, and I wasn't on it.

Again. In fact, there wasn't one fat white bald guy on it. Not even Marlin Fitzwater!

George Clooney was named the Sexiest Man Alive. (Although I think there was a write-in for Sir Isaiah from the Queen Mum.) What does Clooney have that I don't? I mean other than his fabulous Batman suit, a starring role on *ER*, chiseled good looks, and a coterie of drooling babes?

(But how about his mind? Does he know the capital of Missouri? Did he ever play Yahtzee with Sir Isaiah Berlin?)

People also named its runner-up ten, divided into categories. Sexiest Explorer: someone named Jerry Linenger, whose apparent qualification is that he spent 133 days aboard Mir, and none of the toilets exploded while he was up there. Sexiest Businessman: The guy from Virgin Atlantic, Richard Branson, photographed in a terry-cloth robe that he apparently picked up at Hugh Hefner's pad. Sexiest Royal (a short list): Prince Felipe of Spain, who's pictured wearing a puka shell necklace. (Phil, sweetheart, it's the '90s. Don't they have calendars in Spain?) Sexiest Anchor: Matt Lauer, who ought to thank God for his spinal cord, or else his head would float away like a balloon. Sexiest Author: Serial Shirt Remover and Tree Cutter Sebastian Junger. Etc.

So I'm not sexy. And though I talk a lot, nobody has ever called me a "sought-after conversationalist." Often at home when I begin talking, the room clears out. I am human Glade.

I do have my own radio show. Hundreds tune in. My audience is full of deep thinkers and beguiling conversationalists. Here's an example.

Me: You're on the air.

Caller: Yeah, I wanna fire the football coach. He's a moron. I hate his offense. I hate his defense. He's a moron. A monkey could come in here and do a better job. My dog knows more about football than this moron.

Me: I gather you think he's deficient in some areas.

Caller: He's a freaking moron.

Me: And what qualifies you as a football expert?

Caller: I drive a beer truck.

I used to imagine ways of making my résumé more urbane. All the news about the British au pair last week reminded me that I used to think that having an au pair was an extremely sophisticated thing. My main reason for having children was so I could hire an au pair. I loved saying "au pair." It sounded so continental. I believe it means "jailbait" in French.

I would set very high standards for my au pair. Education, ambition, and love of children would be important, of course. But foremost, my au pair would have to be Scandinavian. She'd also have to answer a detailed questionnaire, including "What I want to do most in America is . . ."

Correct answer: ". . . fold underwear in the basement with the man of the house."

So where am I? What's my obit going to look like?

"Anthony Irwin Kornheiser died a broken man, trying to be the next Isaiah Berlin. He never went to Oxford. He was never sexy. He never had an au pair. And the only person who ever called him 'Sir' was a kid working at McDonald's."

Go Ahead, Make My Career

A dam Clymer, you lucky dog.

Clymer is the *New York Times* reporter whom George W. Bush called a "major league [rhymes with glass bowl]" into a live microphone on a campaign stop.

How great is that?

Not only does the possible next president of the United States know your name—but the guy says you're major league. Major league! Wow.

"I didn't know there was a league," my friend Cindy said.

It was all most people wanted to talk about last week. Day after day there was another story about Adam Clymer. What Clymer said in rebuttal. What Clymer's friends say about him. How the journalistic community is reacting to this attack on Clymer. It's a career maker. One day he's just another stooge with a notebook, and the next he's major league. From now on, Clymer will be everywhere. First Elián. Then Darva. Then Rich. Now Adam Clymer.

Enough already about Clymer.

How do I turn this into something about me?

I've got the credentials.

I'm a *gaping* glass bowl.

Ask my friends. Ask my kids. They'll tell you. They'll sign affidavits.

I don't know if I'm major league, but I'm damn sure Triple-A.

I'd give anything to be insulted by the next president—Bush or Gore. I don't care. Though it's beginning to look like Gore, isn't it? (I mean, as long as Clinton keeps making long trips to Gabookistan, or some other chicken-poop-intensive Fourth World paradise.) Suddenly, Gore *looks* presidential. It's time to give Naomi Wolf props for this alpha male jive. It's not easy for a fifty-two-year-old man to put on blue jeans and a polo shirt and not look like a fat yuppie poseur. It's scary when Joe Lieberman does it. His shoulders sag. He wears his belt so high you might think it was a heart monitor. Lieberman looks like he's going to Seniors Singles Night at a condo in Boca Raton. Gore is genuinely studly. Who knew? In the end it may turn out the most important choice he made wasn't his vice president, but his personal trainer.

On the other hand, Bush is shrinking before our eyes. He's looking small and pinched. And Dick Cheney—what a toady. It's one thing for George W. Bush to call Clymer a major league glass bowl. Bush is the big banana. But for Cheney to pipe up like Rootie Kazootie, "Oh, yeah . . . big time" is snarky. All Cheney did was pile on. Come on, Dickie, find your own journalist to smear.

Like me!

I'll tell you this: If one of these guys ever sprayed the magic word in my direction, I wouldn't respond with restraint like Adam Clymer. He was so far up the high road, the oxygen masks deployed. All Clymer said was, "I am disappointed in the governor's language." And this was after Bush refused to apologize for calling Clymer a glass bowl—only that anybody heard it!

I don't know jack about Clymer. (Or should I say, I don't know him from Adam?) I've never met him. Maybe his hands are tied by working for the *Times,* and he can't milk this fat cow. But I would.

I'd sell T-shirts with my face on the front, and on the back a picture of my backside, and the words MAJOR LEAGUE. I'd write a book titled *From One . . . to Another.*

I always envied the journalists who made the Nixon "enemies list." As a veteran sportswriter I've had run-ins with athletes. In a rage, a player for the New York Yankees once threatened to cut off a sensitive part of my anatomy—which he identified as my "tentacles." (This same genius once confided to me that he feared contracting "vizerial disease." I assured him that only happened to viziers.)

But let's face it, being abused by athletes is only one slimy step above being abused by reporters. Just the other day in *The New York Times Magazine* I was referred to as "a kvetching columnist for *The Washington Post* who had gained a surprisingly strong following for his show on ESPN Radio."

Kvetching? Me? How can anybody say that? Do I strike you as a chronic complainer? Show me a single column I've ever written that expressed the slightest dissatisfaction with anything. I'm Mary Freakin' Sunshine. Calling me "kvetching" is ludicrous.

("Maybe it was a typo," my editor said. "Maybe he meant to write 'fetching.' ")

And how about the phrase "surprisingly strong following"? Like I'm a complete no-talent, and anybody who listens to my show must be the first person in his family to walk upright.

But being insulted by some freelance writer won't get me anywhere.

I need some kahuna to go after me like Bush went after Adam Clymer.

The closest I've come so far is that some years back at a formal dinner George W. Bush's mom, Barbara, called me "Mister Porthauser." I didn't think she meant anything bad by it. But in retrospect perhaps she did. Like mother, like son? Maybe she called me a "major league Porthauser."

It's all coming back to me now. I recall President Bush speaking to me next, and this was right after Barbara made the "Porthauser" comment. All these years I thought he'd said, "Care for some wine?" But he probably said, "Oh yeah . . . big time."

Food for Thought

After careful consideration, I have decided to pursue other employment.

(What will you miss most? My charm? My wit? The crotch jokes?)

It's not that I dislike being a professional sportswriter and (alleged) humor columnist. I am happy in my work. But my dream job has recently come open.

Phyllis Richman, *The Washington Post*'s distinguished restaurant critic, is retiring.

And all I can say is: Let the big dog eat.

Being a restaurant critic is a physically demanding job. Virtually every night you need to stay awake through long dinners at fine restaurants. You need to have good teeth to chew USDA choice steak. You need to be ambidextrous to use either hand to signal your waiter to bring another expensive bottle of imported wine. Occasionally you are even called upon to speak and say things like "More gravy, hoss."

Herewith is my application for the job of restaurant critic. My sample restaurant review, in twenty-five words or fewer:

"The waiter brought the bread, which was impudently crusty without being overbearingly crispy. The warm butter was irresistibly insouciant, reminding me of a French girl's . . ."

Oh, well, that's twenty-five.

I can't say that I have been encouraged in my pursuit of the restaurant critic's job. One objection seems to be the notion that I don't know jack about food.

Look at me. I weigh 215 pounds, 165 of which are gathered

around my middle like a goiter. Of course I know about food. I eat five meals a day. Not including the bags of Cheez Doodles.

Another objection stems from the fear that I will be too easily recognized. Restaurant critics are supposed to blend in and not be known, so they'll pay the same prices and get the same service as any schmo walking in off the street.

How stupid is that?

I *want* to be recognized in the restaurant. I want to be FEARED by the staff when I walk in the door. I want people to bend over backward to cater to my every whim. I am ANTHONY IRWIN KORNHEISER, dammit, and you had better valet my car and treat me like I hold your genitals in my hands. Got that, food boy?

The essence of my reviews wouldn't be to tell you whether a restaurant was good enough for a schmo like you. Why would I care if you liked the place? I don't know you. You can eat at Sac o' Burgers, for all I care.

The essence of my reviews would be: Was this place good enough for ME?

I want my friends to drink and eat with me, and get rowdy and smash wineglasses against the walls. What is the point of being a restaurant critic of a major metropolitan newspaper if you can't trash the joint and get your friends free food? There are two words a big-shot restaurant critic should never utter: "Check, please."

(This reminds me of the time I went to the Palm, and some up-tight gastroenterologist told me that my friends and I were making too much noise for him to hear the medical lecture in the next room. What a putz. And what a scam—trying to get a tax write-off for a pricey dinner by claiming, "I attended a medical lecture!" If I had been the restaurant critic, I'd have gone straight to the maître d' and insisted that the doctor and all the members of his party be immediately stripped to their shorts and tossed into the street or I'd tell *tout* Washington that the Palm's baby asparagus lacked a certain je ne sais quoi. That's power, baby.)

The one thing that worries me about being a restaurant critic is that I like to go to bed early. I don't really want to be eating dinner past eight o'clock, and unfortunately that's when they serve it. I'm sure the better restaurants will have no objection to just dropping their food off on my porch so I can eat it at my convenience.

So you don't think I know nothing about food, I asked my friend Nancy to give me a pop quiz. Here it is:

1. What is demi-glace?

Demi Moore's sister.

2. What is a galangal?

Another easy one. Those scenes in certain movies that men really like to watch despite the fact that no male actors are involved.

3. What is pho, pronounced "fuh"?

I didn't know that. I told Nancy to phogettaboutit.

At this point, I probably should state my philosophy of restaurant reviewing. I plan to have a rating system that incorporates up to twenty-five smiley faces—because I can't imagine anything more embarrassing to a really expensive restaurant than having to display a favorable review that awards large smiley faces.

Pay attention: I'm not crazy about restaurants that are obsessed with "presentation." I've come here to eat, not decorate my house. So when I order a chicken dish, don't bring me a plate with a piece of chicken the size of a guppy surrounded by a "drizzle" of drops of some fruit sauce. Look, I don't care if the plate looks like it's spent the last six weeks hanging in the Louvre—just bring me some damn food! And another drink too, okay, honey?

And another thing: I will review only steak houses. All I eat is steak. Maybe an occasional prime rib for variety. But mainly steak. Oh, and bread with real butter. Not a foo-foo flavored whipped butter. Who do I look like, Niles Crane? Real butter. Lots of it. Chop-chop. You can keep the vegetables. Give them to homeless people. They need the vitamins. It's tough sleeping on a grate.

So I will review steak houses. Downtown steak houses. I don't go to the suburbs. You think Mister Tony is going to eat in a mall? Phogettaboutit!

I won't review foreign restaurants either. I feel inadequate in foreign restaurants that insist on printing the menu in their native language. I once went into a Greek restaurant and said to the waiter, "Oh, this looks good." And it turned out I'd ordered the "coat check."

Honestly, I can't see eating blood sausage or soup made out of bird saliva. And who am I to judge that one cat tastes better than another? Let their own people do that is my feeling.

That's it.

Let's eat.

Double Jeopardy

I can't talk to you now.

I'm busy talking to Herb Stempel, who you might remember was a celebrated quiz show contestant of the 1950s.

I mentioned Mr. Stempel in a recent column about the megahit quiz show *Who Wants to Be a Millionaire.* And it seems I was not, technically, totally accurate in referring to him. So I called him in New York City to apologize.

"I wrote 'Stemple,' with *le* at the end," I said.

"It's S-t-e-m-p-e-l," he said.

"I also wrote that you appeared on *The $64,000 Question*," I said.

"No, it was *Twenty-One*," Mr. Stempel said.

"There's one other tiny item."

"Oh?"

"I, um, I said you were dead. Hahaha. Isn't that a riot? Um, Mr. Stempel, you're not laughing."

Let us review:

I spelled the man's name wrong. I got his claim to fame wrong. And I said he was currently dead when he was alive. I hit the trifecta!

Oh, baby. Do you want to hand me my Pulitzer now, or will you mail it? That's K-o-r-n-h-e-i-s-e-r.

Anybody can spell a name wrong. As a matter of fact, the reason I misspelled Stempel's name is because my friend Gino peeked at the column as I was composing it and tried to save me embarrassment by telling me, "You've got the guy's name wrong." At the time, I was calling him "Herb Stuckler."

Gino said, "It's Stemple, you idiot."

My friend Nancy warned me I had the wrong quiz show, and though I generally value Nancy's counsel enormously, I figured she's just a chick. What does she know?

The thing about Herb being dead? That was all *moi.*

A lot of you are probably wondering how a prizewinning columnist could make such a stunning series of mistakes. You're probably saying: "Jeez, Tony, don't you check anything?"

What do I look like, a freakin' database?

I should explain the sophisticated journalistic process I go through while producing this column: I write something I think might be true, such as, "Herb Stemple made a bundle of dough on *The $64,000 Question,* and now he's dead as a doornail." Then I walk outside my office and I yell at whomever is around, "Hey! Anybody? Herb Stemple, the guy on the quiz shows forty-five years ago—alive or dead?"

I literally mean "anybody." It could be somebody fixing the copy machine, or a Japanese tour group. I don't care. If nobody says, "Alive! He's in my bowling league," then I go with my gut, and my gut said: Dead.

I mean, come on, the guy was on TV in the 1950s. The sets looked like *aquariums.* Nobody got out of those alive.

True, I have access to up-to-the-minute online resources. I could get most of the information I need from my own computer. But I'm so pathetically technophobic I don't even know how to score porn! So I have perfected an open-the-door-and-holler approach to research. I am well known for this. In fact, my friend Tracee keeps a list of some of the questions I have asked recently, which include, and I quote verbatim:

"What was an event before the 1600s that was famous and that involved only one person, like Martin Luther nailing the proclamation to the church door—but not that?"

"Who's blind that you can make fun of?"

"You know the thing that goes, 'Mine eyes have seen the glory yada-yada-yada'? What's that called?"

My mistakes about Herb Stempel could have been far worse. It would be inexcusable, for example, if I ever identified Joan of Arc as "that minx who drowned in a motorboat accident in the Yucatán."

But what I did was bad enough to warrant this embarrassing correction. (Of course, I'd prefer to be writing a correction like: "Lord Alfred Beckwith DeBootay, the English nobleman whose descendants invented cream cheese, was mistakenly referred to as the eighth Earl of Shropshire. He was the seventh.")

I've thought about trying to wiggle out of this. I could say, "What's the big deal? So I had some guy dead, and he's alive. So sue me! Hahaha. Hey, I'm a humor writer. Nobody believes the crap I write. Here, I'll demonstrate: Woodrow Wilson was gay."

Or I could say, "So what if Herb Stempel is alive? I was talking about Herb *Stemple*! Have we heard from *him* yet?"

And, of course, I thought about claiming David Broder wrote it.

I have to admit this whole episode has humbled me, made me more tolerant of imperfection in others. I used to go ballistic when anybody made a mistake at *my* expense. I won't be so quick to judge people again. Oh, excuse me for a second—that's my doorbell.

"Hey, hold on, pal. This is pepperoni. I ordered *green pepper*. What, you were smoking so much dope you grabbed the wrong box? Green pepper. Got it? Maybe remembering both a color and a food group was too tough for you. Now go back and get me the pizza I ordered before I call your parole officer!"

Hi, I'm back. Where were we?

Anyway, I called Herb Stempel, and he was great. We chatted for a while. I asked him about the quiz shows nowadays.

He told me about watching *Jeopardy!* a year ago and being appalled at how easy the questions were: "For a thousand dollars they asked, 'What is the capital of Paraguay?' That was a romp!"

There was silence on my end.

"Asunción," Herb said.

Oh, yeah, sure.

"*TV Guide* called me recently," Herb continued. "They gave me sample questions from this *Millionaire* show. For a million dollars they asked: Who was Sissy Spacek's cousin? And the choices were: Cliff Robertson, Wilford Brimley, Rip Torn, and Jack Lemmon."

Herb paused. He might have been waiting for me to answer. But I was still trying to spell "Asunción." I thought the capital of Paraguay was Paraguay City.

"It's Rip Torn," Herb said. "They're both from Texas."

Who didn't know that?

I thanked Herb for his time, and apologized again for my mistakes.

"I guess I got you confused with Charles Van Doren, who is dead," I said.

"No he's not," Stempel said.

Hey! Anybody? Charlie Van Doren, dead or alive?

Optical Delusions

For some years now my eyesight has been declining to the point where I am unable to read anything in close range—and by "close range" I mean anything in the same room with me. I suffer from a condition known as presbyopia, an ophthalmological term for "Willard's going to be announcing your birthday soon."

I am still excellent at reading large green overhead road signs, so you can take me on trips. Sadly, they don't print the dosage instructions for Zantac on large green overhead road signs. So last year my friend Nancy gave me a pair of nonprescription reading glasses (referred to technically as "old-people glasses") that she had bought for herself off a rack in a drugstore. They made me look like a member of a bowling league in Akron, but at least I could read typefaces smaller than TURNPIKE NEXT EXIT 1 MI.

When those glasses broke I went for an eye exam to get real glasses. And I was introduced to an "eyewear fashion consultant," who said she would design glasses that would be "customized to my face shape, coloring, and lifestyle needs."

"How would you describe your face shape?" she asked me.

"Like a potato," I said. "Or possibly an eggplant."

"How would you describe your lifestyle?"

"I spend most of my day obsessed with my own tedious problems, my fear of failure, and looming death," I said. "You got any glasses that will make me look like Woody Allen in *Annie Hall*? Or perhaps somewhat Norwegian?"

I tried on roughly 681 frames. Amazingly, no matter what their shape or color, I still looked like a fat, white, bald guy in glasses.

"I see you in something sleek and intellectual," the consultant said.

"You mean like a Lexus with a Harvard sticker?" I said.

She chose frames that were almost square, with a kind of an up-sweep "to match the contour of your face." (That turniplike contour, I think she meant.) They had that Elaine Benes stylishly small feel. I decided to order the blue-tinted lenses that get darker in sunlight, because I thought they were really cool, and they might make me attractive to a fifty-year-old woman with astigmatism. I also made my consultant promise to send me a customized "idiot chain," so I could wear the glasses around my neck. That way I wouldn't misplace them, sit on them, and squash them within an hour.

She said my glasses would arrive in the mail within a week. But they never came.

Six months passed. My vision got worse. One night I was watching television, holding what I thought was the remote. Much to my children's amusement, I was trying to change channels with a Nokia cell phone.

So I called and asked, "What happened to my glasses?"

"You never got them?"

"No."

"Are you sure? Have you looked?"

"Have I looked? Even if they *were* in my house, at this point I couldn't see them anyway."

Turned out, the original glasses were lost during delivery. So now I was going to get that pair and a new pair—two pair for the price of one!

When they arrived, I proudly modeled them for my pals at work. I stood in front of my friend Nancy, eager to see the look on her face—except when I put the glasses on I couldn't see her face. It was a blur.

"Those glasses are hideous," she said. "And they don't seem to be helping you see."

I moved backward to try to get her in focus.

From a certain distance, at a certain angle, the new glasses helped me see more clearly—but I had to cock my head the way my dog does upon hearing dry food being poured into her dish.

Nancy stared at me, shaking her head slowly.

"It's not you," she said. "It's just not you."

"Who is it? Is it someone better than me?" I asked hopefully.

My boss, George, came out of his office to get a look. George wears glasses with the approximate thickness of a bridge abutment. George's eyes are so bad that he doesn't actually see things, he sniffs them.

George was wiping his glasses as he looked at me in my new glasses and pronounced them "good."

I smiled at Nancy in triumph.

Then George put on his glasses, looked at me, and began laughing in wild, uncontrollable seal barks.

I felt awful. They hated my glasses. They hated my dainty ebony-link idiot chain. ("Where are the rhinestones?" Nancy asked.) They hated my Hollywood blue-tinted lenses.

"I'll have you know these glasses were picked out by a woman who's a fashion consultant," I told Nancy.

"Really? Well, she picked out very womanly glasses for you. You look like Mrs. Doubtfire."

(Actually, as my friend Gino later remarked, "Mrs. Doubtfire's glasses are more manly than yours.")

I pointed out to my colleagues that I was getting *two* for the price of one.

"How much did they cost?" Nancy wanted to know.

"Two hundred forty-one dollars," I said.

"You're a complete sap." Nancy took off her glasses and handed them to me. "Try these."

They were perfect. Womanly, yes, but I was used to that by now—and I could *see*. I didn't have to cock my head like a deaf beagle.

"Ten bucks," she said. "Aisle four, near the shampoos. You can't miss it. There's a huge overhead sign."

On the Line: My Reputation

Here's the highlight of my week: I was a lifeline on *Who Wants to Be a Millionaire.*

I was a "phone-a-friend" for a guy who not only isn't my friend, I don't even know him! His name is Ken Krantz, and he reads my columns. Out of the blue I got a fax from him asking me if I'd be his "phone-a-friend" in sports, an area where he felt weak. (I didn't know how weak. This is how weak: I asked Ken what he thought of a possible Michael Jordan comeback. He said, "He's never been the same since leaving Tito, Jermaine, Marlon, Jackie, and La Toya.")

Apparently you're allowed five "phone-a-friends," designated in advance.

This got me thinking whom I would choose to be my "phone-a-friend." Obviously, Catherine Zeta-Jones. I don't care if she doesn't know squat. This is my only chance to get her home phone number. If I got a hard question on "international political leaders," I'd certainly call George W. Bush. The leaders would be fresh in his mind, since he's just recently learned their names. Oh, and I'd make sure at least one of my "phone-a-friends" dialed directly into an escort service. Regis: "Hello?" Phone-a-friend: "You've reached Sorority Sluts." Hahaha.

I called Ken: "You're crazy to ask me to do this. I can't be trusted. What if I deliberately give you the wrong answer and you lose everything?"

He said, "Then the next column you write will be published posthumously."

So I felt good, at least, that we'd established parameters.

Ultimately, I agreed to do it. In a couple of days I got a call from a woman who briefed me on the rules:

On the day that Ken was going on *Millionaire,* I had to be available by phone from 4:00 P.M. to 7:00 P.M. There was no guarantee Ken would make it to "the hot seat." But if he did, I had to camp near my phone.

"What if I need to go to the bathroom?" I asked.

"Can't you hold it in?" she said.

(Good thing for her Ken's phone-a-friend wasn't Marion Barry.)

Between 4:00 and 7:00 I had to let my phone ring three times, and then pick up.

"You'll receive a call that your friend is in the hot seat," she said. "The next call will be from Regis. When you answer, say, 'Hello.'"

(So *that's* how it works. That explains why when Regis says, "Hello, this is Regis Philbin calling from *Who Wants to Be a Millionaire,*" nobody says, "Yeah, right, Jocko, and I'm Kathie Lee.")

"Can I make small talk with Regis?" I asked.

"What???"

"Can I tell him a joke? You know: A rabbi, a priest, and Frank Gifford are in a spy plane over China, and—"

"No. Don't tell Regis any jokes," she said. "Pay attention to the question. If you don't know the answer, or if you're making a guess, tell your friend. If you're certain, let him know. After thirty seconds the call will be automatically terminated. Do you understand?"

"I'm scared I won't know the answer," I said.

"Oh, come on, Mr. Kornheiser, you're a professional sportswriter. Most of our sports stuff is simple. Here's one from last week: 'Who holds the Olympic record for consecutive bulls-eyes in the women's rapid-fire-prone rifle event?' Heck, you probably know the answers to *all* the riflery questions, not just the easy ones."

(*Gulp.*)

"Well, sure, I'm a professional. But let's say I inexplicably have a brain lapse. Can anyone be in the room with me to help?"

"Sure. You can have as many people as you want. But you only have thirty seconds. And only you can speak over the phone."

I thanked her for her patience. Then I went to towel off. I had enough water running down my spine to irrigate the Negev.

I went through the sports staff at *The Washington Post* and lined up eight experts to help. The plan was I would say the question out loud, recite the possible answers, then look to them for the correct answer.

"We could look it up on the Internet," someone said.

"We only have thirty seconds," I said. "That's not enough time to do a search."

"Can't you buy some more time?" someone asked.

"Buy some time? Like *Wheel of Fortune*? 'Oh, Regis, excuse me, I'd like to buy another thirty seconds.' Of course not. God, I'm sweating like a pig."

"Tony, you *are* a pig. How well do you know this guy?"

"I don't know him at all. He's a fan. He called me blind."

"Well, who cares then? No matter what, just tell him 'B.' Then let's order some Chinese."

I sat by the phone. Each time it rang, my heart stopped. At 5:00 I got the call from *Millionaire*.

"Ken is in the hot seat. The next call could be from Regis. Are you ready?"

"Am I ready?" I said. "I was born ready."

Then I threw up.

I gathered everybody in my office. At 5:30 the phone rang. I picked up on the third ring and said strong and clear, "Hello."

I heard, "Tony?"

And I said, "Regis, how are you, buddy? How's that dopey solid-color shirt-and-tie thing working out for you?"

Except it wasn't Regis. It was a guy from *Millionaire* calling to tell me, "Ken used his lifeline, so you're free to go."

"He used his lifeline? On what?"

"On a music question. That's all I can tell you."

I was crestfallen. I *know* music! Gerry and the Pacemakers,

"Ferry Cross the Mersey." Little Millie Small, "My Boy Lollipop." I even know the long-lost third Righteous Brother, Olaf. Ken could have called me.

The show was taped, and it airs this Tuesday. My dear friend Ken was sworn to secrecy, and I have no idea what happened. So I'll be watching. Um, if you know which one Ken is, point him out to me.

Something Special in the Air

As most of my faithful readers know, I'm somewhat anxious about flying. I recently made a list of things that scare me most about flying, and I narrowed it down to three: takeoff, landing, and the part where we're in the air. Other than that, I'm fine. I'm a hoot at curbside check-in, for example.

My friends who frequently fly tend to complain that airlines don't treat you with civility. They don't like it when airlines make you suffer through long delays without explanation, or when you check a two-suiter and they return it as mulch. And, oh yeah, when airlines sit you next to a dead man.

Excuse me, Tony, when you say "dead man," do you mean like someone who drank too much and passed out?

No, I mean a dead man. As in rapidly decomposing.

As in, "I don't think you have to worry about *this* guy snagging the last Budweiser."

Newsweek recently had a cover story on "Seven Ways to Fix Air Travel." Fairly high on that list I think would be: Make Sure the Passenger in 16-B Is Breathing.

This happened recently on a Continental Airlines flight from Bali to Hawaii: The plane put down on a remote island in Micronesia and took on a middle-aged man in a hospital gown and two attendants. Seated across the aisle was the Beaulieu family from British Columbia: Donna, her daughter Teresa, and son-in-law Dale Alexander. According to an account in the *Gazette* of Montreal, Donna had a hunch the man wouldn't make it through the flight. Donna said, "I got to see him choking and gagging and frothing and everything."

(Hey, that's *my* bit! I usually begin to froth before they complete the oxygen mask demonstration. By the time we're on final approach, they could use my accumulated froth to coat the runway in case of an emergency landing.)

Where was I? Ah yes, the patient was choking, gagging, and frothing. "And his leg kept coming out into the aisle beside me," Donna said. "We were trying to push it back so the food cart wouldn't run over it."

(Gasp.)

Let's back this up a bit.

1. What is this guy doing in an aisle seat? If anybody can be moved to a middle seat, it's a dead man. It's not like he's going to complain about lack of leg room. At this point you can stuff him in the overhead.

2. They're *serving*?

"Oh, miss, can I have some extra cashews? They're not for me, they're for my friend here, when he wakes up (*wink, wink*)."

Reportedly, the man died after three hours on the flight. (Actually that's not bad longevity for coach class.)

In a written complaint to Continental, Dale Alexander said he had to go to the back of the aircraft and persuade flight attendants the man had passed away. Well, sure he had to persuade them. The in-flight movie was *Dude, Where's My Car?* Most people closed their eyes and tried to sleep through it. Only the lucky ones actually died.

Donna Beaulieu said airline personnel returned the dead man to an upright—and locked?—position and proceeded to serve the meal: "They sort of propped him up with a pillow under his head, and tucked him in like he was having a nap." (What, they should hang him up front, where they put the suit bags?)

Okay, Tony. This really has gone too far. Don't you think this is insensitive—even for you?

Wait. I got one more: So I pictured him belted in there, with the food still on his tray—and me in the seat next to him, saying, "Hey, you gonna eat that?"

The worst part would come when the flight was over, and the passengers started filing out. They'd pass this dead guy and start wondering, *Hmmm, I had the chicken. Did* he *have the chicken?*

(I have to confess: Every time I hear an airplane horror story involving serving the meal, I'm reminded of that Wall Street executive who got drunk on a flight from Buenos Aires to New York some years back. When the flight attendants cut him off from any more liquor, he jumped up on the food cart, pulled down his pants, and—how shall I say this tastefully?—rolled a log on that bad boy! Afterward, one of the exec's pals said in his defense, "It seems so out of character for him." Really? Who the heck doesn't it seem out of character for?)

I told my friend Mike the story about the man on the plane dying. Mike's a frequent flyer, and he said, "There are a lot of advantages to flying while dead."

"Like what?" I asked.

"Turbulence doesn't bother you, for one thing."

The Beaulieu family is seeking compensation for discomfort they endured during the flight.

The discomfort ought to be worth *beaucoup* upgrades, huh?

The only reason anyone flies now is to get upgrades to first class. Nobody in first class would have cared if there were *ten* stiffs up there with them—as long as they got the hot fudge sundae and the leg room.

Personally, I'd welcome flying next to a dead man. Next time I book a flight, I'm going to ask, "Got any dead guys on this flight?" It's like finding a mouse in your yogurt, or finding that glorious chicken head in your Hot Wings.

It's a gold mine. It's upgrades out the wazoo.

I'd kill to sit next to a dead man.

In last week's column I wrote about being a "phone-a-friend" for contestant Ken Krantz on *Who Wants to Be a Millionaire*. I wrote I was miffed that Krantz didn't use me as a lifeline on a music question. It turns out the question was: "Who won a Pulitzer Prize for musical composition?" The choices were: Duke Ellington, Charles Mingus, Miles Davis, and Wynton Marsalis. It's a good thing Krantz didn't phone me. After thirty-one straight years of losing, whenever I hear the word "Pulitzer Prize," I froth. P.S.: Krantz won $250,000 on the show. And I *am* the weakest link. Good-bye.

State of the Reunion

I'm back from my "guys only" high school reunion in the Catskills, and I have learned two important things about myself.

1. I don't snore, which is a huge plus when you're sharing a room. I was in great demand because I didn't snore. Across the hall, John sounded like a moose trapped in an elevator. Two different guys tried to trade their roommates for me. I was the Ken Griffey Jr. of sack time.

2. I'm tall.

I never thought of myself as tall. I'm six feet even. But I guess everyone in my high school class has already started shrinking, because I seemed to be the tallest one there—I was even taller than the guys who were on the basketball team! I could eat off their heads (which in the Catskills is considered "brunch"). I was waiting for the guys to start singing, "Follow, follow, follow, follow, follow the yellow brick road." I couldn't figure out how we ever won a game. Who did we have on our schedule, the Harmonicats?

I am looking at a photo of the twenty-five guys who attended the reunion, and I can honestly say not one of us looks a day over sixty—and I surely hope that's true ten years from now when most of us will actually *be* sixty.

It was a weekend reunion at a hotel. We all ate together, played some ball, and hung out in a conference room, smoking cigars, drinking Scotch, playing poker, and telling *fabulous* stories from our lives. Here's one: Stanley had this dog, a total loser, and it was always running away and winding up in a neighbor's yard. Stanley was routinely called in the middle of the night to pick up the dog—whom he hated and would've happily let loose on the Long

Island Expressway. So this one time the dog bolted, and after it was gone for two weeks Stanley gratefully gave it up for dead. Then one day Stanley's wife was out walking, and she swore she heard the dog barking at her, faintly, from Beyond. "I know this sounds crazy, but I think Scooter is calling to me," she said. Lo and behold, it turned out the dog was in a manhole. He had been wandering underground through the town's sewer system for two weeks. Vet bills for the beast ran into thousands of dollars, including delousing. A few weeks later, in the dead of winter, the dog ran away again, and this time they found it in a neighbor's pool, frozen stiff as Al Gore's butler.

You think that's funny, Tony?

I guess you had to be there. (And drinking heavily.)

This one is better, I think: Stanley made a lot of money in business, employing hundreds of underpaid laborers. One day he bumped into another of our classmates in New York, whom he hadn't seen in twenty years.

"So, what do you do?" Stanley asked Dave.

"I'm a union organizer," Dave said. "What do you do?"

"Um, nothing," Stanley said.

When I got home from the reunion the first thing my kids asked me was: "Had your high school classmates changed?"

Well, that's not quite true. The first thing my kids asked was: "Can we go out to dinner?" The second thing was: "How come I have to take out the dog? I took the dog out last night. Make Michael take out the dog."

My kids never actually asked me anything about the reunion. I'm not sure they even knew I had been away. How would they know? It hadn't been announced on *The Simpsons*. But the point is: Other than adding a few pounds and losing some hair—and in one notable case replacing the lost human hair with something that appeared to have been ripped from a yak's underbelly—the guys hadn't changed much (except for the one who now, to everybody's amazement, looks exactly like Bea Arthur). The funny ones were still funny. The quiet ones were still quiet. The boring ones were still boring. And not everybody had become a rocket scientist.

For example, at one point we were discussing where to hold our next reunion, and Steven said, "Let's have it in Puerto Rico, because that's one of the few states I haven't been to."

Wait, it gets better.

Steven then said, "How many states do we have now? Fifty-two, right?"

And I said, "Yeah, the continental forty-eight, Alaska, Hawaii, and then in the last few years we added Puerto Rico and France. It was in all the papers."

Later in the evening the scholar-athlete of our class, as smart and handsome as the Robert Redford character in *The Way We Were,* turned to me and asked, completely serious, like he has been living on the third moon of Jupiter, "What team does Cal Ripken play for? Is it the Cubs?"

"He came *up* with the Cubs organization as a baritone," I corrected, "but was traded to the Utah Jazz for Wayne Gretzky and Wallace 'Two-Ton' Twombley. Later he played for the Topeka Oysters in the Negro Leagues, and finally retired to Poughkeepsie, where he runs the numbers racket."

"Oh," was the reply.

That picture we posed for was taken on the steps of the dining room of the hotel our last evening there. We'd been together for forty-eight hours by then, and you can see the joy in our eyes. But there were some scratches at the edges. At our age the curve is no longer going up. Every one of us had our triumphs and our tragedies, too. Parents were gone. A sister. A wife. There were children born with terrible defects. There were operations, chemotherapies, divorces, business reversals. The gift of the reunion was the chance to reconnect, however briefly, with the friends we'd known in happier times.

I look at the picture and smile to see that we've become our fathers. We're fat, old, bald, and loud. Some of us have even started driving Cadillacs. Fifteen years from now they'll have to wake us up for the next picture; we'll be sleeping off dinner in the easy chairs in the lobby. I'll be the only one not snoring.

You Camp Go Home Again

This past weekend I went to my camp reunion. Camp Keeyu-mah was in business twenty-five years, from 1949 to 1974. (Official motto: "Send Us Your Child for Eight Weeks, and If We Don't Send You Back Your Child, No Sweat, We'll Send You Somebody Else's.") About two hundred people showed up, ranging from their forties to their seventies. Because I'd gone to camp for sixteen summers as a camper and counselor, I knew almost all of them, though their faces had changed; now they had the fuller, weathered faces of their parents that I remembered from Visiting Day thirty-five and forty years ago. It was like something out of Stephen King—if Stephen King loaded up on downers.

In the main, the women had aged better than the men. I say this because some of the men were so fat they could have been entered in the Pennsylvania State Fair. Women are quicker at recognizing the perils of aging. For example, women usually know when it's time to stop wearing halter tops. Men blithely continue to wear form-fitting shirts even when their "form" now resembles a big ol' sack of feed. Women would never be so blissfully ignorant. Like the woman in her mid-forties who showed up with spectacularly platinum blond hair, and when a man said she looked like Marilyn Monroe, she responded: "Do I look more like Marilyn Monroe when she was alive or dead?"

The reunion's organizers planned a surprise Color War break. Color War is a (mostly athletic) competition in which campers are divided into teams according to camp colors; my camp's colors were blue and white. Typically, the announcement of Color War—the "break"—is done in some off-center way; maybe by painting colors on campers' faces while they're asleep, or, you know, marauding through the bunks and tying every third child to the rafters.

This "break" was by helicopter. The local veterinarian has flown his own chopper to get to his patients for forty years. Now as we stood around the flagpole for the welcoming ceremony, he passed low over the camp, dropping blue and white streamers. Except the streamers didn't drop cleanly—they hung over the runners of the helicopter. As the streamers began swirling wildly, all of us on the ground had the same terrifying thought: The streamers are going to get into the rotor, and the chopper is going to crash and kill us all! I began to fantasize the first sentence of my own obituary: "Tony Kornheiser, who was afraid to fly and preferred his feet on the ground, died yesterday when a helicopter fell from the sky and crushed him." Fortunately, the vet flew off without incident.

At that point, we did what any reasonable group of middle-aged adults whose lives had just flashed before their eyes would do: We ate lunch. It was the traditional camp picnic lunch we had forty years ago, hamburgers in the basket. They tasted just as we remembered them: like death warmed over. I don't want to say the meat was tough, but some of the hamburgers had tattoos.

After lunch people wandered around camp, and ultimately gathered around the main softball diamond for the traditional Color War game. The score went to 8–7 Blue, and White was down to its last batter with a runner on third base. The White captain, my friend Keith (who wanted someone else to drive in the tying run, so *he* could drive in the winning run), spotted me watching the game and said, "Tony, get up there and hit." I declined, saying I hadn't swung a bat in twenty years.

"Get up there and hit," he said. "Do it for your children."

"My children don't speak to me," I said.

"Then do it for *my* children," Keith said.

I went to the plate and swung, missing the ball by a "Dukakis-like" margin. I missed the second pitch, too. Keith called time and walked into the batter's box. He said to me, "Stevie Wonder would come closer than that." Then Keith put his arm around me and said, "Okay, Tony, let's go—just like we did it in practice." That cracked me up. Our last practice was in 1966.

I swung and hit a line single to right. Unfortunately, I pulled a groin muscle running to first and needed medical attention. (Though at my age the good news was that I even had groin muscles.) That was my one moment of glory.

But as much as a reunion—any reunion—is about glory and camaraderie and reliving the best moments of your life, reunions are also about time gone by and friends lost. When you go fifteen, twenty-five, thirty-five years without seeing somebody, sometimes it's too late. These were people I spent every summer of my youth with, people I loved in a place I adored. And lately I've begun to count the wrinkles and the bald heads and the artificial hips, and I know there's more time behind us than ahead. You come together on occasions like this, aging and slowing, and you don't know whether to cry or laugh.

At the end of the reunion, we gathered at the lake, where people made small speeches about the campers, counselors, and staff who had passed on—then we lit candles that were fastened to paper plates and cast them out onto the water. One of the people we mourned was my Aunt Shirley, who died recently. My Aunt Shirley and my Uncle Arnie owned the camp and were beloved by all who went there. Arnie, now in his eighties, was the last to place a candle on the lake.

I loved being there, rocking in the cradle of my childhood, seeing dear friends, deceiving myself into feeling momentarily young again. But every step I took I saw my aunt, and I felt the presence of my mother and father, coming one last time to visit me. Mostly I wandered around alone, standing silently in old, familiar places, inhaling the aromas, and trying to press every square inch of the camp into my mind's eye like flowers in a book.

There would be other reunions, but I guessed I'd never be back again. The book of the dead would be too long. So I wanted to memorize this one perfect day and hold on to it forever. And I stood on the shore and looked out at the lake, crying gratefully as the tiny flames bobbed in the water.

Fast Women

Did you read the news story about a driver's ed teacher in North Carolina who got so angry when someone cut him off that he ordered the student who was driving to speed up and catch the guy? And when she did, the teacher got out of the car and punched the offending driver in the nose!

Is this really the kind of behavior we want from a teacher? Is this really the lesson we want to be giving the youth of America? I mean, if you have the dirtball cornered, shouldn't you kick him in the groin, too?

Okay, okay, I admit that this guy was probably not the world's best role model for containing road rage. Hiring him as a driver's ed teacher would be like hiring a personal fitness trainer who weighs four hundred pounds, slugs bourbon from the bottle, and chain-smokes cigars.

This story got me thinking about my own driver's ed teacher from high school. His name was Mr. Cmaylo (pronounced, I swear, "Mister Smile-O!"). Mister Cmaylo never smiled. He seldom talked. He was never big on driver's ed theory. The only actual rule he ever imparted, to the best of my recollection, was: "Never run over a cardboard box, because a kid could be inside it."

Mr. Cmaylo was a big, beefy taciturn man who would sit in the passenger's seat reading a newspaper while we drove, as if he didn't have a worry in the world. A lot of students were grateful for Mr. Cmaylo's calm demeanor; they interpreted his reading the paper as a sign of confidence in them. I realized he just was a rabid fan of the Jumble. There were three of us in the driver's ed car. Me, Tina, and Susan. Tina was wild and exotic. She ran with an older crowd, many of whom left on sabbatical from time to time to attend prison.

Being in the driver's ed car with Tina was really different. There were always two lessons going on simultaneously: driving and anatomy. Tina wore skirts the approximate width of a wedding band. By the time she was sixteen she'd already been driving for four years. I didn't know why she was taking driver's ed; she should have been giving it. I assumed Tina's earliest driving experiences involved getaway cars.

Susan wasn't nearly the polished driver Tina was (neither was Shirley Muldowney). In fact, the only time I ever saw Mr. Cmaylo put his newspaper down was when Susan was driving. Susan didn't inspire confidence when she got behind the wheel, perhaps because she appeared to be legally blind. Her glasses were so thick they came with a defroster. And she was scary pale and terribly sensitive, and tended to become flustered when the slightest thing went wrong—for example, if she found out that people in Yemen were starving, she would throw her pasty hands in the air and begin to cry, which, as Tina and I told her, wouldn't have scared us as much had she been in the backseat and not behind the wheel at the time.

Once, when Susan was supposed to shift from park to reverse, she dropped it into drive by mistake, and when she felt the car going forward, she panicked and floored it. We shot forward like John Glenn on the launchpad. The G-force made our cheeks flap. And since we had all turned around to look out the back window, our heads nearly snapped off. Mr. Cmaylo slammed down so hard on the dual-control brake that I thought he'd go through the floorboards. When we came to a stop we were so shaken we all asked Tina for a cigarette—Mr. Cmaylo, too.

The first time I ever drove the driver's ed car, Mr. Cmaylo had me park it on a busy street in the commercial section of town. I signaled that I was going to pull over to the right, and I guided the car to the curb and pulled easily behind another parked car.

At that point I was supposed to switch from the front seat to the backseat, so Tina could drive. (Tina liked to drive because she could use the rearview mirror to put on her makeup.) I carefully checked the street for cardboard boxes—all clear—and flung open the driver's side door, and *bam!* These were narrow streets, and a huge tractor-trailer sheared off the door!

One instant the door was there, and the next it was gone. The force of the impact pushed the door one hundred feet up the street. This is my first time ever behind the wheel. And I see the truck driver running toward the car, screaming about how I shouldn't be allowed to drive even a little red wagon. And I begin to shake because I didn't even have a license yet and already I'd been in an accident. And I looked at Mister Smile-O, hoping he'd say something reassuring.

And he said, "Mmmph. I guess I better drive back to school."

(Makes you feel warm all over, doesn't it?)

And I got into the backseat, next to Tina, who was wildly excited because of the violent, random, and idiotic nature of the crash. And you know, it could have been worse.

The Fighting Hasidim

After fifty-three years of proudly being called the Colonials, my alma mater, Binghamton University, recently rated by *Der Spiegel* as one of the "better schools" in south-central New York state (motto: "We're Only 207 Road Miles from Yale"), has decided to change the nickname of its athletic teams.

No, this wasn't some political-correctness fix. Colonials isn't a hideously embarrassing racial slur, like, say, Redskins—if there could possibly be somebody insensitive enough to use *that* as a name for a sports team. Colonials is a benign term, meaning either "a member or inhabitant of a colony" or, as I've just learned, those pathetic buckle shoes nobody has worn since the time of the Pilgrims, with the possible exception of Elton John.

(Jeez. All this time we were named after *shoes*? Whose idea was that, Judy Garland's?)

Binghamton decided to dump "Colonials" for a much more practical reason: "Colonials" wasn't moving T-shirts. End of discussion.

Name changes are nothing new to my school, which was originally Triple Cities College and then—when I went there—Harpur College. When people asked me where I went to school, I would say "Harpur" very fast and deliberately slur the pronunciation to see if I could fool some dopes into thinking I went to "Harvard."

Later, it became SUNY—Binghamton. Now it's simply Binghamton U. In a few years, it'll probably be a Starbucks. (I took my daughter up there a few years ago, showed her the familiar red brick neo-penal architecture, and she said, "Daddy, it looks like a drug rehabilitation center." I smiled and told her, "Sweetie, you don't know how close you are.")

I have to laugh when I think back to the athletic teams we had when I was in school. We were not a jock school. There was no football team. The center on our basketball team was only six feet two; he had a terrific view of the opposing center's armpits. After his junior year, he left to join the circus! Everything you need to know about the state of Harpur College athletics is embodied in the name of one of the school's legendary stars: Jack "the Shot" Levine.

We never won anything. It wasn't just that your guys could beat our guys; your *girls* could beat our guys. The piccolo section of your band could beat our guys.

Along with a new nickname, Binghamton wants a mascot, too. When I was at Harpur, we never actually had a mascot the students could relate to—I'd have suggested a cuddly stuffed animal who sat immobilized for five hours playing the first side of the *Moby Grape* album and babbling about how if you cut open a Cheez Doodle, the colors were *really far out.*

It's okay with me if they want to change "Colonials" to something else, but I must express my outrage at how the new nickname was arrived at.

A marketing company was hired to prepare a list of thirty names. I quote from the alumni newsletter: "The following qualities were considered in selecting the name: gender-neutral, non-offensive, powerful, aggressive, dignified, and marketable."

(So I guess "Big Hairy Chicks on Crack" had no chance.)

What kind of nickname can you get from that commercialized, politically correct crap?

I asked my friends at work to brainstorm a name using those guidelines. Here's what they came up with:

The Smelt
The Binghamton Empowered Persons
The Bisexuals

The Binghamton Bada-Bing!

The Bolivian Swarming River Rats

The Golden Geldings

The Binghamton Crosbys

The Fighting Beiges

The (Name of Your Corporation Here)

The Binghamton Bacilli

The Fighting Hasidim

And my personal favorite: The Swiss.

But for some reason, Binghamton picked Bearcats.

There's no such thing as a bearcat. It's a mythical animal. A fraud.

My friend Tammy, who has two cats, points out quite correctly: "Of course, it is mythical. I am absolutely, positively certain my cats would never, ever, like, *do it* with a bear."

(Tammy also asks, "Why aren't there beardogs?" But that is a question for another day—and possibly another galaxy.)

The alumni journal praises the choice of Bearcat: "A cross between the power and ferocity of a bear and the cunning and quickness of a cat."

Well, if what you want is power and ferocity, and cunning and quickness, why not choose a nickname like Psychotics With Chain Saws? You think *that's* not marketable? That's got big-time *WWF Smackdown!* potential!

The University of Cincinnati has been the Bearcats for one hundred years. And Cincinnati is a good athletic school. Its basketball team is number one in the country now. Everyone will assume that Binghamton stole the nickname from Cincinnati. And, let's face it, stealing from Cincinnati is about as desperate as it gets. I mean, what a dump. If Binghamton is the way your foot smells, Cincinnati is the way your foot *tastes*.

If you're going to steal somebody's nickname, steal something with power and majesty. Call yourselves the New York Yankees.

(The Smelt is looking better, isn't it?)

Not only isn't "Bearcats" original, but the logo they picked is almost exactly the same as that of the NHL's Florida Panthers. So we've got a phony-baloney animal and a rip-off logo. It's all schmutz.

As an alumnus in good standing (well, okay, an alumnus *still* standing), I am herewith ripping up the $50,000 check I had just written to the Binghamton Alumni Association.

And they can forget about a major donation until they come up with a nickname that stands for something. Something that says it all. How about the Binghamton Balding Kornhuskers!

I Dig a Pony

When I was a kid reading comic books, I used to see an ad in the back for something called White Cloverine Brand Salve. There were pictures of swell things you could get, depending on how many tins of salve you sold. Stuff any nine-year-old would want: an Army helmet, a pail, a penknife to kill Hitler with.

Most of the gifts you could get for selling fifty to one hundred tins. But under a big picture of a happy, towheaded boy in a cowboy hat petting a pony was the magic number: eight hundred. Sell eight hundred tins of salve and get a pony! While the other kids walked to school, I could come gallivanting in on a horse. That was my first real fantasy. Hey, I was nine.

I would gaze at the picture and think: Man, that kid must be Dale Carnegie combined with Dwight Eisenhower to unload eight hundred tins. I couldn't imagine selling White Cloverine Brand Salve to anybody with an IQ higher than a head of lettuce. To this day, I've never seen a single tin of salve in anyone's home. I doubt that I've even heard the word "salve" since 1962. It went out with Fabian.

Everybody in my family was big on getting something for nothing. My mom used to save S&H Green Stamps. We only bought groceries in stores that gave stamps, even if it meant we had to buy the disfigured potatoes stamped "Disinfect Before Cooking" and dented cans of waxed beans. I can't remember what we were saving for—no doubt something impractical like a vacuum cleaner, instead of a pony. It was my job to lick the stamps and paste them in books. The stamps tasted like the backseat of a Studebaker. I used to wonder how many books I'd need to get a new tongue.

Anyway, that was in a simpler America, an America where a guy named John Glenn was about to blast off into outer space, an America where your president wasn't playing hide the White Owl with an intern. (But who knows? He may have been playing it with Marilyn Monroe.) Back then, when you got gifts in return for opening up an account at a bank, you got an alarm clock or a scratchy horse blanket—not a pretentious bottle of oak-barreled Australian chardonnay. (Your old man would've said, "Gimme the clock. I don't want anything made from grapes some kangaroo stepped on.")

This may be a more complicated America, but the gimmick never changes. The lure of getting something for nothing has been going on all my life. Today, the gimmick is "points" you accumulate for using a certain credit card, or staying at a certain hotel chain, or choosing a certain long-distance carrier.

I have one credit card where for 15,000 points I can get a cordless drill; for 59,500 I can get a PalmPilot. Oh, did I mention that to get each point you have to spend one dollar? So I can get this PalmPilot for almost $60,000, or I can drive to a store and buy it for about $500. I guess it depends on when I need it—now, or in the year 2525.

The problem with these gift programs is that I don't need any of the junk they offer. I already have a cordless drill. Give me something I need. How many points for a hair transplant?

Or a hip replacement?

How about a night at the Mustang Ranch?

I also have all kinds of miles on airlines, but airline tickets are wasted on me, since I hate to fly. It's like offering free antlers to an Oldsmobile.

My neuroses are killing me in today's travel-oriented gift market. I once cashed in enough hotel points to get a six-night stay in Florida, and the hotel chain threw in a free airplane ticket (afraid to fly), a free cruise ticket (afraid of boats), a free amusement park package (afraid of roller coasters and other airborne rides), a free hang-gliding lesson (you gotta be kidding me), and two free dinners at the hotel restaurant. (I should drive all the way to Miami and eat in the hotel?)

My sportswriter colleague Michael Wilbon informs me he has 1.6 million miles with American Airlines. I believe this entitles Wilbon to actually *fly* the plane. But that's bupkus compared with the number of miles John Glenn must have accumulated over the last thirty-five years in order to get a free trip on the space shuttle.

My editor Rich says he wants to earn points toward a "guaranteed majestic afterlife." Rich wants a reincarnation card. "I don't want to come back as a dung beetle." (Actually, people who know Rich think it would be a step up for him to be a dung beetle.)

I want to go back to the old days, when "something-for-nothing" meant you really got something. Before the Real Estate Agent from Hell came up with the idea of a "free" weekend in a resort community, with golf, boating, and gourmet dining—and all you have to do is attend a "brief seminar." So you drive two hundred miles, and after three hours of being trapped in a room with a guy trying to sell you a time share in this mudhole, where the mosquitoes are as big as Al Roker, you flee for your life without even picking up the free bonus gas grill.

My friend Nancy remembers clipping coupons from the back of cereal boxes that got her land in Alaska. This was in the '50s, before they discovered oil, when nobody thought of living in Alaska, not even Ted Kaczynski.

"I'm guessing somebody has built on *my* land," Nancy said.

How much land do you think you have?

"I think you got one square foot per cereal box," Nancy said. "So I probably have eight square feet. But it could be right on the pipeline. I could be the next Jed Clampett!"

She can have Alaska.

I'm fifty. I don't have much time left.

I want the pony.

The Kornheiser Papers

Note to readers: The following manuscript was discovered in a doorway in an abandoned building on Fifteenth Street, where it was being used as bedding. Apparently, the document was written by Tony Kornheiser during his "vacation period" last August. Presented to literary historians, the "Kornheiser papers" have been tentatively authenticated (pending DNA tests on the suspicious stains) and published here for the first time. Now we ALL have something to be thankful for.

My doctor, Lester, likes to introduce me as his "marginally famous friend."

I once asked him to define "marginally famous," and he responded, "Do you remember the Turtles?"

I did. They had a few hits in the '60s, including "Happy Together," which featured these unforgettable lyrics: "We're happy together . . . How is the weather?"

"Well," Lester said, "now, thirty years later, you might be more famous than their drummer."

So I am marginally famous. How marginal became clear to me when I was a "celebrity" in a golf tournament recently featuring former great athletes like Bo Jackson, Dave DeBusschere, Yogi Berra, Jerry Kramer, Bobby Thomson, and Ralph Branca.

As the golfers gathered by the first tee, I walked over to the people in my group and introduced myself.

"I'm Tony Kornheiser," I said, thinking that was sufficient.

There were four of them: Gene, Edgar, Jeff, and Ryan. Four players and one celebrity is the usual format.

We stood there a while, the five of us, and then Edgar asked Gene, "Who is our celebrity?"

I said softly, "Um, I am."

They regarded me curiously, the way they might regard a big bowl of cranberry sauce on a city bus.

"What do you do?" Edgar asked me.

I explained that I write a column that appears in many fine newspapers throughout North America, including the *Rhinoceros Times* in North Carolina, the *Sebring Shopping Guide* in Florida, and the *Daily News* of Prince Rupert, British Columbia. I also do a daily radio show for ESPN, and I am occasionally on TV. I offered to provide Edgar with references.

Edgar gave me a blank stare. "I've never heard of you," he said.

I felt like I was the mystery guest on *What's My Line?* and the panelists were still stumped even *after* they'd removed their blindfolds. Or maybe I was the million-dollar question on *Who Wants to Be a Millionaire* (Who is Tony Kornheiser?) and not even Regis Philbin, who had the answer in front of him, was confident.

"I was hoping for Yogi Berra," Edgar said.

I got prepared for a long afternoon, but after a few holes it all smoothed out. Edgar pulled out a cell phone and called his sister in Washington, where I am widely known as a media whore, and she'd heard of me, so I was aces with Edgar. More important, Gene turned out to be a partner in the famous steak house Smith & Wollensky, which just opened downtown, and he gave me his card and told me to be his guest. What good would that have done Yogi Berra? At his age, he shouldn't eat red meat.

To show the flip side of marginal fame, the next week I went to Syracuse, New York, to do my radio show from our affiliate there, and I was treated like a god. I was chauffeured around in a stretch limousine. The Hotel Syracuse put me in the Governor's Suite— and it's a good thing the governor wasn't there, because it could have gotten very crowded in the bathroom, *bada-boom.*

The greatest honor of all was: I was asked to throw out the first pitch before a Syracuse Sky Chiefs baseball game. I heard I was chosen ahead of the bass player from the Turtles. The Sky Chiefs are a farm team for the Toronto Blue Jays, and the best part was I got one of those satin warm-up jackets the players wear. It's blue with red sleeves and SKY CHIEFS is written in script across the chest. But my eyes are so bad I thought it said "Sky Chefs," and I assumed the team was sponsored by an airline caterer.

When I got to the ballpark, I panicked that I wouldn't be able to reach home plate from the pitcher's mound. So I began throwing baseballs in the tunnel leading to the dugout. I was horribly wild. A couple of Sky Chiefs walked by and looked at me—fat and fifty, straining to throw strikes in a satin jacket—and one said to the other, "Man, this geezer better not give up his day job."

After five minutes, I had completely thrown out my arm, of course, and I was estimating how much rotator cuff surgery would cost me when I was led to the dugout and introduced to the Syracuse manager. I told him I was afraid I might be so wild that my pitch might sail past the catcher and hit the screen behind home plate. He laughed and said, "You'll fit right in. Most of my pitchers do that." Then he told me, "Stick around, I might use you in the late innings."

I heard the public address announcer call my name, and to my great relief some people cheered for me—the others weren't saying, "Booooo," they were asking, "Whooo?" I walked out to the pitcher's mound and waved to the crowd like I imagined a real celebrity, someone like Leeza, would.

As the catcher knelt at home plate getting ready for the pitch, I wound up—and hummed a fastball at the mascot, a grown man dressed like a fuzzy parrot, who was standing twenty feet up the third-base line. I popped him in the stomach, and he took an elegant pratfall. Folks in the stands laughed, which was music to my ears. The only discouraging word came from the mascot, who said, "I was hoping for Yogi Berra."

A Genuine Anthony, and What a Bargain

Okay, here is my drawing. Actual size. I call it *Cat on Lined Paper*. How much am I bid for it?

I show you my drawing because the other day a drawing of a horse by Leonardo da Vinci, a drawing not much bigger than my stunning *Cat on Lined Paper*, went for $11.48 million.

This set a record for works by Leonardo. And I quote from *The Washington Post* story now: "It also tied the record for Old Master drawings, established just last year for Michelangelo's *Study for the Risen Christ*."

"Old Master" drawings? This is an official category? There's like, what, an "Old Masters" committee that meets and votes these guys in?

"I'd like Old Masters for five hundred, Alex."

Who else is in the Old Masters—other than Jack Nicklaus?

No, really, someone actually came up with an official art category "Old Masters"? How old do you have to be to be an Old Master? Is it very stringent, like "Dead, buried, rotted, to dust"? Or can you be automatically notified of your membership with a form letter, like with AARP?

"Congratulations, Mr. LeRoy Neiman, over the protests of art critics everywhere you just achieved Old Master status."

Now I understand that art is a specialized taste. A lot of people skim right over the art stories. When I mentioned that some small drawing by Leonardo da Vinci sold for big bucks, my friend Cindy shrugged it off, saying, "Big deal. It's not like it's a Leonardo DiCaprio." But my position is: We can all use a little more culture.

Not that money should be the reason we artists—Leonardo and I—draw. But I feel compelled to report that this particular drawing, which will now line art historian J. Carter Brown's pockets with 11 million simoleons, was originally bought by Brown's father for $2,800. This is known in the art trade as "letting the big dog eat." Incidentally, the drawing was purchased by an anonymous buyer who reportedly said he was "looking for a small horse thing to hang in [his] den, near the lithographs of the dogs playing poker to, you know, pull the whole room together."

After the sale, Brown described himself as "beaming from ear to ear." Duh! Brown said he would have liked to give the Leonardo to a public institution, but it represented too big a portion of his estate. I understand completely. That's why I sell my used pants.

Let me continue with the news story: "His tiny drawing, only five inches by three, may not be the 'great world masterpiece' that Michelangelo created in his *Risen Christ*. It isn't one of Leonardo's top ten drawings, as one expert pointed out. It may not even be in his top forty, or one hundred."

Hmmm. "Only five inches by three."

This is not a size we generally associate with art; this is a size we generally associate with MotoPhoto. Maybe I'm old-fashioned, but when I spend $11.5 million on a drawing I don't expect it to be the size of some cheesy Dale Earnhardt commemorative stamp from Mordovia. Come on, three by five? I have refrigerator magnets bigger than that. This thing is the size of a Post-it. When Brown's father originally bought it, did he use it as a coaster?

You know what most people call a three-by-five-inch drawing on paper?

A freakin' doodle!

I can do that. I did do that. See *Cat on Lined Paper*.

Now what about the assessment that this particular Leonardo drawing of a boy on a horse—a horse that isn't completely finished, as opposed to my fully realized cat—"isn't one of Leonardo's top ten drawings . . . may not even be in his top . . . one hundred"? (There's a list of Leonardo's top one hundred drawings? Where does the list run, *USA Today?*)

I can assure you *Cat on Lined Paper* is in my top ten.

And *Cat* . . . is not a sketch for another painting, like this Leonardo: "The drawing is a study for a figure in the background of Leonardo's *Adoration of the Magi.*" I'm not giving you cheap background-filler figures here. You get the whole cat. And you get it on paper just like Leonardo. Plus, I will personally deliver it to your home, with an order of kung pao chicken. Let's see Leo do that.

And here's what people who know art have said of my work: My friend Sally, a sophisticated New Yorker who ate lunch on the steps of the Metropolitan Museum of Art every Thursday for four years while attending the Clara B. Spence School for Young Ladies (motto: "You'll Wear These Kilts and Like 'Em, Missy"), called *Cat on Lined Paper* "a work of casual magnificence . . . emblematic of Mr. Tony's oeuvre." She added: "It shares with Leonardo's masterpiece an unstudied nonchalance."

And when I asked her, just for the historical record, of course, "What will future generations make of my cat?" Sally said without hesitation, "They'll look back and see the art that was concealed within your art."

So there.

Let's start at $2 million.

You Get
What You
Vote For

Dubya's Dumb Luck

Hi, I'm George W. Bush, and I'm running for president.

Admittedly, my campaign has been in trouble lately. Near as I can figure, the criticism boils down to three things: I'm distant and I'm dumb.

I'm going to change all that.

I have a new strategy. I'm not going to be distant anymore. I'm going to let America see me for who I am. I'm just like you, a hard worker who learned his business from the ground up, by starting out as the humble owner of a major league baseball team.

So I went on *Oprah*.

Wasn't I great?

I didn't even fall for that trick question she asked me: "What's your favorite sandwich?"

Are you kidding me? Take a look at Oprah. Like Oprah could care what anyone else likes to eat. She was just hoping I'd brought a sandwich *with* me.

I had only one slip-up. I told her my favorite song was "Wake Up Little Susie" and that Buddy Holly sang it. But I quickly corrected myself and said it was the Everly Brothers. Everyone knows Buddy Holly sang "Chances Are." Even Adam Clymer. I love the Everly Brothers. I'm told they played a concert at the Birchmere a few weeks back. I don't want to say the crowd was old, but when they gathered around the stage to try to get the Everly Brothers to do an encore by lighting matches, their oxygen tanks exploded.

Did you see the coverage I got with *Oprah*? I was on the front page of *The Washington Post* and *The New York Times*! The *Post* had a photo of me smooching Oprah! Take that, Al and Tipper. (I wonder if I should have slipped Oprah some tongue?)

Hmmm, I'm just thinking out loud here. But if I get the front page of *The Washington Post* by kissing a black woman, maybe I can get the cover of *Time* by kissing Connie Chung. And since the Olympics are going on, maybe I should go to Australia and kiss me an Aborigine! I'm drawing the line at *Will & Grace,* though. I'm a compassionate conservative, but I'll reach out just so far.

My new strategy is to go on all the TV talk shows. I'm tired of seeing Al Gore with Letterman and Leno, and Joe Lieberman getting big laughs with Conan O'Brien. I've got to give Gore credit, though. That Jew thing is working. Man, I was so wrong to pick Dick Cheney. What a lox this guy is. I should have picked a Jew, too. Maybe Whoopi Goldberg.

The more talk shows I do, the less I have to debate. Debating is so boring. They ask you questions that never come up in real life. Like "Who's the president of England?" What's the difference as long as both countries can work together on issues of mutual concern, like, you know, what really happened to Princess Di?

It's not that I'm unwilling to debate. In fact, I'm looking forward to it. I'm hoping somebody asks Al Gore about the claim he made that his dog and his mother-in-law were taking the same kind of arthritis medication—and his mother-in-law's cost three times as much as his dog's. But maybe he made an honest mistake and confused his dog and his mother-in-law. I do that all the time. It's just hard for me to believe that his dog and his mother-in-law take the same stuff. What HMO do the Gores belong to, Schnauzer Permanente? When they examine his mother-in-law, do they stand her up on an aluminum table and hold her snout shut?

Anyway, to get back in good graces with women voters, my plan is to go on *Leeza*. And *Jenny Jones.* And *Sally.* And what about this *Queen Latvia* show? I don't know how the Queen of Latvia got her own show in America, but if I go on with her maybe the press will stop writing how I don't know any world leaders.

I'm tired of people saying I'm dumb.

How dumb can I be? I graduated from Yail.

I will admit, though, that I've been watching the Olympics for over a week and I'm still confused by the time difference. I know it's fifteen hours. My staff explained to me that if the little hand is on the 6 and the big hand is on the 12 in my office, it's 9 in Australia. But is it yesterday, today, or tomorrow there? And if it's today here and tomorrow in Australia, wouldn't that mean they'd know everything that happened here before we do? So am I president yet?

I haven't been watching the Olympics that much. It's too anti-climactic. By the time we see the events, the medal winners are eligible for Social Security. NBC's announcers say, "Stay tuned and we'll see if the U.S. beat Kuwait in baseball." We'll see? By the time they run tape, it's been so long since the actual game that we could have *invaded* Kuwait!

Um, W., the U.S. PROTECTS Kuwait, it doesn't invade it.

Whatever. My point is that the Olympics may be reality based, but they're not reality. It's like *Survivor*—but with a bigger torch and lower ratings. If you want to know the truth, I think the Olympics are already over. All the athletes have been flown to Hawaii and sworn to secrecy, and NBC will string out the results over the next three years, or until George Clooney comes back to *ER*.

I tried to watch the first week, but there was too darned much swimming. I've never been all that interested in water, except as a chaser. And with all that churning water you couldn't tell which stroke they were swimming, or whether it was a qualifying heat or the final—with the full-length bodysuits you couldn't even tell if it was men swimming or women. Call me old-fashioned, but when I look at someone in a bathing suit, I don't want to have to guess if it's a man or a woman.

Anyway, I'm George W. Bush. I'm running for president.

Unless the election is already over.

Al Gore's New Stand: A Slouch

Let me see if I have this right: Al Gore, who is running for president on the grounds that he is a regular guy who's in touch with the people of this country, has hired feminist author Naomi Wolf to advise him on his campaign. Ms. Wolf, a big-haired cutie, is perhaps best known for her views on sex. She advocates teaching teenagers masturbation, mutual masturbation, and oral sex—a subject in which, she brags in her book *Promiscuities,* she was rather adroit.

Hey, now!

To use Gore's own slogan, there's "A Change That Works for Working Families."

Not to put too fine a point on the recent, um, forthright exchange of positions in the Oval Office, but wouldn't you think any Democrat would go for garlic and a wooden stake if an adviser even mentioned oral sex?

As the father of two teenagers, the last thing in the world I want the schools to teach my children is how to masturbate. Heck, let 'em be self-taught, like their father. (As political performance artist James Carville proclaims, "I must have been a prodigy. I learned it all on my own.")

Of course, I might sing a different tune if I could sign up for remedial adult education. Just out of curiosity, how would one teach a course on masturbation? "In an offhand manner," suggests Don Imus's cohort, Charles McCord.

Wolf says teaching kids sex in this way "is as sensible as teaching kids to drive."

Whoa, dollface! Where were you when I wrote *that* column?

Before he hooked up with Naomi Wolf, Al Gore's standard

campaign speech was about greenhouse gases. I take it that will change.

It has been reported that in an attempt to make Gore appear less like a Doric column, Wolf has relaxed his wardrobe and told him to speak from the heart. It shows how far we've come as a culture that Wolf is an "adviser," because long ago, in a universe far away, women who picked out a man's clothes and told him what to say were called "nags."

Wolf's concern is that Gore is a "beta male," and he has to become more of an "alpha male." (For purposes of identification I am classified as "overnight mail.")

Apparently, it's Wolf's belief that Gore has to get more in touch with his masculinity to win over the electorate. People like Wolf and her fellow babe-ette, writer Susan Faludi, have created an industry based on the conceit that men are horribly conflicted and confused about their masculinity.

Personally, I suffer no such agony. I wear leg warmers because I like the way they feel on my soft, bare skin. You got a problem with that?

Anyway, it's not just famous politicians who have to deal with this masculinity issue. Did you read about the women's rugby team from Ohio State University who took off their shirts on the grounds of the Lincoln Memorial? *The Washington Post* published a photo of the women from behind, who were apparently responding to the common taunt, "Show us your backs!")

What could be more confusing to men?

1. Rugby is a masculine sport. Why are women playing it?

2. Not only are women playing it, but they're TAKING OFF THEIR TOPS! Talk about psychic whiplash. Am I going to need a V-Chip in my set for the next women's gymnastics championship?

I have to say I agree with the U.S. Park Police spokesman who said that while the team's action was legal, "the Lincoln Memorial is not the appropriate place" to bare one's breasts. Okay. How about my office?

I had a masculinity question the other night myself. About

twelve of us had gathered at the Palm to celebrate my boss George's good fortune at receiving a very prestigious award here at *The Washington Post*. We were in a private dining room, separated from another private dining room by a large wooden screen (which, come to think of it, bore an uncanny resemblance to Al Gore).

We couldn't have been there more than fifteen minutes when the maître d' said to me, "There's a man who would like to meet you."

He introduced himself as a gastroenterologist. I wasn't surprised. I've got fans in all the digestive subspecialties.

I said something incredibly witty, like, "Heavens, is my large intestine hanging out?"

The guy begins to tell me how he's in the room next to ours listening to a lecture with a bunch of other gastroenterologists, but the noise from our room was so loud it drowned out the lecturer, and he had to stop.

Excuse me?

First of all, what is he doing going to a lecture in a steak house? That's like holding a wedding at a construction site and asking the guys using the jackhammers for a little courtesy while the DJ cues up the "Wedding March." This is the loudest restaurant in town. You couldn't hear the person next to you if he was blasting for bauxite. Men bring their wives here so they don't have to even *pretend* to listen to them. We should be quiet so these gasbags can hear a lecture on *bile ducts*?

Second of all, this is red meat with huge mounds of hash brown potatoes. These guys call themselves physicians? This food'll *kill* you. Your arteries will clog up like the Beltway after a tanker of Mazola Oil splits open.

"I wanted you to know you were very, very loud," he said.

"What?" I asked, cupping my hand to my ear.

And then it came to me: Al Gore could instantly become an alpha male by stepping out from behind that wooden screen and using those new earth-toned cowboy boots Naomi Wolf picked out to kick some girlie-man gastroenterologist butt.

And then he could take off his blouse and run a victory lap.

Down for the Recount

My advice is to grab a Snickers bar. We're not going anywhere for a while.

The Democrats have already asked for a "hand count" of the Florida ballots. (Imagine if the person counting *forgets* whether the last number was 5,243,241 or 5,243,242 and has to start over again!) Later they'll ask for a finger-and-toe count. Eventually, Bush will ask for a standing-eight count. (Have you seen the photos of Bush since the election was put on ice? His brow is furrowed. His lips are pinched. Bush looks so confused—like he's holding one of those Palm Beach ballots.)

This whole mess began on election night when the TV networks prematurely declared Florida for Al Gore. Their emphasis on being first to award states to one camp or another has led to sloppy reporting. For example, even before the polls closed the Sci Fi Channel declared, "A sudden voter surge from the Andromeda Galaxy has all but ensured a Buchanan presidency."

Let's calm down, back up a minute, and show the public that the media can be responsible. Let's get it right this time.

I think we have enough solid information to declare Franklin Delano Roosevelt the winner in 1932 and 1936. There's some question, though, about 1940. Also, about the name of FDR's dog.

Can you believe this? Can you believe it's November 12 and I'm still writing election columns? I haven't made a Florence Henderson plastic surgery joke in *weeks*. The woman could have gone through three more face-lifts in that time. That would get her close to Cher territory.

On Election Night I became so bleary-eyed watching the colors swirl and change on the TV maps I thought I was back in college taking mescaline. I guess I drifted off to sleep. When I woke up in a state of delirium ("ABC can now project the state of Delirium to Bush") the first thing I saw was Wolf Blitzer's white beard. I thought he was Santa Claus and he had come down my chimney to deliver Florida to *me*.

I actually felt sorry for some of the TV talking heads who were so sleep deprived their face-lifts exploded like Firestone tires. There came a point where they had to ditch the pancake makeup and use the hard stuff—wall spackle.

Let's be honest: After it became clear the election hinged on Florida, and there wouldn't be a winner for days, what was left to say? How many times can Dan Rather explain how the electoral college works? By 4 A.M. the only one listening was George Bush; previous to this when he heard "electoral college," he wondered which fraternity there had the best parties.

Reportedly, Gore called Bush twice—the first time to concede, when Gore thought Florida had gone over to Bush, and the second time to withdraw that concession.

That's when they got in a catfight! Gore wound up mewing, "Don't get snippy about it!"

Don't get *snippy*? Who talks like that? Somebody must have stopped taking his alpha male pills.

What could have made Bush snippy? Maybe he misunderstood some complicated word that Gore used, like "transubstantiation" or "cat."

I'm sick that it all came down to Florida and I didn't vote there. I could have, since I inherited my dad's condominium in Broward County. Broward was one of the places where ballot boxes were misplaced. If ballot boxes were lost in Dade County, they could be anywhere. (I'd look in Marisleysis's house, in the closet with the fisherman.) But in Broward, I know exactly where the ballots were dumped: by the salad bar during the early bird at Catfish Dewey's. *Everything* in Broward stops from 3:30 to 6:00 for the early bird.

Nobody over the age of sixty-five voted during those hours. They ate a five-course meal for $6.95, left no tip, and told the waitress, "Be a dear and pack up the rest of my boiled chicken—and the leftovers on that table over there as well." No doubt somebody got confused and took home the ballot boxes thinking they were filled with chopped liver.

Gore's probably thinking: *If only I'd spent more time at the assisted-living facilities. If only I'd spoken to the residents' issues.* (One is getting hearing aids free from Medicare; Gore would have to SPEAK REALLY LOUD.) *If only I'd promised them five-mile-an-hour speed limits and a law allowing them to make left turns from the extreme right lane.*

I'm not sure what is the fairest way to settle this election. It's not like soccer, where at the end of a lot of overtimes they have a "shootout." You wouldn't want to announce a "shootout" in Miami. Trust me on this.

Surely there's a remedy for thousands of yentas in Palm Beach County who wanted to vote for Gore, but got confused with the ballot and wound up voting for Pat Buchanan. *Oy, vey iz mir!* They'd sooner vote for Colonel Klink than Pat "What If I Don't *Want* It on a Bagel?" Buchanan.

The problem, obviously, is that none of them could read the ballots. The last few times my dad voted he couldn't even see the giant sign that said POLLING PLACE. When they drew the curtain on the voting booth, my dad took off his clothes and waited for the doctor to come in.

I thought of my dad again when I saw Gore's campaign manager, Bill Daley, yapping about "wanting to protect the Constitution and the will of the people," when what he really meant was: "Before this is over I'm going to press so many suits you'll think I'm a tailor."

Daley's Dad was Richard Daley, Chicago's mayor-for-life. *There* was a guy who could deliver the votes. Daley's people voted early, and often—not to mention posthumously. (So many dead guys voted in those days that there were Democrats elected to the House who should have rightfully dropped the "D-Cook County" designation and gone with "D-Composition.") If Richard Daley was around, Gore would have won in Florida by fifteen thousand votes on Tuesday. Five of those votes would have been from my dad.

The Good, the Chad, and the Ugly

Hello. My name is Tony. I'm an electionaholic. And I have a confession to make:

God help me, I don't want this to end.

I love the smell of churning chads in the morning.

The hanging chads. The dimpled chads. The pregnant chads.

(Sigh. All this talk about Chad, and none about Jeremy.)

Chads are a sore point for my friend, the brilliant comic writer Norman Chad. "There's a pregnant Chad?" he asked in horror. "It's not mine. I never touched her. I'll take a blood test."

Imagine my delight that my desire to prolong the election puts me at odds with James Baker, who insisted from the start that the election must be certified now, this very moment, "for the good of the American people." Of course, by the American people Baker means himself, the Bush family, and the membership at River Oaks Country Club in Houston.

But what's the rush? Is Baker afraid that if the deadlock goes on much longer, his boy will get tired of filling his imaginary Cabinet and move on to other imaginary activities, like getting all the way to three hundred dollars on *Who Wants to Be a Millionaire* without using a lifeline?

But admit it, you'll miss Baker when he's gone. The country will be in far worse shape when this whole mess is over and Baker, Warren Christopher, and Florida's Secretary of State Cruella De Vil are off the air. We'll all have to go back to watching *The Michael Richards Show*. That show is enough to make you take the ballot puncher to your own eyeballs.

I love watching Baker's briefings. Since he stopped being secretary of state, I'd forgotten how commanding he can be. You can almost see the steam rising off his head every time he's forced to *once again* explain exactly how the world should function. "Hello? Hello? Don't you people get it? If we actually counted *all* your votes, we'd lose."

Baker, at least, cuts a powerful figure. Warren Christopher, on the other hand—what happened to this guy? He appears to be melting. And what is he talking about? Every time any Florida court has ruled against the Democrats, Christopher says it's a great thing for Al Gore. If the Florida Supreme Court had said Gore wouldn't get a recount even if he crawled through the Everglades muck on his hands and knees, Christopher would have gleefully announced, "Florida justice obviously supports the vice president's environmental initiatives." (Tell the truth: In those natty British suits don't Christopher and Baker look like aging actors doing *The Importance of Being Earnest* at a dinner theater?)

I had to smile when Christopher mentioned he'd "run into Baker at breakfast the other day." How great is it that these patricians are stuck in the same motel in Tallahassee, a place where a "gated community" is a trailer park surrounded by razor wire! Normally, Warren Christopher and James A. Baker III wouldn't be caught dead in Tallahassee, and now they're fighting over cold rubber French toast at the Motel 6 breakfast buffet.

Not since the O.J. trial have we had this kind of continuous boffo tort TV. Jeffrey Toobin! Dan Abrams! Soul Sister No. 1, Doris Kearns Goodwin! And wall-to-wall Greta Van Susteren! They're swooning at Harvard Law School, fainting at Yale.

And how about my man William "You Want a Piece of Me?" Daley, who I couldn't help but notice has a head that could float above Fifth Avenue on Thanksgiving Day. What I like most about Daley is that he remains unimpressed with the fact that George Bush's daddy was the president, because his daddy was the Boss. (That's right, his real name is William Springsteen.) When Daley gives a briefing, it's all he can do to stop from slugging everyone in the room. I mean, everything about this guy screams, "Don't

[mess] with me, pal, I'll plant you like a tulip bulb." When this is over Daley is going straight to *The Sopranos.*

For days, Al "Mulligan" Gore and George "Jeb, You *Promised*" Bush almost disappeared. (If they could have just kept it up for four years, the problem would have been solved.) Gore was seen transparently pandering to Camelot nostalgia by playing touch football with his family. Bush spent time on his Texas ranch with his dog Spot. Yes, Spot. The dog is actually spotted, so there doesn't appear to be any saving irony. It's altogether possible Bush actually thought about a name for the dog and came up with Spot! Do you believe this guy?

The two finally did speak up midweek. When Gore offered to meet Bush, he was so geeked up, his head kept bouncing around on his neck, like one of those dashboard dolls. Later, Bush turned Gore down and insisted on no more recounts. Did someone say snippy? Bush gives more snip than a vasectomy clinic.

We should hand Bush this, though: The guy can really wear jeans and a suede ranch jacket. He's exactly what our president should *look* like. But as one of my wickedly funny friends says about George W. rather than Jeb running for president, "It's like Don Corleone picked Fredo over Michael."

But the real star of the show has been Florida's Ballot Babe, Katherine Harris, the Junior League Blind Date from Hell!

In an arena chock full of secretaries of state, Harris is the one who appears to have been lost in the woods as a baby and raised by Tammy Faye Bakker. I don't want to say Harris wears a lot of eye shadow, but it looks like she's applied enough paint to refinish the Wilson Bridge. How does she put it on? Fire hose?

Harris is the one who carefully considered the written requests to conduct hand recounts—or *would have* carefully considered them if she hadn't already fed them to wild goats. When Gore campaign officials suggested she was acting as a Bush partisan, her measured response, as a responsible public official, was, in its entirety, "Bite me."

In politics they call this "respecting the will of the people."

In Chad they call it "Must-See TV."

Someone Get the Hook

Dear Al:

I can call you Al, right? I feel like we're on a first-name basis, because I see you on TV every night begging for votes. You're like somebody from Pledge Week. How can I get you to stop? More to the point, if I agree to go to Florida and vote for you, how many ballots do I have to dimple before you send me a CD? (Not a tote bag, dammit.)

Not that I could actually get my hands on a ballot. I saw them trucked up to Tallahassee from Palm Beach with a police escort and news vans following behind, TV helicopters overhead. It was so eerily reminiscent of the O.J. low-speed chase I was waiting to hear David Boies on a CB radio saying, "I'm in the Ryder. I've got Al Gore with me. I'm bringing him in. But back off. He's got a loaded chad pointed at his head."

Anyway, Al, I know that a lot of folks are asking you to drop out now. Some are asking you to do this, quite frankly, because they can't stand watching you on TV. Half the time you're flapping around like a great heron. Honestly, can't you keep your head still? What are you doing, auditioning for *The Exorcist III: The Recount?*

Most people who want you to drop out, though, are saying you should do it for the good of the country.

Country-schmuntry.

Do it for *me.* Al, baby, two words: Bor-ing!

This election is, like, sooo over. If I had the clicker, I'd be way past your channel by now.

Seriously, what is your problem?

I mean, you don't really think you're going to be president, do you? The dope won. You lost. Get over it.

I understand you have to keep up the pretense of winning. And I know it's killing you that Bush has asked Katherine Harris for the first dance at the Inaugural Ball and Dick "Large and in Charge" Cheney is itching to change all the locks on the White House. But isn't setting up your "transition team" a bit out of a reach? What positions are you offering in the (*wink, wink*) Gore administration? Ambassador to Remulak?

I see footage of you sitting there, pathetically speed dialing everybody in town. You look like a telemarketer. You gonna go from trolling for votes to selling Ronco Inside the Shell Egg Scramblers? Hmmm, you think you could do any volume in Semi-Lifelike Al Gore Action Figures®.

The meter's running, Al. This thing has already taken almost FOUR WEEKS. Carmen Electra's marriages don't last this long.

You know, I think I may be to blame for all this. A couple weeks back, I was telling everyone how I wanted this to go on and on. Al, I was *joking*. I'm a humor writer. What, you thought I was David Broder?

Not to put too fine a point on it, but how many times must *Friends* be interrupted for a special bulletin about which court you plan to petition next so you can get a recount in West Eckveldt, Florida? (Some of these judges you've got—where'd you find them, at a bus terminal?) You're just not that important, Al. You had a good run, but it's not like you're Matthew Perry.

I'm glad you think that there's a great civics lesson being taught here—that every vote counts. But where I live, in the District of Columbia, for years they didn't actually count *any* votes. They just threw them in a pile marked FOR MARION BARRY.

Of course you don't want to give up: If you don't win, you don't have a job. And with your recent, um, overeager performances on TV, it's not like Ted Koppel has anything to worry about. For that matter it's not like *Bernie* Koppel has anything to worry about.

Go home, Al. Kiss your wife. (Not like *that*.) Play touch football. Do whatever it is that fifty-two-year-old rich white men do when they're out of work: Learn to paint, trade online, download porn.

Don't make us have to pry the chads out of your cold, dead fingers. First you went to the Florida Supreme Court. Then you brought the election to the U.S. Supreme Court. What's next, the Supreme Soviet? How many Supremes are left before you get to Diana Ross?

I'll bet if we could vote again, the results would be a whole lot different—I mean now that we've seen how you guys react under stress.

You're a train wreck.

Lieberman never met a spotlight he didn't like. You light a match near this guy and he'll do the first act of *Annie*.

Cheney had a heart attack.

Bush's face was visited by boils.

(I know you're trying to make it sound like it's not personal between you and Georgie, but tell the truth. When you see Bush squinting at the TelePrompTer from his Texas ranch, and he purses his lips and his face starts to twitch and he makes that same robotic speech about how he's won like a zillion times already, and if there's another recount he's going to hold his breath until his face turns blue, don't you get the sense that he's so lost that Cheney and Baker ought to be dropping bread crumbs? No wonder Bush's numbers go down every time he tries to look presidential. It only reminds people that when all the fun is over, this guy is actually gonna be president!)

By the way, am I the only one who's bothered by the fact that Bush refers every question to Baker? What did I miss? Did Jim Baker get elected something?

Speaking of very former secretaries of state, what did you do with Warren Christopher? One day he's out front, the man on the podium, and the next day he's vanished. Poof. Where's Warren? Did he molt? Is he wrapped up in a cocoon somewhere, waiting to emerge as a butterfly? Quick, somebody call 911 and put out an alert for an old guy with Mr. Potato Head eyebrows and a $5,000 British suit.

It's your show now, Al. You're everywhere. Wasn't that you on *BattleBots*? I *know* I saw you being interviewed by Claire Shipman on NBC. You tried to appear calm, as if you haven't been thrashing around since November 7 like someone possessed. You said, "I sleep like a baby."

Yeah, I know.

Rosemary's.

Bush-Whacked by Gore Groupies

We begin this week with a note to the readers:

I have received many letters and calls protesting last week's column about why Al "Do You Think Boies Could Sell Them on a *Foot* Recount?" Gore should put a sock in it, already.

Readers apparently thought I tilted too far toward George W. Bush, who has already begun the arduous task of tagging and color-coding his jogging outfits for the move to Washington, while Dick Cheney and Jim Baker pick the cabinet and make plans to declare war on Indonesia for the thrill of testing some cool new bombs we have.

I'm somewhat stunned by the allegation that I'm pro-Bush, since in that column I referred to Bush as "a dope." Of course, I meant it in the most complimentary sense—okay, maybe not as smart as Phoebe on *Friends,* but certainly smarter than meat tenderizer. I suppose we shouldn't fret that when Bush was asked what impressed him most about Condoleezza Rice, he said, "It cooks up in a minute."

I have to admit I'm beginning to like Bush more, because the longer he sits on that ranch, the more big, fat Republicans show up in giant cowboy hats and tight blue jeans. They look like huge, overstuffed chew toys. Every time I see Trent Lott, whatever I happen to be drinking explodes out my nose.

I was chastised for suggesting the election be ratified before all the ballots were recounted by hand, using special spectrographs, electron microscopes, and the Hubble telescope to examine chads; and if that didn't work, placing direct long-distance calls to the Psychic Friends Network to assess voter "intent"—maybe even picking up a few votes from disembodied spirits and ancient Egyptian pharaohs, who surely would have voted for Al Gore because he invented embalming.

And I was chastised for writing it was Gore who carried the case to the U.S. Supreme Court, when it was actually Bush. My mistake was seen as proof that I am, in the words of an angry caller, "completely and totally prejudiced toward a man who would cut your taxes and the taxes of your rich media friends, while babies starve in the streets." I assume he meant Bush, because Gore would never let anybody starve in the street when he could bore them to death in front of their TV sets.

Okay, I apologize for getting some of the legal minutiae wrong. You thought I was Greta Van Susteren? I thought the first step in "tort reform" was roll the dough into a ball. Hello? Hell-o. I'm writing jokes here. I have no political influence whatsoever. I have political *flatulence*. I should take Beano before writing these columns.

Come on. Do you think there's any bench Gore wouldn't have appeared before to keep his hopes alive—up to and including Johnny Bench? Gore would go to Judge Judy if he thought there was a shot of getting a recount.

(I don't think Gore ever plans to go away. I think he'll end up setting up a government in exile in Palm Beach County. Sort of like what Chiang Kai-shek did in Formosa. It'll be called Formatzoh.)

I may not be Tim Russert, but I do have something going for me. Because I am a man, I can pay attention to weighty political subjects, such as Dennis Hastert, with only half my brain—while women need to use all their brains to follow along.

That's right. A recent study at the Indiana School of Medicine (motto: "That's Right, We're the Indiana School of Medicine") was conducted on men and women who listened as a novel was read to them. Brain scans indicated the women used their entire brains to listen, while men used only *half* their brains! This allowed men to continue to scratch themselves during the experiment.

"Somebody read *Jane Eyre* to the men, and their right brain was listening, and their left brain was imagining Jane Eyre naked," my friend Tracee concluded.

I suggested men might listen with *both* sides if the novel had been *Sorority Sluts Get Wicked*.

I saw pictures of the brain scans. Men have one small spot on the right side of their brain that is engaged—maybe it isn't a spot, maybe it's a gnat or a piece of lint. Women clearly have spots on each side engaged in listening.

Tracee explained the apparent disparity this way: "The right side of a man's brain is still functioning because that's the remote control hand. The left side is dead because that's the side they fall asleep on in the recliner."

I disagree. The problem is that men aren't interested in droningly tedious topics—defined here as anything a woman might choose to talk about. My friend Tom says he often reaches moments of crisis during long soliloquies by his wife, in which she's relating a story some friend told her that involves a long list of characters he can't possibly keep straight, and he has to remind himself to "remember a few key phrases in case she asks a question when she's done."

This happens to all men. They begin to glaze over when women talk to them.

"Men don't listen to women," a woman friend of mine lamented, "because they are completely incapable of any meaningful exchange of emotion that doesn't involve sports on TV or checking out the waitress. Men are *always* thinking about themselves. I can't tell you how frustrating it is to have these one-sided conversations."

"Huh?" I said. "Did you say something?"

Taking a Shine to Sheen

It's one thing to put these debates between Al Gore and George W. Bush on TV as a public service for viewers who would otherwise be forced to undergo surgery without an anesthetic. But it's quite another to preempt *West Wing* to do it.

West Wing is the best show on TV. Why would anybody want to see Gore and Bush clumsily trying to act presidential, when they can see Martin Sheen elegantly succeeding?

And speaking of anesthetic, what sort of megadose was Al Gore on at the debate Wednesday night? I can't recall such a drastic change in anyone's personality since Grateful Dead fans stopped taking drugs and realized: Jeez, this music is *terrible*!

In their first debate Gore was all over Bush, hectoring him. Plus, because of his multiple layers of makeup, Gore looked so waxy that you wanted to strap him to the top of your car and yell, "Surf's up!" But the other night Gore was barely alive. Obviously, Gore's handlers told him to "try to be a little less annoying—even *we* want to slap you." Gore was so tame I thought Bush would give him a biscuit and pet him.

And is it just me, or does Bush always look like he's struggling to read the cue cards—except there aren't any cue cards. You just know he's thinking, *Dang. I knew this stuff yesterday.* During Wednesday's debate he actually said, "Africa is an important continent." (Which in a way relieved his handlers, since earlier in the day Bush had also identified Africa as "an important food group.") When Gore finally came to life and hit Bush with bad stuff about Texas, Bush sat there pursing his lips as if he were undergoing a proctological exam. I'm not saying the president always has to be the smartest guy in the room. But Bush may not even be the smartest guy in a phone booth.

Is there any doubt who would get the most votes for president in a three-way race among Gore, Bush, and Sheen? Sheen would win in a landslide. What's not to like about Martin Sheen—except those two dopey sons of his, Emilio and Charlie, the Chang and Eng of schlock.

I'd also take Sheen's vice president over either Dick Cheney or Joe Lieberman. If Cheney were any more of a fat cat, he'd campaign in a window box, sunning himself. And Lieberman has taken so many new positions, it's hard to tell if he's running for national office or posing for *The Kama Sutra*. On the other hand, Sheen's vice president is Tim Matheson, who was Otter in *Animal House*! It was Otter who was comforted by Fawn Leibowitz's sorority sister in the backseat of Flounder's car after that terrible kiln accident. It was Otter at the toga party who bagged Dean Wormer's boozy wife. Remember how he debonairly took off her mink coat and hung it on a hook? But there was no hook there, and the mink dropped to the floor. That was so cool. That's what we need in a vice president. A frat boy who can score boss chicks. (Yes, Mr. President, the *vice* president.)

Playing the president in recent years, we've had lots of actors I'd vote for ahead of Gush and Bore—excuse me, Bush and Gore. Actually, the only actor who really stank as president was Ronald Reagan.

I'd vote for Michael Douglas from *The American President*. He *looks* like a president. Also, Catherine Zeta-Jones for first lady is the only domestic policy the man would need.

I would vote for Kevin Kline, who played the president in *Dave*. Kline is funny. And when people laugh at him, it's because he's actually *trying* to be funny. Not because he says things like "Al Gore's plan is so prescriptive we'll need IRA agents" to figure it out. *IRA* agents? And where would we get them, Belfast? Hello? Hello, is this on?

I'd vote for John Travolta, the president in *Primary Colors*.

Imagine Travolta dancing at state dinners the way he did in *Saturday Night Fever* and *Pulp Fiction*. Now imagine Al Gore doing the macarena.

But Martin Sheen is the one I'd most like to see in the Oval Office. On *West Wing* he has a way of speaking from the heart, even when it's going to hurt him in the polls. Sheen doesn't lie—unlike Gore, whose October surprise is probably that he invented the new Redskins defense.

In the face of mounting criticism of his overblown claims, Gore said he would "take responsibility for getting some of the details wrong." For example, if Gore claimed that after a hurricane he flew a plane loaded with food and water to the hurricane site, and toured the affected area with the governor, then cooked hot meals for folks whose homes had been devastated—and it turns out that in fact Gore stayed home watching *When Shaved Poodles Go Psycho IV* on Fox—well, Gore would take responsibility for getting "some details" wrong.

Sheen's president is always very forceful; he knows what he thinks. Unlike Bush, who seems to be in a perpetual fog, like he's trying to figure out how to pronounce "Dahomey" and use it in a sentence other than "Gimme a gin and tonic, and give Dahomeys whatever they want."

It's distressing when your choices for president are so uninspiring. Perhaps that's why in its current issue *American Journalism Review* asked a panel of respected journalists: "Which journalist would you like to see run for president?"

I won't bore you with the pathetic choices, but a genius, Ken Fuson of the *Des Moines Register,* said the following: "My pick for president is Tony Kornheiser. He writes columns. He hosts a popular sports radio show. He appears on ESPN's *Sports Reporters* show. He can write sad. He can write funny. He can go short. He can go long. And he golfs! The future of the free world would be safe in his hands."

Modesty forbids me from saying anything other than: "Damn right."

A Rhyming Shame

For years now, I have phoned in my last column of the year by stealing everybody else's jokes. (You give and give all year long; what's wrong with coasting a little at the end?)

But even I can't justify doing that anymore. All jokes are Internet jokes nowadays. It's gotten to the depressing point where you don't have to be a licensed professional humorist to steal jokes. Any freakin' amateur with a laptop can do it.

I gave considerable thought to how I could still produce a column that required no thought whatsoever. I toyed with the idea of simply presenting punch lines from old favorites.

Like: "Do I know it? Madam, I *wrote* it!"

God, that joke cracks me up.

But I decided against that, because, strange as it sounds, not everyone is familiar with such classic lines as: "Now hold on, sometimes a good sheep will do that."

So in looking for one good joke to tell, I decided to again tell the story of the biggest joke of the year 2000: No, not John Travolta's ludicrous *Battlefield Earth,* although that's way up there. It's the presidential election, stupid.

(And for some reason, it came to me in the form of an epic poem.)

Maestro, if you will . . .

The Florida Sec'y of State,
Ms. Harris, whose friends call her Kate.
Eye shadows she gathered,
Her peepers she slathered,
To certify Bush by said date.

And that was the start of it all.
When Kate left her job at the mall
To do her sworn duty,
This Junior League beauty,
Who craved an inaugural ball.

'Twas Florida that was the site,
Of the bitter electoral fight.
The anchors descended,
CNN never ended,
Until Greenfield bid Greta good night.

It relentlessly kept us on hold.
Constitutional scholars were polled.
Floyd Abrams, Jeff Toobin.
(How I longed for a Reuben,
And a couple of beers that were cold.)

There was Albert, the Prince of all Gore,
His undoing, his penchant to bore.
George Bush played the foil,
And developed a boil,
Wore a bandage that could cover a floor!

Those butterfly ballots, egad!
Machine counts were all breaking bad.
It's Palm Beach Gore needed,
His advisers conceded.
"You must count and then recount the chad."

Bush trotted out trusty Jim Baker,
Who accused Gore of plotting a caper.
"He will count till he wins!
"Do not let this begin!
"Think of Poppy! There's so much at stake here."

Gore won lawsuits, and Bush won some others.
(Although Bush got squadoosh from his brother.)
Bush's best hired gun
Was a Democrat's son.
Barry Richards, that's one mother-%%$@!*!

Theodore Olson and foe David Boies.
Both presented their cases with poise.
To Judge N. Sanders Sauls,
(Who's got a big pair of . . . um, gall!)
As my rabbi said, "What's with those goys?"

But the Gator high court went with Gore.
And Bill Daley let out such a roar.
(Richard J. would be proud
Done a jig in his shroud.)
Tipper looked for some champagne to pour.

Karen Hughes cried the court did Bush wrong.
Ari Fleischer sang the same song.
Dick Cheney said little;
He had tubes in his middle.
From his ranch Bush said, "I'm gonna kill Jeb."
No! No! He said, "My faith is still strong."
(Yeah, that's it.)

All the way up the ladder it climbed.
To the U.S. Supremes, who were primed.
Souter, Breyer, and Stevens,
Day O'Connor and even
Chief Rehnquist, who's out of his mind.

Scalia, of course, took the lead.
He said, "Nobody messes with me."
Clarence Thomas said zippo,

Not even a quippo.
It's like he was catching some z's.

The majority had to be five.
But when would the verdict arrive?
Rather, Brokaw, and Koppel
Feared the awful debacle:
They'd announce it on Larry King Live*!*

They ultimately called it for Bush
(Whose brain I've described as soft mush).
The recount was ended.
That's how Bush ascended
Minus an actual putsch.

Bush met Clinton, and then met with Al.
It was tense; they are hardly good pals.
Gore had partied till dawn,
His eyes red, his face drawn.
In Spain they'd say Al was muy mal.

And now soon they'll inaugurate George.
A presidency somehow to forge.
I don't want to sound bitter,
But all things considered,
We'd be better off with Victor Borge.

Stupes to Conquer

It has recently come to my attention that George W. Bush is the president of the United States. Apparently, Bush has been in office for *months*! You could have knocked me over with a feather. I was still on the edge of my seat, awaiting the results of the tense recount in Florida.

Guess I fell asleep.

It wasn't only me, apparently. It seems to have also just dawned on the American people that George W. Bush is actually president. (Well come on, nobody looked up from *Survivor*! And then there was the *Friends* wedding. And then *Sex and the City* came back on. How much information can they expect us to absorb?) In recent days Bush's approval rating has plunged like one of J-Lo's Grammy necklines. Bush is down eight points in a month. Bulletin to the President of the United States: This ain't T-ball, pal. In real life, they *do* keep score.

Republican strategists (and congratulations to those of you who screamed out, "Oxymoron!") believe that Bush's decline in popularity can be directly linked to the growing awareness that he is president. Bush was at the height of his popularity when he was being confused with George Bush, W's father; Jeb Bush, W's brother; and Rosebush, W's boyhood sled.

As always, Bush's greatest hope lies in the American people, the majority of whom is dumber than a bucket of hair. Despite the growing numbers of people who "can pick Bush out of a lineup," in a recent national survey only 28 percent of respondents knew "Bush" was president; 24 percent said "the other guy, the guy with those stupid alpha-male open-collar shirts," was president; a surprisingly high 16 percent identified Jim Jeffords as president, but many explained that Jeffords recently resigned the office "to go back to Vermont and run a Ben & Jerry's." (Oh, you think Americans aren't that stupid? Well, a *New York Times* story about the movie *Pearl Harbor* quoted opinions on the real Pearl Harbor offered by Americans on *The Tonight Show* that bear repeating: "It was in 19, like, 67. The Chinese people invaded America. Didn't they?". . ."It was bombed. By the Hawaiians. I think the Hawaiians won.". . ."It started World War II. In 1924." The scary thing is, I think I recognize my daughter in that group.)

It's been pretty much straight downhill for Bush since being appointed president by Big Nino "Knuckles" Scalia. Here are the highlights:

1. Life savings were lost as the stock market cratered.

2. Life savings were lost as gas prices soared.

3. Our spy plane is being sent back to us in 4 million easy-to-assemble jigsaw pieces.

4. Republicans lost control of the Senate.

Gosh, Tony, the Republicans must feel awful about numbers 1, 2, and 3.

You are the weakest link. Good-bye.

Republicans aren't concerned with people who lose their life savings; Republicans don't need life savings—they have equity. Nothing that happens to the economy can hurt Republicans. It's essentially a question of whether in any given administration they are merely "disgustingly rich" or "have more money than God." Nor do Republicans care about reassembling spy planes. That is labor. Republicans are management.

Ah, but losing control of the Senate. That stings. Because that means a loss of committee chairmanship, and with the loss of chairmanship comes a loss of limousines and office space. Now the Republicans don't have the corner offices, and they are freakin' steamed. They hate Jim Jeffords like Firestone hates Ford. Like Philip Morris hates juries.

Trent "Thanks-a" Lott in particular hates Jeffords. Lott is in lock-and-load position over Jeffords's defection, since that bumped

Lott from "Majority" to "Minority" leader. So here's Lott, in need of intravenous Prozac, saying that Jeffords taking a walk away from the party was "a coup of one that subverted the will of the American voters who elected a Republican majority."

Excuse me? What happened to the will of the American voters who gave more popular votes to Al Gore than to George Bush? What do they have to show for it, Trent, besides T-ball on the South Lawn? Or didn't you read the report of the U.S. Commission on Civil Rights that said Florida's conduct in the presidential election was marked by "injustice, ineptitude, and inefficiency"? And that was just in the application of eye makeup.

And if it wasn't bad enough that Jeffords left, John "I'm Gonna Get You, Sucka" McCain is on the verge of declaring himself a free agent. Bush could be down two in a month. You know what they do in baseball to pitchers who can't hold a lead? . . . Actually, they pay them about $4 million a year. But that's another column.

On the plus side, Bush *looks* great. He's working out two and three times a day. He's the first president who, in listing priorities for his administration, began with: Run seven-minute miles and bench-press two hundred pounds. Bush gets up in the morning, hops on a treadmill, and memorizes what Uncle Dick has written out for him. It's like being Peter Jennings, without the European tailoring. It takes all kinds, doesn't it? Bush is pumping iron. God knows what the guy before him was pumping.

W's Theme Song:
"Heart and Soul"

Normally, I don't go back to the same well week after week, so George Bush should be safe for a while. But did you see what Bush said after his recent meeting with Russia's President Vladimir "Ras" Putin? Bush met with Putin for ninety minutes and declared the former KGB agent a righteous dude. Bush explained: "I was able to get a sense of his soul."

See, right there is proof of the high quality of a Yale education. All Bush needed was ninety minutes to go metaphysical. Imagine if he'd hung out with Putin the whole afternoon. We all might be levitating. What's next, the Vulcan Mind Meld?

I'm delighted Bush could peer into Putin's soul. Maybe he was like Woody Allen, who said he was once charged with plagiarism on a metaphysics exam because he'd peered into the soul of the student next to him.

I'm curious about the size of Putin's soul. How much soul does he have? More than, say, Sam and Dave? More than Luther Vandross? Barry White? As a kid growing up in the Soviet Union, did his homeys say to Vladimir, "What it *is*, bro"?

(I interrupt this column to bring you this item. I quote from the wire service account: "Viagra has been banned from greyhound racing in Ireland after reports that it can make dogs run faster by speeding up their heart rate." Like my friend Denis says, man, if they catch that rabbit now, watch out!)

I hope I'm not the only one besides Crazy Ol' Jesse Helms who finds it uncomfortable that the president of our United States meets with an elite commie spy for an hour and a half, and pronounces him "honest, straightforward, and trustworthy." (Is Bush a fish or what? Half an hour with Robert Hanssen, and Bush would probably make him Postmaster General.)

I mean, it's one thing for Bush to get out of a meeting with Putin and say, "I met with Mr. Putin, and we reached consensus on a wide range of aims. True, we still have some serious cultural issues to bridge. Like that hideous beet soup the Russkies eat. One swallow of that slop and I'm all over Mr. Putin like my daddy was all over the prime minister of Japan a few years back. But on a personal level, Vlad's my dawg; ya know what I'm sayin', boyyyyyee."

But for Bush to say, "I was able to get a sense of his soul." Excuse me, who did we elect president, Shirley MacLaine?

Of course, the president wasn't the only one with unexpected insight this week. A check of Barbra Streisand's Web site revealed America's Diva is urging Californians to conserve energy by hanging their wash out to dry on a clothesline.

Let me ask you something: You think Barbra Streisand hangs her wash on a clothesline?

Are you crazy?

Babs pinning up bras and panties? With those nails? Bite your tongue.

She has people (who need people) to do her wash. (They're the luckiest people in the world.) The closest Babs ever gets to a line of clothes is Versace. Barbra Streisand couldn't find the washing machine in her own house without a Coast Guard search-and-rescue operation. She thinks All Temperature Cheer is what she gets when she steps onstage at Caesars Palace when the AC is on the blink.

Barbra probably hasn't done a load of wash in thirty years. It's a misty watercolor memory of the way she was. I'm betting it's in the prenup that James Brolin does her wash. That's why he's hawking Flex-A-Min, for when his muscles ache from ironing and folding. Seriously, what else is he doing? It's not like when Sir Laurence Olivier died, Marlon Brando stood up and said, "Don't worry, we've still got Jimmy Brolin."

Come on, close your eyes and imagine Barbra Streisand measuring the liquid Tide, hahaha. This is how Babs saves energy on her laundry: She wears something once, then throws it away.

Like these famous actresses in Malibu would hang their wash out on a line to dry. Like they'd string the clothesline between houses. Like one day Babs will lean out her window and call to Cher, "Hey, girlfriend, your wash looks great! Your thongs look so bright. What's your secret? How do you get your whites so white? And your plumage so, um, plumey?"

Like that'll happen.

If word got out that babes like Angelina Jolie and Catherine Zeta-Jones were hanging their wash out to dry? It would give new meaning to the phrase "panty raid." They'd have to post an ARMED RESPONSE sign next to the Clorox.

The gall of Barbra Streisand to call on her fellow Californians to hang their wash on a line when the only thing she knows about manual labor is that "manual" sounds like the name of her gardener. This from a woman who allegedly had it written into her performance contract in Las Vegas that the help couldn't *look* at her when she walked by; they had to avert their eyes. Who is she, Medusa?

I love Babs's Web site. She posts her political tracts, like "Dick Cheney's Record," "Last-Minute Thoughts Before the Election," and "Ten Republicans I Would Boink Even Though They Vote to Make Us Dependent on Fossil Fuel." (Okay, I made that one up.) But she actually does have political tracts. In "A Call to Conserve," she talks about how to reduce energy consumption: "Only run your dishwasher when it is fully loaded and air-dry your dishes instead of using the dry cycle. Turn off appliances and lights when they are not in use . . . seal and caulk doors and windows that leak." What kind of language is that? Is Barbra Streisand channeling the Maytag repairman?

By the way, Babs's Web site also has signature stuff you can buy: Streisand soup mugs, with her name in script; limited edition Streisand champagne; Babs's portrait in Lucite.

I'm holding out for a "Presidential Edition" glimpse of her soul.

Bill, Monica, and a Shooting Starr

Shooting Starr

If I understand the Whitewater investigation correctly, Kenneth Starr is asking women in Arkansas if they've had sex with Bill Clinton. At press time, it was not clear if he was asking *all* women in Arkansas, or if he was working from some sort of list.

I thought Whitewater was about banking, not boinking.

(Actually, I am a little vague on the details of Whitewater. Who wouldn't be? It's either a Ponzi scheme or a log flume ride at a theme park. The investigation seems to have been going on for a very long time with very little progress, like that TV show *Step by Step*, with Suzanne Somers and Patrick Duffy.)

Have you been following this thing? There are several disturbing factors:

1. Starr's head looks exactly like a lightbulb. (How many presidents does it take to change a lightbulb? None. The lightbulb is totally independent, and beyond the reach of presidents.)

2. Starr seems to be on what could be called a fishing expedition, if you fish with dynamite.

3. Starr is so sleazy he is actually on the trail of a Clinton love child! One Arkansas state trooper was reportedly asked whether a certain woman had given birth to a child, and did "it look like" Clinton?

Lessee. Chubby cheeks and face, a nose like Silly Putty. What baby *doesn't* look like Bill Clinton?

Maybe Starr feels he has to do something dramatic because he made such a fool of himself a few months ago when he announced he was leaving Whitewater to become dean of the law school at Pepperdine University, which he described as a "once-in-a-lifetime" job offer.

Pepperdine is in Malibu, California, overlooking the Pacific Ocean. Other schools award Ph.D.s. Pepperdine awards SPFs. Starr may as well have become dean of french fries at McDonald's Hamburger University.

Going after someone important for seemingly minor, unrelated charges is a tried-and-true tactic of law enforcement officials; remember that the feds didn't nail Capone for murder or racketeering—they got him for income tax evasion. But this is ridiculous. Focusing the Whitewater investigation on Clinton's sex life is like going after O. J. Simpson by trying to prove he illegally disconnected the catalytic converter on his Bronco.

Starr's tactics are so cheesy that next to him, Clinton looks like Gandhi.

Starr says his rationale is that a person might spill intimate criminal details during pillow talk. This seems improbable to me. It is hard to imagine the conversation:

"Oh, baby, you make my knees knock. Your teeth are like pearls. Your eyes are like limpid pools. Hey, did I tell you that I just made $230,000 selling a nine-acre tract of barren land in violation of Banking Regulation RM-8750, Subsection 1-W?"

I don't think so. Speaking of the law, you'll remember that last week I wrote that although I was available for jury duty, I hadn't yet been called to the courthouse. Well, this week I was. I was part of a jury pool of about sixty people for a cocaine trafficking trial. The judge explained the allegations and read us a series of fifteen questions. If you said yes to any of them, you then got a chance to explain your answers to the judge and the attorneys for the prosecution and defense. The questions were straightforward, such as: Have you seen the defendant before? Have you seen the lawyers before? Does anybody in your family work in law enforcement? Do you believe the government when it says that no spaceship landed at Roswell, and those aliens were really just crash dummies, even though eyewitnesses said they spoke in a musical cadence and ingested water through their spinal columns?

I answered yes to one question: Were you the victim of a crime in the last ten years? (Yes, my car was stolen a few years ago. And my editor is killing me.) I was worried about the man sitting to my left. He said yes to eleven of the fifteen questions, including: Is there any reason why you could not sit on this jury because you don't believe in the American judicial system? Of all the juries in the world, Che Guevara has to walk into mine.

Anyway, I went to talk to the judge, and I explained that my car was once stolen. And the judge asked me, "Is there any reason that experience would make it hard for you to judge this defendant?" I smiled and said, "Not unless it was him who stole my car."

I explained how the police found my car quickly, and the defense attorney asked, "Do you feel beholden to the police?" I said, "No, but they did a good job." And the defense attorney said, with some irritation, "That's twice you've mentioned the police now." And I said, "Well, they got my car back. I thought I ought to disclose that. Would you feel better if I had said that the local chapter of the United Mine Workers recovered my car?"

At that moment I sensed I was not going to be put on the jury. Guess what? I was right.

Sweatin' the Small Stuff

So far the funniest thing I've heard since the Starr report hit the fan was when Bill Clinton urged the public not to "get mired in the details here."

I love that. It's exactly what I would have said if there was a 443-page report about me, and on 442 of those pages was the phrase "unzipped his pants."

I'd want to go in a different direction, too.

"My fellow Americans, how 'bout Sammy Sosa and Mark McGwire, huh? Man, they're slamming the ball. And those Yankees? Geddoudahere. Thank you, and good night. Drive safely. Go and sin no more."

So let's forget about all those pesky, squishy details. Who needs a nation thigh-high in the spinach dip? (Says my friend Nancy: "I'll never look at spinach dip the same again.")

I've been avoiding reading footnotes ever since college, and this is no time to start parsing Ken Starr's report for references to Altoids and cigars. Does anyone really need to know that Monica Lewinsky had the most torrid relationship with a Cuban since Lucille Ball?

In fact, if I might be, ahem, blunt, I think we've all heard enough about the president's position on young people's tobacco use.

(I can't help it. Every time I hear the word "cigar" now, I think of the line Groucho Marx used on his quiz show to a female contestant who'd borne fifteen children: "Madam, I like my cigar, but I take it out of my mouth once in a while.")

David Kendall, the president's lawyer, has been trying to distract the public, too—with his face. The sides don't match; it looks like something Picasso painted.

Of course Clinton tried to use Czech Republic president Vaclav Havel for cover the other day at their joint news conference. Havel was here to speak about the potato harvest and NATO enlargement. The White House press corps kept questioning Clinton about engorged tubers.

Havel delivered careful, one-sentence answers like he was the Prague Yoda or something. But he got his own laughs. After all, it was his idea to invite Lou "Take a Walk on the Wild Side" Reed to play the White House state dinner.

Clinton will take whatever cover he can get at this point. He has made it known that he's receiving "pastoral care" from a roster of clergymen that grows every day. He's surrounded by more priests than the Notre Dame football team. Except they're protecting interns from offensive lines.

Clinton has suggested there could be a bright side to this whole thing because it could serve as "a learning experience." I know plenty of guys who are ready to enroll at Clinton University. (Syllabus: all the good parts in *Delta of Venus* and *Tropic of Cancer*. School Motto: "Ladies Drink Free.")

And I'm personally ready to pledge his frat, I Phelta Thi.

If you think the release of the president's videotaped testimony will hurt him, wait until porn stars start doing live reenactments of the Starr report on cable access.

Wow. Who in the government would watch that? I mean, besides Clarence Thomas?

But that, at least, would be more exciting than CNBC, CNN, and MSNBC, all of which are rapidly becoming the Impeachment Channel with Greta Van Susteren and Joe diGenova.

Geraldo Rivera has moved the most seamlessly from the days of all-O.J., all the time to all-Monica, all the time. Geraldo sits there, slamming into Clinton like a hurricane for having demeaned the presidency with his cheap sex obsession—the same Geraldo who wrote gleefully in his autobiography that he had sex with the wife of Senator Jacob Javits in her mirrored bathroom and shagged the ex-wife of the prime minister of Canada in a rowboat in Central Park.

The other night political consultant Ed Rollins proclaimed to Geraldo, "I care about adultery. Adultery broke up my marriage."

Geraldo attempted to comfort Rollins by declaring, "You were victimized by adultery. I have victimized by adultery."

Thanks for sharing, guys. Now go back into the forest and beat on some drums.

But the worst revelations lately are the sexual confessions of members of Congress. As kids we thought there was nothing worse than picturing your parents doing it. Now I have to imagine Helen Chenoweth, Dan Burton, and Henry Hyde checking in for a threesome at Plato's Retreat.

Last week Hyde referred to an affair thirty years back as a "youthful indiscretion." He was forty-one when it began. Hank, get outta here, the window on your youthful indiscretions closed during the Korean War! Next he'll ask us to ignore his acid experiments at that rave on his fiftieth birthday.

Right here, right now, I'm personally begging Senator Barbara Mikulski not to be part of this horrifying trend.

But back to Mr. Bill and Miss Monica. As a sportswriter, there are some details my boss George and I have paid considerable attention to. And we have a theory. Notice the dates when Monica says she and the Prez were playing with Mr. Macanudo.

November 15: a Wednesday during football season.

December 31: the day before the New Year's Day bowl games.

January 21: the Sunday between the conference championships and the Super Bowl.

February 4: the Sunday after the Super Bowl. The sex was in the morning, hours before the Pro Bowl, which starts late because it's from Hawaii.

March 31: the day between the semifinals and the championship of the Final Four.

April 7: the Sunday before the Masters.

My point is that every one of these sexual encounters took place when there were no sports on TV to distract Clinton. The man is a total sports geek. Remember where he was at 1 A.M. a few years ago when that small plane crashed into the White House? He was up in the attic watching West Coast college football on ESPN.

The problem is that District Cablevision stinks. You can't get WGN. You can't get WOR. The man simply couldn't get his sports fix.

All Hillary had to do was give him a satellite dish, and this never would have happened.

Let this be a lesson to the rest of you.

A Starr-Crossed Tale

There once was a man named Ken Starr.
In matters of law he went far.
For fame he did reach,
The Big Creep to impeach.
He came close. But, heh-heh, no cigar.

Forty million Starr spent to inquire,
Whether Bill in his lust did conspire,
To obstruct and to lie,
Cover up and deny.
(Did Vernon get Revlon to hire?)

Starr's charges got meaner and leaner.
No high crime, and no misdemeanor.
They centered on sex,
As opposed to bad checks.
Starr spent years to indict Clinton's wiener!

Now the president looks like he'll dance.
He'll avoid doing time for romance.
So Bill's in the clear.
He has saved his large rear.
"Go pay Paula. And pull up your pants."

Ms. Lewinsky was taped by Ms. Tripp,
Saying blah-blah and da-da-dip-dip.
Quoting Babba and Bubba,
And her own stagestruck mother.
It was torture—a slow, steady drip.

They examined the president's id.
With witnesses locked on the grid.
There were Currie and Willey;
Marcia cried herself silly.
And who could forget Sid the Squid?

William Ginsburg defended Lewinsky.
Her pulkes he found quite munchinsky.
But Cacheris and Stein,
Struck a deal so divine,
Ginsburg ended up just a buttinsky.

As I gazed at this noble committee,
I was stunned to see nobody pretty.
There's just mutt after mutt.
Nadler's Jabba the Hut!
Are they voted in just out of pity?

All the randy details Starr compiled,
Delighted his side of the aisle.
Myopic and smug,
A fancy-pants thug,
Starr has substance, but no sense of style.

He glories in being called "Judge."
As if no one could ever begrudge,
His implacable gaze,
His self-righteous ways,
His four-hundred-plus pages of sludge.

Starr warbles as sweet as a crooner.
He sails effortlessly, like a schooner,
As the Democrats grate him,
And poke him, and bait him.
Abbe Lowell tries to grill him like tuna.

On the stand Starr receives much affection.
From Republicans: blanket protection.
But then questions get rough.
And, unsure of his stuff,
He resorts to some navel inspection.

I'd have loved to see Carville alone,
With his singular brand of corn pone,
Foam-flecked and growling,
Baying and howling,
Gnawing at Starr like a bone.

But the White House chose Kendall to clamor,
At Starr's prosecutorial hammer.
He got under Starr's skin.
Which by then had worn thin.
And they hissed back and forth, yam and yammer.

The election has rendered this moot,
There's no juice in the impeachment fruit.
Voters stood up for Bill,
Sent more Dems to the Hill.
Good-bye and good riddance to Newt.

I'm now ending this chapter and verse,
With a thought that's both blunt and that's terse.
Say we're done with the parsing,
And the rest of this Starr thing.
Or just drive me away in a hearse.

The Clinton Show

In defense of Bill Clinton the Democrats deny nothing. They eagerly confirm that the president is a weasel and a liar, that what he did with Monica Lewinsky was "sinful" and "morally reprehensible." Whenever Clinton's name is mentioned, Democrats get a pinched expression and sniff the air nervously, like somebody broke wind.

But of course they wouldn't vote to impeach Clinton. Like Clinton—who's so sorry he should consider changing his name to Brenda Lee—they prefer the option of censure. At this point the president would gladly wear his underpants on his head and run around the Rose Garden if the Republicans would only call this off.

The Democrats say they don't want to put the people through "the horror of what will follow." Impeachment, they warn us, will paralyze the country.

I'll tell you what will paralyze the country: another day of looking at Henry Hyde. Where does he get his suits, Sunny's Surplus? His jackets are so bulky, it looks like if you pulled a string they'd inflate.

What a cast of characters on the Judiciary Committee. Democrat Robert Wexler shouts like a hyena. His district is in South Florida—Heaven's waiting room—and Wexler probably won because he was the only candidate people could understand without a hearing aid. Republican Mary Bono has the lights on, but nobody's home. She makes her late husband, Sonny, seem like Alistair Cooke.

Have you ever heard anything more stultifying than these hearings? It's like being trapped in an elevator with the Japanese cast of

Cats. Republican counsel David Schippers lectured for two hours and forty-five minutes straight. When he was done, the run toward the House bathroom resembled the Oklahoma Land Rush. If that's the way politics is conducted, how could you blame Clinton for taking a "Monica break" now and again?

What's with all the Watergate crawlbacks? It's like somebody set up a Monsters of Impeachment Reunion Tour. Did you get a load of Robert Drinan? He looked like the Creature from the Black Lagoon.

Jack Kevorkian, please pick up the white courtesy phone.

The hearings have been a terrible letdown. All hat, no cattle. It's like the Clarence Thomas confirmation hearings—but without the Coke can.

(Another letdown last week: the Frank Sinatra files released by the FBI. They spend forty years stalking Frank, and they can't come up with a single piece of credible evidence to prove what everyone knows: that Frank personally ordered the murders of Bing Crosby, Dinah Shore, and Secretariat. Kitty Kelley had more on Frank in 40 pages than the FBI had in 1,275. What was J. Edgar Hoover doing all this time, trying on bustiers? And someone dares to call Henry Hyde the chairman? Francis Albert Sinatra was the Chairman of the Board, baby, and don't you forget it.)

Yet as horrifying as these impeachment hearings were, I don't want to see it stop now.

I want exactly what the Republicans want. I want to subvert the will of the people and make a joke out of the national interest by putting the president of the United States on trial for the high crimes and misdemeanors of his ding-a-ling. (Then I want to put Bob Inglis on trial for that smirk of his.)

Look, I didn't sit through all these months of *Geraldo Live* to see it end here—with the last word going to some pompous law professor lecturing me on what the Founding Fathers meant when they allowed for impeachment in the Constitution. (As if this is possible. The Constitution was written 220 years ago. I only saw one witness all week old enough to know what they were thinking: Elizabeth Holtzman.)

I don't want *impeachis interruptis*.

I want a trial in the Senate that lasts for months. And I want to see Strom Thurmond try to stay awake through all of it.

I want Linda Tripp questioned about what she does to collect a $90,000 check at the Pentagon—besides talk all day about bikini waxing with Monica. I want to see Lewinsky's big can on the witness stand. I want to hear her talk about the sex in glorious, graphic Larry Flyntesque detail, so I can be insanely jealous.

Chairman Hyde says, "It's not about sex." Of course it is—that's why we were all riveted to our TVs back in January. When it became about perjury and the law, like this week, we switched the channel to *Sunset Beach*.

The president's lawyer said people don't want any more "salacious muck."

Which people has *he* talked to?

I say: Gimme muck.

I for one am unafraid of the "horror that will follow."

After watching Bob Barr, the Stone Age Republican from Georgia, how could it be worse than the horror that preceded it?

(Seriously, when you see the people we've elected to actually represent us, don't you long for a dictator? A fat guy wearing epaulets and a slew of silly medals on his chest would be so much less embarrassing than, say, Maxine "Muddy" Waters or George "The Geek" Gekas.)

I want to hear from expert sex witnesses. Let's bring in Dick Morris and see him grilled about how he talked poll results with the president, and let his "escort" listen in on White House calls. I yearn to hear Senate witnesses described as "forensic hookers."

As a nation, we need to process the Clinton "sins" so we can get on with the process of healing. But we shouldn't do it hastily. Certainly not before a series of televised reenactments.

The fact is this country needs an impeachment trial. Without it, the cable TV industry as we know it will collapse. Chris Matthews will end up standing at the entrance to the Metro, holding a sign that says: WILL HECTOR ANYONE FOR FOOD.

Put it on during sweeps week, and it'll crush. I'm talking better numbers than the Super Bowl: a 30 rating and a 65 share.

Impeachment could be so big that if the House didn't vote it, Aaron Spelling would have to invent it.

Won't You Come Home,
Bill Clinton?

Perhaps you've noticed that President Clinton has gone to Africa for eleven days. He is being accompanied by his first wife, Hillary.

It is the most extensive visit to Africa by any U.S. president. Apparently, the previous record was two hours, for refueling. President Reagan once *thought* he was in Africa, but that turned out to be a screening of *The Gods Must Be Crazy.*

You may be wondering why the president of the United States would choose to spend eleven days visiting such garden spots as Rwanda and Uganda, when the most beautiful place on Earth right now is here, in Washington, at cherry blossom time.

Why is he in Africa?

a. To bag a zebra on safari.

b. To bag an intern on safari.

c. To buy a phat dashiki to go with his mad-flava Indonesian batik shirt.

None of the above. The correct answer is:

d. Because it's harder for a process server to deliver a subpoena in Botswana than at 1600 Pennsylvania Avenue NW.

At this point, Clinton will go anywhere to get out of Washington.

He would happily climb on the next space shuttle—but John Glenn had dibs.

While in Africa, Clinton offered what was called "a broad expression of contrition" for America's shameful role in slavery.

It was an important, heartfelt moment. But Clinton clearly sees the benefit of staying on the road. And so his next trip will take him to Bolivia, where he plans to spend twenty-one days and apologize for Butch Cassidy and the Sundance Kid. After that the president will be traveling to the Yukon Territory to apologize for whale massacres in the late 1880s. Next he's off to the Marshall Islands to apologize for "all that bird guano." And there's talk that he'll visit the Wal-Mart in Port-of-Spain to apologize that they ran out of the twenty-four-packs of Diet Coke for $4.99.

I don't know about you, but I'm not sure President Clinton is ever coming back.

What's he got to come back to? He doesn't own a home. He lives in public housing with a dog and a cat. And the law is after him. You put that profile on anybody else, and the guys down at Max's 24-Hour Bail Bonds would be getting very nervous.

From now on, Clinton will try to avoid Washington like Marcia Lewis avoids the grand jury. You know how presidents will fly to flood-ravaged areas and help with the cleanup to show how responsive they are? At this point Clinton will helicopter to your home if you call about the standing water in your basement.

In his zeal to get out of town, Clinton appears to have embarked on something that looks like a farewell tour. Which is exactly what you do to shore up a sagging career.

Look at what it did for the Judds.

I'm anticipating a video and a CD, including tunes like "Help Me, Rwanda," "Ghana Get You into My Life," and "Baby, You Can Drive Dakar." I've already seen photos of Clinton dancing, holding babies, and shaking hands. If I didn't know better, I would assume he was running for president of Senegal—which might not be a bad gig, because that way he could continue to claim executive privilege, and also sport a happenin' leopard-skin hat.

(Speaking of the Judds, did you happen to take a gander at Ashley Judd during the Academy Awards? She was wearing a skirt with a belt-high slit, and appeared to have dressed in such a hurry that she plumb forgot her undies. Let me simply suggest it's no wonder Ms. Judd wasn't cast in *The Real Blonde.* Even more shocking was that upon seeing Ashley's display, Madonna and Drew Barrymore didn't peel off all their clothing in some sort of ritualistic Slut-Off. The Judds are an accomplished family. Ashley acts. Her mother, Naomi, is a best-selling author. And her sister, Wynonna, hasn't missed a meal since 1992.)

It's no wonder Clinton doesn't spend any time stateside. I believe we're now into double figures regarding the number of women who are being sought by Ken Starr to testify whether they've had sexual relations with Clinton. (As the boys in the frat house would say: "Double figures. Sweet!")

Soon, Starr will have the records of every book these women have ever purchased. What is this cluck thinking? Does he hope that Monica Lewinsky—thank God I finally got her name into this column; I was running out of time—bought Clinton a copy of *A Night to Remember*? Or *Waiting to Exhale*?

Anyway, while Starr continues to chase his own tail, here's what I predict will happen when Clinton finally returns to Washington. He will be wandering on the South Lawn when a bottle will drop from the sky. It will be one of those new Virgin Cola bottles that the loopy Richard Branson is selling in the surgically augmented shape of *Baywatch* love goddess Pamela Anderson.

Drawn inexorably to that bodacious shape, Clinton will pick up the bottle, draw it to his lips, then hold it over his head triumphantly—as crowds of tourists go wild and hail him as a new prophet.

The gods *must* be crazy.

Bill's Next Gig

One year from today a tall, tanned, silver-haired man, instantly recognizable, stands at a lectern in the Beverly Hilton, washed in the exhilarating sound of applause.

He begins to speak.

"Thank you. It's a pleasure to be with you tonight. Here's a joke my ex-wife won't like: Why did Hillary always like to mess around very early in the morning? [*Pause.*] She wanted to be the first lady."

Bada-bing.

"Hey, how about that Bob Livingston, huh? He gets caught playing Hide-the-Gavel and has the honor and decency to resign. I say, give that man a cigar."

Bada-boom.

"Take my franking privilege. Please."

A former president has to make a living, doesn't he?

Remember, just last week it was Henry Hyde who suggested: "The president would be welcomed around the country at groups who would love to hear him speak."

But who knew it would come so soon?

It's time to consider what President Clinton will do when he leaves office—which, judging by my wristwatch, may be as early as Wednesday.

By bombing Iraq, Clinton was able to DeLay impeachment by a day or two. (DeLay: Get it? And as Dave Barry might say, don't you think the Dick Armey is a great name for a punk band?)

In fact, I imagined Clinton sitting in his office last week, writing:

Dear Diary,

Holy cow. It worked!

". . . Caught between Iraq and a haaarrrddd place."

I'm glued to CNN. But the night-vision gizmo makes it look like I'm staring into a frog pond. And I keep seeing a car driving down a street—it looks like the same car all the time. Maybe it's like what Keanu Reeves did in Speed, *where he ran the same loop to fool Dennis Hopper and get everybody off the bus. . . .*

Hey, that Christiane Amanpour's a babe.

Hmmm, now what? Can I possibly keep bombing until the new Congress gets in?

Note: Need Albright to get me a list of countries I can bomb and nobody will make a big stink.

Belgium, duck! Hahaha.

Ah, but victory for our Commander in Briefs was all too brief.

By Friday, Congress was back deliberating impeachment, and Clinton had to consider what to do next. What best becomes an ex-president?

Richard Nixon became an author. He wrote grave, numbingly boring books about his life, his presidency, and his foreign policy. The books were outsold 100 to 1 by the *Where's Waldo?* series.

Gerald Ford played golf and tried not to kill anyone by skiing into them. Somewhere, Ford has a presidential library with his important paper. Jimmy Carter became a handyman. You can phone him, and he'll go to your house and fix your toilet and put your door back on its hinges. The man wears overalls. It's pathetic. (It's impossible to believe these men were actually presidents. What happened to us in the '70s? What were we thinking?)

Ronald Reagan, of course, became an airport.

George Bush has gotten much more interesting since leaving office. All of a sudden he has a wild side. He jumps out of planes! (The only thing I can imagine Clinton jumping out of is the second-floor window of some honey's town house.) I fully expect to see Bush rolling down Wisconsin Avenue on a street luge.

Bob Dole never was president. But he took a critical first step upon entering the private sector: He got a face-lift. So instead of looking seventy-five, he looks seventy-one. Clinton simply has to get "blephed." (Blepharoplasty, silly, an eye job to get rid of those horrible bags; he's carrying enough lower-lid luggage to be a bell-boy.) Now Dole's touting Viagra—he spends half the night keeping Liddy giddy!

Sex and lying seem to be what Clinton does best. Surely there's some job he can find that rewards these attributes. Should he open up a public relations agency with Dick Morris? They could do PR for Larry Flynt's new *Smokin' Hot Congressional Quarterly*.

Funny how Republicans see a Democrat who has admitted, under duress, to having an improper relationship with a woman not his wife, and they want him removed from office. But when these same Republicans see Republicans who have admitted, under duress, the same thing—they praise them like the '72 Dolphins. What am I missing here? The only reason these people didn't lie about their affairs under oath is because nobody asked them under oath.

Okay, what else could Clinton do? He can write his own tell-all book. I can see it now: *Inside Monica*.

He could be on the senior golf tour. A McDonald's manager. Dry cleaner?

I know. Clinton can construct crossword puzzles. That way he'll be able to tell us what the definition of "is" is.

Better yet: He ought to call up his Hollywood pals and start producing movies. I can see him green-lighting his first feature: *Saddam, You've Got Mail.*

Forgotten But Not Gone

To: William J. Clinton
President of the United States
Washington, D.C.

Dear Bill,

Jeez, what the hell has happened to you? You've, like, disappeared. You and Chuck Mangione. I keep thinking I'm going to
see you on a milk carton. *Bada-bing!*

Everywhere I turn I see John McCain, George W. Bush, Al
Gore, and Bill Bradley. But not Bill Clinton. I mean, really, what
does the president of the United States of America have to do just
to get a little publicity these days—marry Darva? (Did you ever
hear of such a thing? A TV show where fifty women parade past
you in bathing suits, competing to be picked out and whisked off?
Hey, will ya listen to me. *Hear* of it? You probably *pitched* it.)

But the point is, even if you did, nobody cares. You are such
non-news you may as well be secretary of agriculture. Remember
in the good old days when you'd go jogging, and all the TV networks sent camera crews? Now you could *streak* and you couldn't
even raise a minyan. You're a stealth president. You could fly right
into CNN and nobody would see you.

I saw where recently you convened a summit of Internet security specialists to talk about how to stop hacking. This is what it's
come to? Bringing a bunch of techno-geeks to the White House to
discuss how to erect a computer firewall? What's next, Bill, a *Star
Trek* convention?

I feel for you. You're rattling around in the White House like the Ghost of Christmas Past. Your daughter's back in college. Your wife has gone to New York on, um, business. We both know she's never coming back.

She's calling herself simply "Hillary" now. Not Mrs. Clinton. Not Hillary Rodham Clinton. Just Hillary. Like Wynonna. One day she'll be campaigning in a small Upstate town, like Binghamton, and she'll pull out a guitar and start singing C&W. Gaaack.

It's just you and that dumb dog now. (The cat's gone, right? I mean, it's too pathetic to contemplate—a middle-aged man alone in a big house with a cat.) Face it, it's over. Al Gore's got more juice than you. Al Gore! Hey, did you see where Al's thinking about making "Love Train" by the O'Jays his official campaign song? Remember that? *Très* lame. "People all over the world, join hands. Start a love train." Oh, please, Al start *this*!

Talk about the end of the ride. Billy, bubbeleh, your *name* doesn't even come up! The other day in Albany, Hillary and Al had a joint campaign stop; they hugged and kissed and made slurpy speeches about each other. You they didn't even mention by name. They referred only to "our president," like you were stuffed, and in mothballs somewhere, like Trigger. They sure as hell don't want you to campaign for them. Everybody admires your political skill, but nobody wants you anywhere near them. You've become Dick Morris!

The days of wine and health care are over, Bill. And that cute thing you do when you bite your lip? Forget it. Leonardo DiCaprio did that in *Titanic*. It belongs to him now.

Last week I mentioned your name to my pal Frankie, and he said, "Is he *still* president?"

Hmmm, what could you do to get some attention?

Ooops. Sorry I asked.

Here's the problem. You're forgotten, but not gone.

AND YOU'VE GOT TEN MONTHS TO GO!

You must have built up sick days, right? Maybe you can take them all at once. You throw in your vacation days and comp time, and you duck out by October. Maybe catch the Series. Or go to Cannes and party with Matt and Ben.

Look, I understand your situation. You feel useless. You feel like nobody's listening. You feel you're the sound of the tree falling in the forest that nobody hears. I know that sound. I *make* that sound. I prepare my annual State of the Household Address, and before I even clear my throat, my kids ask:

1. Do we have to listen?

2. Are you done yet?

It's okay. It's nothing a little Johnnie Walker Blue and some cashews can't fix.

I empathize, Bill, so I'm inviting you to hang with me. You can sleep in the attic. (It's probably nicer than where Hillary made you sleep.) If your wife calls, my seventeen-year-old daughter will take the message.

She'll tell you, "Oh, some woman called for you a few days ago. I wrote it down, but I don't remember where. Can I have some money to go to Montgomery Mall?"

You'll ask what the name of the woman was, and she'll say, "I don't know. But it was like a weird name."

"Was it Hillary?" you'll ask.

"Uh, *no*! Hillary. That's random. . . . Gee, you ask a lot of questions."

Look, Bill, you love sports. I'm a sportswriter. I've got cable. I know all those guys at ESPN. You love good conversation. I'm a radio talk show host. You love to eat. I've got the Ronco Rotisserie; we can cook four whole chickens at a time! You love interns. I, um, know a good internist.

Hey, if we get tired of hanging around the house, watching March Madness and *When House Pets Go Mental,* we can go check out Saks. When was the last time you went to a high-end department store in the middle of the week? I'm telling you, it's a total babe-o-rama. It's like some exotic little game preserve. A couple of Big Bwanas like us, who knows what could happen? (Short of actual impeachable offenses, I mean.)

Then we can go completely nuts at Cinnabon.

Don't worry. When we get back to the house, my daughter will have a careful accounting of any important messages.

Like: "A man called. It was urgent. Something about briefs in a suitcase. Or maybe coats and a briefcase."

You mean *codes* and a briefcase?

"Yeah, right, whatever."

Uh-oh.

Lay It on Me

Hiya, hiya, hiya. Is everybody having a good time? Is everybody ready to laugh? Put on your party hats, here comes Mr. Tony.

Not that I'm bitter. I only mention it because I've sacrificed the best years of my life to give you a smile. Even when something catastrophic happens—when a volcano erupts and kills thousands, or, um, my cable goes on the fritz—I'm still thinking about how I can make you laugh. See, it doesn't matter how much I have to suffer, as long as *you're* happy.

I'm sure after all these years of mirth, you must be wondering how you can say, "Thank you, Tony."

Here's how: Say it with home furnishings.

I've taken the liberty of establishing the Tony Kornheiser Gift Registry. You can access it at my Web site, Thankyoutony.com, where you can show your appreciation for my years of public service by giving me what the pros call "your generous contribution to the White House."

I want what Bill and Hillary got.

Everything.

The nation was anticipating the Clintons finally leaving the White House. And technically, they *did* leave the building. They just didn't leave anything in it.

I wish I had a picture of Bill and Hillary walking from the White House to the moving van, their clothing bulging with swag. The flatware in their pockets jingled so loudly, people thought they were the Marine Band.

Check out Bill's golf haul. He got four drivers—one from Jack Nicholson! (And don't ask how many mulligans it comes with, because you can't *handle* the truth)—four putters, two sets of irons, and a golf bag. That's enough equipment to open a driving range. Plus, the Clintons got $71,650 worth of artwork, including "two Mongolian landscapes," which puts them two up on me—and everybody else outside of Ulan Bator—and a $300 "painting of Buddy," their dog, smoking a cigar and playing poker, I hope.

They took $21,819 worth of china.

Yeah, sure, they plan on entertaining. But they now control more china than Li Peng!

They took $17,966 worth of flatware.

This is like calling Crate & Barrel and instead of ordering "service for twelve" you order "service for New Jersey."

They took $52,021 worth of furniture.

That leaves, what, the Lincoln footstool? When Bar and Poppy drop over for an evening of highly competitive cribbage, what are they going to sit on—Jeb?

I guess the Clintons figured: Hey, we've just bought two houses. *Somebody's* got to furnish them.

The Clintons' position was that "good friends" had sent them all this stuff and meant for them to have it. I believe that. Over the years I, myself, sent Bill autographed copies of two books I wrote. In retrospect, I feel bad sending books. The way the guy's scrounging around, I probably should have sent him a leg of lamb and a lob wedge.

Lately I've tried to put myself in the Clintons' place. What would I want from my many generous friends?

I would want a Mercedes-Benz S600.

Black, thanks.

Of course, if I were in the Clintons' place, and I'd just gotten an $8 million advance on a book the way Hillary did, I could easily afford to buy the Benz myself. But like the Clintons, I'd enjoy it so much more if *you* bought it for me.

That's the part that gets me—the eight big ones Hillary just reeled in. And it's not like Bill's begging for spare change on Pennsylvania Avenue. He's pulling down $150,000 a speech. (And a great speech it is: "I did good, didn't I? Okay, there was that messy thing. But ten years from now who's gonna remember? Take Al Gore. Please. You believe what a putz he was, not running on my record? Talk about blowing it, er . . . hey, who's ready for me to play 'The Girl from Ipanema' on my sax?") The Clinton family income will probably be $15 million this year. They can't afford flatware on that? What are they making flatware out of these days, weapons-grade plutonium?

Plus, Clinton's getting this primo office space in midtown Manhattan. Originally, the approximately $800,000-a-year rent was supposed to be absorbed by taxpayers. But Clinton has recently committed to contribute $300,000 with funds from his charitable Bill Clinton Foundation (motto: "Oh, Please, You Don't Expect Me to Live in Arkansas, Do You?").

Some folks, I've read, are angry at the Clintons for leaving nothing in the White House but the doorknobs. Not me. I'm impressed. I'd love to live in a fancy, furnished house, rent-free, for eight years, and then haul all the furniture out with me. That's so cool. It's like they cashed in 750,000 Marriott Rewards points.

Ultimately, whether you think the Clintons acted badly is a matter of perception. Take what happened at the Miami Seaquarium the other day. A big sea turtle met an untimely death, and while everyone felt terrible about it . . . well, let me quote from the Associated Press: "Flesh from a protected species of sea turtle that died . . . was turned into stew and eaten by some of the facility's workers." Hmmm. Maybe they ought to change the name to Miami Seaquarium and Chowder House.

I concede there was probably a better way to dispose of Mr. Turtle. But if it had been a chicken, would anyone be squawking? (Except the chicken. *Bada-bing!*) Of course not. The bad part wasn't that the workers ate the turtle. What were they supposed to do? Let it lie in state and then give it a Viking funeral? The bad part was that people found out!

It isn't illegal to make turtle bisque, but it presents what the pros call "an image problem." Now, any time a lobster dies in that aquarium, everybody's going to sniff the guards for lemon and butter sauce.

Essentially, what happened to the Clintons was: They were caught eating the sea turtle.

I Logged Lewinsky

White House Log. December 11, 1996: M. Lewinsky arrived, seeking meeting with president on "a matter of grave economic importance." Spent fifteen minutes in Oval Office with door closed. Upon leaving Lewinsky was overheard saying, "Then I can put you down for two boxes of Thin Mints, two Samoas, and a box of Trefoils?"

White House Log. April 14, 1997: M. Lewinsky arrived for "Cabinet-level discussion of troop deployment in Bosnia." Had one question before private meeting with president. "How do you spell 'Bosnia'?"

White House Log. July 13, 1997: M. Lewinsky cleared to enter after confusion at security gate, where she claimed to have a package for the president. "Actually," she clarified, "I *am* the package for the president."

Don't ask me how I obtained the annotated "Lewinsky Logs." All I can say is it was rough. Rougher than being Linda Tripp's hairdresser.

According to White House records, Monica "The Sweetheart of Rodeo Drive" Lewinsky made thirty-seven visits to the White House between April 1996 and December 1997. This was *after* Lewinsky left her job at the White House for her job at the Pentagon. That's a lot of return visits to the White House for an intern. That would be about thirty-seven more than Warren Christopher.

"It doesn't seem high to me," Lewinsky's lawyer, William Ginsburg, said of the number of visits.

Maybe not if she was working for Domino's.

White House Log. June 9, 1997: M. Lewinsky arrived for the seventh time in the last two weeks. "Hee-hee, I came back because I left my Tic Tacs in my desk," she said. (*Note from Betty Currie: Even though the door was closed, I heard everything, right?*)

I'm sure there are many explanations besides sex why Monica Lewinsky had such free and easy access to the president of the United States.

Um, just give me a second here.

Ummm.

Oh! Ginsburg has asserted that his client and the president were "colleagues."

White House Log. November 2, 1997: M. Lewinsky arrived and identified herself as having "served the president in a variety of positions." She was wearing a long T-shirt dress and carrying a book of poetry she said was given to her by "The Creep." (*Note from Betty: Is this when she turned the gifts over to me?*)

Of course, it's possible that Monica wasn't there to see the president at all. Kenneth Starr has twice called White House valet Bayani Nelvis to testify. Nelvis is said to have been fast friends with Monica; the two reportedly dined together and exchanged gifts. (Was Monica an intern or a catalog rep for Lillian Vernon?) Maybe it was Nelvis whom Monica went to see thirty-seven times.

White House Log. November 10, 1997: M. Lewinsky departed abruptly when informed, "Nelvis has left the building."

I realize that by concentrating on an inconsequential scandal that I am giving terribly short shrift to political issues of great importance. For example, last week President Clinton presented the nation with its first balanced budget in thirty years. Wow. That's swell.

Now back to Monica:

I worried about her being so cooped up here in Washington. I worried she wasn't eating correctly. ("Who's Feeding Lewinsky?" was actually a suggested *Washington Post* "Style" section story.) I worried she'd blow up like the *Hindenburg* if all she ate were the Dunkin' Donuts her Watergate neighbor Bob Dole brought over.

I worried she wasn't able to do much of anything—except, apparently, tell everybody in the world that she was having sex with the president of the United States. She told her high school friends. She told her college friends. From everything I read in *Newsweek* and *People,* the last two folks in the country to know were me and Hillary.

So I was glad to see Monica return home to Beverly Hills this week, in search of what her lawyer called a "normal" life. I think just about everyone in America thinks of Beverly Hills as a place where you can live a normal life—after your cosmetic surgery scars have healed and you've undergone laser hair removal and colon hydrotherapy, of course.

"She wants to go shopping," Ginsburg said.

Of course she does. She needs some new outfits for the impeachment proceedings.

It's great that Monica's back in her element, and, like, what an element it is. Here is what Monica's classmate at Beverly Hills High, Eden Sassoon, daughter of Vidal Sassoon, told *People* magazine: "If we had, like, parties, Monica would be there. But, like, I wouldn't call up Monica and be, like, 'Hey, we're going to do this and that.' "

Thank you, Eden, I know it was difficult to, like, string as many as four words together in, like, English. Now go get yourself a Frappuccino before somebody from *The New Yorker* asks you to spell "cat."

I'm glad Monica's at home with her dad and her lawyer-on-a-leash. The only one I worry about now is Monica's mom, Marcia Lewis, the author. The two are supposedly very close. One story I read said they shared everything.

White House Log. February 8, 1998: M. Lewinsky arrived at White House gate in long T-shirt dress, showed hopelessly outdated photo ID. Upon interrogation, visitor confessed to being Lewinsky's mother, Marcia Lewis. Asked to see president despite having no appointment. Bragged, "If he liked my daughter, he'll love me."

Courting Monica

Where's Monica, already?

I'm ready for her. We're all ready for her.

She's the grand jury's star witness. It's time for her oral presentation. (Forgive me, a poor choice of words.)

Why shouldn't Monica talk to the grand jury? She told everybody else on Earth she was having an affair with the president. She told her mother, for heaven's sake. Doesn't that beat all? In my day a girl *kept* sex secrets from her mother.

A letter came to my house addressed to: "Mr. T. Kornheiser or Current Occupant," which starts out: "I'm Monica Lewinsky, and I've been authorized to offer you 4.9 percent APR on a new Visa card—and, by the way, I'm boinking the president."

Others she e-mailed. *Newsweek* even printed some messages Monica allegedly sent to serial tapist Linda Tripp. Monica refers to "the Big Creep's" wife as "Babba," which may be the female version of "Bubba"—or it may indicate Monica thinks Bill Clinton is married to Barbara Walters.

I'm tired of White House aides, Secret Service officers, and presidential scut boys parading in to testify. Like Steve Goodin, a Clinton aide described in print as "tending to a variety of largely menial duties, like carrying [the president's] coat, briefcase, and water glass." Why bring in that guy? Bring in the guy who carried the president's pants.

I'd like to hear more from Monica's mom, Marcia Lewis, but she won't be testifying again anytime soon—unless they get a dehumidifier in the courtroom, because the air in there is just mangling her hair. And Kenneth Starr probably won't be calling Monica's dad to testify, since Bernard Lewinsky last week compared the special prosecutor to Joseph McCarthy, the Spanish Inquisition, and Adolf Hitler—not exactly the Three Tenors.

Hearing from Kathleen Willey might be fun. Suppose Willey arrived at court disheveled, with her blouse untucked and her makeup smeared, and it turned out she wasn't groped by anyone, that's just her look—early Madonna! (How great would a story like this be: "A high-level administration source, speaking on the grounds of anonymity, said yesterday that Kathleen Willey often pads through the White House with hat-head, her shirttail hanging out, and her lipliner off target. 'This babe must get dressed in the dark,' the source said.")

But it's Monica's moment. I want to see her march into the courthouse—and as she goes in I want to hear that boxing announcer say, "Let's get rrrrreaadddddy to rrrrrrruummmbbbllle."

But it's secret grand jury testimony, Tony. You'll never hear it.

Oh, dear, you're right. No one will ever divulge what Monica says. There'll be no leaks at all. Well, then, I guess this is the end of the story. I'd better stop here and start writing a column about how we're backing off bombing Iraq and have decided instead to install a huge boombox on the Kuwait-Iraq border, and blast Spice Girls songs at top volume until Saddam Hussein kills himself.

Please.

Secret testimony? With Monica's lawyer William "Testing: One, Two, Three" Ginsburg? Are you kidding me? This guy will do thirty minutes into a red light on Connecticut and K.

The second Monica is done talking, CNN will have her testimony word for word. Wolf Blitzer will be reading it so quickly, he'll look like the guy in the sign language circle.

Then we'll know exactly what White House spokesman Mike McCurry meant when he said that the relationship between Mr. Clinton and Ms. Lewinsky could turn out to be "a very complicated story."

How complicated?

More complicated than the story that's in everybody's head now? The perfectly innocent one about the nice old duffer who took a professional interest in the perky young intern, and left her a few voice mails on her home answering machine, and gave her a few small gifts—and let her drop by his office, um, thirty-seven TIMES.

Here's what could really complicate that story:

If that *was* the story.

My feeling is the president would be better off with the "Stalker Nymphos from Outer Space" story, in which an alien lands on Earth in the guise of a White House intern, with only one purpose: to drain the very life force out of the leader of the Western World.

McCurry says of the Clinton-Lewinsky relationship: "I don't think it's going to be entirely easy to explain maybe."

Why not?

The president said he had no sex with "that woman." Simple, right?

Why do I think in a couple of weeks somebody in the White House is going to say, "Oh, *that* woman, Miss Lewinsky? No, no, I thought you were talking about *this* woman, Tara Lipinski. I can't speak for Lewinsky. The president never had any sexual encounter with Lipinski. Or this *other* woman here, Mrs. Kaczynski, Ted's mom."

I like the "alternate story line" some of the president's men are floating, that Monica Lewinsky was seduced by the animal magnetism of the president, but that she is fantasizing about the carnal nature of their relationship—and that the president was simply being kind to someone who is a very needy person. Bill Clinton's whole career indicates that he reaches out to the needy; he feels their pain.

Thirty-seven visits.

Remember the neediest.

A Coupla Chicks Talking

It's Linda like you've never seen her before: Linda Tripp, beauty consultant: "You in red. Yes. [But] just because you wear a red sweater does not mean you have to wear red lipstick."

Linda Tripp, code master: "You can tell your grandchildren you had an affair with the you-know-what of the you-know-what."

Linda Tripp, comforter: "It's a taint on your integrity and your reputation and your character, all of which is so richly undeserved."

Linda Tripp, special friend: "And this outfit makes you look thin and beautiful."

Linda Tripp, she-wolf of the SS: "I really am finished, Monica. Share this sick situation with one of your other friends, because, frankly, I'm past nauseated about the whole thing."

Linda Tripp, blushing phone-sex apprentice: "You're so good at it. No wonder he likes phone sex with you. . . . You're just like a little Marilyn Monroe vixen. I know, in my wildest dreams, I could never have phone sex."

"Oh yes you could," Monica promised.

It's Monica as you've never dared dream.

Monica Lewinsky, biker chick: "He had a big scar on his forehead. And I like that."

Monica Lewinsky, hopeless romantic: "Why can't he just say, 'Look. Go enjoy your life, and in three years we'll get married'?"

Monica Lewinsky, realist: "My mom would vomit if she saw him."

Monica Lewinsky, minimalist: "My lawyer. He said, 'Did you ever have a sexual relationship, da, da, da?' And I said, 'No.' 'Was your job, da, da, da, da, da, ever connected with?' 'No.' 'Nah, nah,

nah?' 'No.' . . . I said, 'Well shouldn't we put something there like I was twenty-two at the time? You know? Like, hell-o?' "

Monica Lewinsky, super-sleuth: "You know what's really weird? I keep hearing these double clicks."

"That's my gum," Linda said.

"Oh, okay."

These tapes are what all the fuss was about? This is what we get for $40 million?

A couple of lonely fat babes yapping? This is like a bad Wendy Wasserstein play.

Linda and Monica weren't the only things dumped into the public trough last week. There was also Sidney Blumenthal's exchange with Hillary Rodham Clinton, in which he talked to the first lady about Monica, and Hillary assured him the president was "ministering" to a troubled young person.

Oh, is that what they call it?

Who do I have to call to get ordained?

As conversations are revealed, words come back to haunt people. When Hillary did an interview on *Today* last January, host Matt Lauer asked about reports that the president had given Monica gifts. Praising her husband's generosity, Hillary said, "I've seen him take his tie off and hand it to somebody."

His *tie*? Hahaha.

As long as people are piling on Clinton, let me say for the record that like the Big Creep, I am outraged at the notion that anyone would think the president's latest offer to pay Paula Jones $700,000 would in any way imply that he was guilty of any wrongdoing in their relationship—which, as I interpret it, was very brief and consisted of only a couple of words and a physical gesture indicating Mr. Clinton's pants were constricting him as he continued to do the people's business.

What's this country coming to if the president can't give some big-haired honey $700,000 just for the fun of it?

If Mrs. Jones doesn't want the money, sir, I do.

After reading these transcripts, I feel terrible for Monica. Between her testimony to the grand jury and her conversations with Tripp, there doesn't seem to be anything left to tell us. Nobody wants her book. How's she going to make a buck off this, like everybody else? Now that Oprah's turned her down, she'll have to get in the pig pile with Roseanne: I can see it now: "Pooky and Baba: Hands Off My Man!"

All this new information will do, of course, is carve the political battle lines even more deeply. Even though recent polls indicate that a significant majority of the American people don't want Clinton to be impeached (notwithstanding the percentage who want him "strapped to a La-Z-Boy and forced to watch *That '70s Show* until he screams for mercy"), Republicans continue to press for impeachment. House Judiciary Committee Chairman Henry "Mack Daddy" Hyde is getting ready for his star turn by trying to disassociate himself from his claim that having an affair between the ages of forty-one and forty-six was a "youthful indiscretion." (Hyde's new position: "Dr. Jekyll did it.")

Sensing it may be a tough sell to force a president from office for mere "ministering," Senate Majority Leader Trent Lott lowered the bar. "Bad conduct, frankly, is sufficient for impeachment," he said the other day.

Bad conduct?

You mean like shoving in the lunch line?

Impeach him? Shouldn't they just give him a time-out?

What's the next threshold after bad conduct, bad manners?

I don't remember the Democrats trying to impeach George Bush after he puked all over the prime minister of Japan.

Where does it end? Bad pores? Bad posture? His lawn's overgrown?

As the Republicans agitate for impeachment, the White House has attempted to paint Clinton as your basic guy next door—if you live next door to the Booby Trap Strip Club. Congressional Democrats, though, put the kibosh on a major effort to air TV spots that would have shown Clinton in a positive light, going about his daily chores in the Oval Office—all tastefully shot from the waist up, of course.

Clinton did get a great run from an exclusive interview with butt-kicking journalist Trude Feldman last weekend, in which he was asked a series of provocative questions, such as: "What is the name of your dog?"

White House officials were so pleased at how well Clinton did with Feldman that they have scheduled an interview with Toni Morrison, whose piece in the current *New Yorker* asserts that Clinton is a black man—which is a surprise, admittedly, but not nearly as big a surprise as if she had said Al "Master Freakblaster" Gore was black. Morrison is expected to ask the president: "If you could be any member of the Temptations, who would you be?"

I've already put in my request for an interview with the president. Here's my question: How desperate would you have to be to have phone sex with Linda Tripp?

Oral Hygiene

I have a confession to make.

Linda Tripp has me on tape.

I dated Linda Tripp. It was four hairdos ago. (Hers, not mine.) Before the frizz, before the straight cut, before the French braid. At the time Tripp was wearing her hair where it belonged—under a hat.

And I know she's got me on tape, because whenever I would lean over and whisper, "Look in my eyes," she would say, "Talk into my brassiere."

We broke off our relationship because we disagreed on the definition of a good friend. I said a good friend was someone you loved and cared about. She said a good friend was "somebody vulnerable who confides in you, then you use that information to land a huge book deal, and then you shed your good friend like a rattlesnake's skin." To which I said, "Oh." And then, "Check, please!"

Any day now Kenneth "That's Not a Lightbulb, That's My Head" Starr is going to subpoena me. He's already called in every live woman in the country to talk about President Clinton's sex life, and he's seeking a court order to exhume Eleanor Roosevelt. It doesn't seem to matter to anybody that Starr has spent $30 million and three years investigating Clinton and the closest thing he's ever had to evidence was Monica Lewinsky's laundry—and it turned out not to include the smoking dress. If Starr were in charge of NASA, we'd be lucky to land a man on New Hampshire. Yet more people are drawing a paycheck from Ken Starr than from the Pentagon these days. If Starr ever wraps up this investigation, half the country will be out of work—including President Clinton, of course.

So now we've got Gennifer Flowers, Paula Corbin Jones, Kathleen Willey, and Monica Lewinsky on the docket. Where are they going to impanel the grand jury? At Hooters? How much worse is this going to get for Clinton? Is there any chance he'll show up on SpectraVision? (Seymour Hersh must be dying. He wrote about the *wrong* president.)

The president's defense, so far, consists of sending Hillary out to the talk shows to foam about a "vast right-wing conspiracy" that includes a secret alien mind ray that has somehow turned Mike McCurry into Shecky Greene. If that doesn't work, Bill's lawyers are working on establishing that he and Vernon Jordan were chipping golf balls on the White House lawn during all the nights in question.

I can't wait to be deposed. I want to give my view on what constitutes sex.

Like most men, I don't believe that oral sex is sex. I also don't believe that oral history is history. And I certainly don't believe that Orel Hershiser is . . . going to win twenty again.

You're probably tired of this sex scandal already. You're probably asking, "Tony, why are you writing about this?"

I'm weighing in because it's good for my career.

It's a natural impulse. Every time CNN runs a picture of Monica "90210" Lewinsky, stage mothers all over the country smack their foreheads and say, "Why didn't *my* daughter think of that?"

I'm completely envious of my pal, *Newsweek*'s Michael Isikoff, who's on TV twenty-four hours a day now. It's Isikoff-O-Rama. He makes Wolf Blitzer look like D. B. Cooper. (One of his coworkers said in *praise* of Isikoff, "He has the stomach to go after stuff nobody else would touch because it's in such bad taste." Gosh, that's like praising the biggest horsefly on the pile.)

The more dirt you can dish on Clinton, the more in demand you are. The other night I watched Larry King interview the comely Gennifer Flowers, doyenne of the big-hair, big-teeth babes. Larry asked her, "Do you think Bill Clinton has been a good president?" And Ms. Flowers, who the last time I checked was a lounge singer, said: "I think Bill gets too much credit for the good economy. I think Alan Greenspan did most of the work." Well, thank you, Marilyn vos Savant, and would you do us a favor and sing "Feelings" in the next set?

Later I was watching *Meet the Press* and the distinguished panel included Matt Drudge, who writes a gossip column on the Internet. The Internet, for heaven's sake, where half the folks who log on believe—from reading the Internet—that if you go into a bar in New Orleans someone will slip you a Mickey, and you'll wake up in a tub of ice with one of your kidneys surgically removed. And Mr. Drudge was asked about the relationship between Clinton and Lewinsky, and he said something in a breathless way that made him look like a Doberman on a choke chain. And then the next question about Clinton went to William Safire of *The New York Times,* one of the most erudite journalists in the country. Teaming Safire with Drudge is like Sir Laurence Olivier sharing a stage with Tony Danza.

Then there's that ponytailed wing-wang Andy Bleiler, who's only one set of hot curlers away from being Linda Tripp. Bleiler was Monica Lewinsky's drama teacher at Beverly Hills High and then supposedly had an affair with her while he was married and she was at something called Lewis and Clark College, where I guess she majored in maps. "I couldn't in good conscience just sit on this, and not tell the authorities what I know," Bleiler said. Oh, really? Hey, Stanislavsky, sit on *this.*

This is what we need, more maggots coming out of the woodwork. Like Dick Morris! Now he's speculating on the chilly nature of Bill and Hillary's sex life. I'm sure they can't wait to hear more radio advice from Dick the Love Doctor: "First, you put on a dog collar. Then you get Mistress IIse to spank you with a rolled-up copy of *The American Spectator . . .*"

Hunkering down for the siege, Clinton has called in some old loyalists: Mickey Kantor, Harold Ickes, Harry Thomason, Clemenza, Tessio. I'd say that the president was prepared to go to the mattresses, but I'm afraid that's how this whole thing started.

I'm reluctant to pick up the paper because all the great lines are taken before I can make them up. On the front page last week, a former White House colleague of Lewinsky's described her thusly: "She'd take little things and blow them up."

I wouldn't touch that one with . . . well, never mind.

Speechless

By now we know everything about Monica Lewinsky. We know about her parents, we know about her former lovers, we know about her taste in clothes and books, we know who does her hair, we know what she eats. We've seen transcripts of her conversations. We know how she thinks.

There's only one thing we don't know about Monica Lewinsky.

So far she hasn't said one word in public. But inevitably Monica is going to look out over all those microphones, from beneath that preposterous eggplant of hair, and . . . say something.

We have no idea what she sounds like.

Jeez, what if she sounds like the Nanny?

"Oh, my Gahhhhd, will you look at all these cameras. I'm like totally plotzing here. Oh, Mister Ca-cherrrrris, be a doll, and get me a hankie and some water. Can you believe this? My grandmother would just DIE to see this. Not to mention a certain Miss Robin Eileen Goldblatt from Beverly Hills High School with the size five dress and size twelve tuchus she should get a heart attack from envy."

Or what if she sounds like Kerri Strug?

Monica, please, don't speak.

Look what speaking out did to Linda "Testing: One, Two, Three" Tripp. After not saying a word for six months, Tripp took center stage the other day and declared herself "an average American. . . . I'm you. I'm just like you."

Excuse me?

You are not like us. We do not always seem to be chewing on a rancid anchovy. We do not always feel underdressed unless we are wearing a wire. And if we strapped a microphone on our inner thigh so the FBI could listen in on our close friend yammering away about excruciatingly embarrassing details of her sex life, and then we sort of copped a smoke when they burst in and hauled her into a back room and tried to scare her witless, igniting a nightmarish national scandal in which that close friend is ridiculed as a liar and a trollop, we would probably feel really, really bad.

Also, our closest confidant isn't the unapologetic Lucianne "The Gaboon Viper" Goldberg. Moreover, we do not ride a broom.

No. Linda, you are not just like us.

Up until now Monica has been Greta Garbo. Her mystery has been her allure. But once Monica opens her mouth, so to speak, her mystery is gone.

From the moment we actually hear from Monica, her career will head straight downhill until she inevitably lands on the set of *Leeza,* sitting between the girl who played Cindy Brady and a woman who used to do the nails of Victor Borge's real estate agent.

What can Monica tell us that we don't already suspect? That she had sex with Bill Clinton? Oh, hold page 1! Look, nobody—nobody!—believes Clinton's story that he didn't have sex with this woman. People who believe in flying saucers don't believe this. People who believe *O.J.* don't believe Clinton's story.

Actually, the conversation between Monica and Ken Starr is not the one I'm most eager to hear. The one I want to hear is the one that will take place somewhere down the road, probably at a Bloomingdale's, when Monica inevitably runs into her old pal Linda. That ought to be a doozy. I'm figuring Monica's opening line will be: "Love what you've done with your hair. It looks a little less like a deceased hyena."

By the way, I'm still trying to figure out what transactional immunity is. It sounds mildly dirty, like protection from sexually transmitted diseases. But transactional immunity seems to be the crème de la crème of immunity. As I understand it, so long as Monica tells the truth, she can testify about anything and not be prosecuted for it, ever. I can imagine Monica arriving before the grand jury with a carton of shoplifted Gap T-shirts, a stash of pot, and six years of old tax records (". . . and in 1994 I took my mother's Shih Tzu, Wallace, as a dependent . . ."). I'm assuming transactional immunity is connected to a type of psychotherapy that was popular in the 1970s called Transactional Analysis. The key phrase in Transactional Analysis was "I'm okay, you're okay." So I guess in transactional immunity it's "I'm immune, you're immune."

I wonder, though, why Starr granted Monica's mother transactional immunity, too. How does it work? Is it like a family pass at Kings Dominion?

Does everybody get to ride free?

You'll forgive me if I seem a little blasé about this scandal. It's hard to get excited about whether a president is lying to cover up his sex life, given what presidents have lied to cover up in the past. This seems so Mickey Mouse.

Give me a good White House scandal. Give me Watergate. That was a scandal that gave us more than we could have ever expected. And what a cast of characters—Katzenjammer Kids Haldeman and Ehrlichman, John Mitchell, Martha Mitchell, John Dean, Smokin' Mo Dean, Anthony Ulasewicz, Jeb Stuart Magruder, that whack job Liddy. There were Cuban defectors, political dirty tricks, laundered money. Watergate was a tour de force. In your wildest dreams did you imagine that everything was on tape in the Oval Office? A smoking gun!

Don't you think the lack of a smoking gun is what, shall we say, stains this scandal?

All Aboard!

The Lewinsky Bandwagon. Week 5:
   A week without red meat.

The dish is getting pretty thin out here on the front lines of quality journalism.

No Monica. No Monica's mom. No Monica's mom's emergency medical treatment team.

The only Monica news all week was that mystery tie she bought.

What color was the tie? How much was the tie? For whom did she buy the tie?

Help, Ken Starr, help! I'm being subjected to an avalanche of *Ties*!

Excuse me, Tony, but six sentences ago you called this the Lewinsky Bandwagon.

Yes.

We remember your hideously boosterish Redskins Bandwagon a few years back. Week after week you wrote the same self-indulgent columns. They were puke! Does this mean we're stuck with endless Lewinsky columns as you fasten yourself to her like a Victoria's Secret undergarment?

The most beautiful sound I ever heard. All the beautiful sounds of the world in a single word.

Lewinsky.

Say it loud, and there's music playing. Say it soft, and it's almost like praying.

Lewinsky, I'll never stop saying Lewinsky.

Lewinsky, Lewinsky, Lew-in-sky!

Hey, why can't I further my career here? Why should William

Ginsburg be the only one to get famous off of Monica's service to the country?

What else can I do? What else is there to be funny about? There's no war with Iraq. How many laughs can I get after I've said "Kofi Annan" sounds like a flavor at Starbucks? Oprah udderly outflanked the Mad Cow Police. Where else should I turn? Ruthann "Honey, I'll Cook Dinner Tonight" Aron?

So I'm stuck with Sweet Monica the Harmonica and her lawyer, (Oh No, It's) Mr. Bill.

The zenith of my week was a phone call from Lucianne Goldberg, the New York literary agent who got the ball rolling by encouraging Linda "8-Track" Tripp to enter the lucrative field of character assassination literature. Ms. Goldberg's reputation for being a shark is such that I thought of holding Richard Dreyfuss's picture up to the phone.

Being a crack investigative journalist, the first thing I quizzed Ms. Goldberg about was her client's ratty hair. "How about *my* hair?" she replied. "When this thing broke I hadn't had my roots done, and I had to give a press conference with two-inch black roots! I was mortified."

She hasn't gone on TV since, though all the network hotshots are plying her with flowers. "This place looks like a well-kept grave now," she said.

That's because you're to die for, Lucianne.

During our chat, she revealed that she'd like to sign Monica as a client. "I'd represent her in a heartbeat," Goldberg said. "Her book would fly out of the stores."

I wonder who'd ghostwrite it?

Maybe a former journalist like . . . Sidney Blumenthal!

Blumenthal was part of the parade of nonentities who trudged in and out of the grand jury last week, including folks who worked with Lewinsky at the White House. But it was the appearance of the condescending Sid "The Squid" Blumenthal that made all working journalists cry foul, because they felt that the First

Amendment was being abridged when a White House aide could be hauled in and made to spill the names of the hacks he was talking to off the record. The issue of exposing confidential sources is a very touchy one in my profession. The last thing we want is for a grand jury to ask who the "source" was on that $150 expense account dinner at the Palm.

All this played out amid the backdrop of the ongoing hissy fit between the White House and Ken Starr, Sheriff of Nottingham. Starr, who's so thin-skinned it's amazing he can shave in the morning and not bleed to death, is flinging subpoenas at a rate that is going to single-handedly provide a new S-class Mercedes for every lawyer in town. Imagine getting paid five hundred dollars an hour just for sitting outside a grand jury room. It's enough to make college kids stop wanting to write *Ally McBeal* and try to *be* Ally McBeal.

So just as this was turning into everything I dreamed for—a story that would allow me to use the phrase "oral sex" in every paragraph!—it has become a lawyer's story.

Now it's about subpoenas and executive privilege. Or maybe it's about the privilege of the executive's subpoenas.

So the spotlight's on the lawyers, especially Mr. Bill, who now goes everywhere with his new best friend, Wolf Blitzer. I've heard they're planning to do *La Cage aux Folles* in summer stock.

Sadly, Mr. Bill is feeling the pinch. Last week he set up a legal defense fund for his client, begging the public to kick in. "My poor little girl can't pay her bills. We have no money," Ginsburg moaned, noting that Monica's dad, Dr. Bernard Lewinsky, had already paid "as much as he had."

Perhaps it is chintzy of me to point out that a couple of pages away in the same newspaper where Mr. Bill was lamenting that the Lewinskys have run out of money, Mr. Bill himself was pictured getting into a limousine. Take the subway, pal. Or get Tim Russert to drive you.

And the very next night Mr. Bill and Monica ate dinner at

Morton's, a steak joint where it's impossible to get out the door for less than one hundred dollars a person.

So if you're contributing to the Monica Defense Fund, make sure to include an additional 20 percent for tips. And three dollars for valet parking.

Another Pizza My Heart

The Lewinsky Bandwagon, Week 6:
    Rollin', rollin', rollin'.

The response is in, and it's overwhelming. Everybody loves the Lewinsky Bandwagon.

For example, reader Cindy Curtis from Reston, who writes: "Tony, Tony, Tony—enough is enough. How much interest can you squeeze out of Lewinsky? I remain your loyal reader. But *ugh*!"

So for loyal readers like Ms. Curtis—and my new best friend, Mr. William Ginsburg, Esq.—and perhaps dozens more, the Lewinsky Bandwagon rolls on toward its ultimate destination: the E. Barrett Prettyman Courthouse in Washington, D.C., the site where Monica Lewinsky may someday testify. And perhaps even deliver a pizza, like she did to President Clinton in the Oval Office, according to his own deposition!

Which brings us to the first question in today's quiz.

Who was E. Barrett Prettyman?

No, everyone knows Mr. Prettyman was the plaintiff in an ill-fated plagiarism suit against Roy Orbison.

Today's first question is:

What toppings were on the pizza Ms. Lewinsky brought to the president?

a. Sausage and pepperoni.

b. Capers, olives, and Kenneth Starr's bloody head.

c. Monica!

(Forgive this intrusion, but I wanted to remind all loyal readers that fueling and caring for the Lewinsky Bandwagon costs money.

We are looking for corporate sponsors compatible with Ms. Lewinsky's new lifestyle. Perhaps a personal shopping service. Or a computer so she can continue to blithely e-mail her days away. Or a deluxe hair tamer. A crate of Häagen-Dazs. Thank you.)

In the same deposition in which President Clinton remembered Monica "Deliver Me" Lewinsky bringing him a slice in the Oval Office, he also recalled having shagged Gennifer Flowers. Once. In 1977. (Once? Oh, please.) It must have been fabulous sex for him to remember it twenty-one years later, considering he can't even remember *meeting* Paula Corbin Jones. You'd think he would have remembered his sack time with Ms. Flowers in 1992 when *60 Minutes* asked him about it. This falls under the administration policy of "telling the truth slowly."

The big fish at the E. Barrett Prettyman Courthouse last week was Clinton's golfing goombah, Vernon Jordan. In recent weeks much has been said about the nature of their private conversations, which have been characterized as "locker room talk."

Locker room talk focuses on:

a. The pleasing aesthetics of the female physique.

b. The type of bath towels available in a locker room, their fluffiness, their absorbency, and whether bar soap or liquid soap produces the richer lather.

c. Are you an idiot? Hooters!

At the conclusion of his first day of testimony, Jordan pledged his unending loyalty to President Clinton, saying, "Ours is . . . an enduring friendship based on mutual trust, respect, and admiration. That was true yesterday. That is true today. And it will be true tomorrow."

Vernon Jordan is so loyal to Clinton that he:

a. Assured him Paula Corbin Jones was "bodacious."

b. Told the grand jury that he, not Monica Lewinsky, was having sex with Bill Clinton.

c. Wears a collar that says, IF FOUND, PLEASE RETURN TO 1600 PENNSYLVANIA AVENUE.

Except for one fancy dinner out, we didn't see much of Monica last week. But her lawyer, "Bill" Ginsburg, was busy. He had a dustup with Ken "I Am the All-Powerful Oz" Starr. He swatted at a TV camera at Dulles on his way to California. And he made news with a bizarre revelation to *Time* magazine that he had "kissed that little girl's inner thighs when she was six days old—I said, 'Look at those little *pulkies*.' "

"Pulkies" is an affectionate Yiddish term for drumsticks. One can only imagine the baffled look on the interviewer's face as Ginsburg scrambled to explain the avuncular innocence of that kiss. *Time* reported the word as "polkas," as if the Schmenge Brothers were in the room, and Ginsburg told me with a chuckle: "Never let a *Time* guy translate."

Yes, Ginsburg told *me*!

He'd returned my call and said about last week's column, "There's no truth to the rumor that Wolf Blitzer and I are doing *La Cage aux Folles* in summer stock. But he's leaving Lynn, and I am leaving Laura—and we're moving in together."

Ginsburg also said, "You're making a mistake picking on me. I'm a nice guy."

Which explains why there's a shotgun seat for him here on the Lewinsky Bandwagon. Just don't hit me, Bill.

My other new best friend, literary agent Lucianne Goldberg—who started the Lewinsky Bandwagon rolling by suggesting to Linda Tripp that she use a tape recorder instead of hot curlers—also reported in to say that she enjoyed being called a shark in last week's column. She faxed me this statement: "When you don't get the royalties you are owed, and the publisher holds all your money as a reserve against returns—who you gonna call? Someone with beautiful manners, or someone with *teeth*?"

Incidentally, to clarify terms in Clinton's deposition, sexual relations were defined as "any contact with someone's groin, buttocks, breast, or inner thigh if intended to stimulate sexual arousal." That lets Ginsburg off the hook for the *pulkies* deal, and it takes Spin the

Bottle out of play. But I'm not sure about those other pizza party games, including Hide the Pepperoni.

Excerpted from the forthcoming best-seller *Fun Facts About Bill and Lucianne*. All rights reserved by Tony Kornheiser, Lucianne Goldberg, and William Ginsburg.

Waiting for a Snowstorm and a Thirty-eight-inch Waist

The Ice Age

After living here for twenty years, I've learned that three things define Washington, D.C.

1. Political scandal.

2. Bad hair. (Not just mine, but get a load of Liddy Dole. Her hair is piled up so high she needs baling wire. Where does she get her hair done, the Cone Zone?)

3. Weather-related panic shopping and hysterical school closings.

That wimpy snow flurry Friday was nothing compared with the previous weekend, when we were hit by the biggest chunk of ice since Boris Yeltsin found out how to make a frozen Stoli margarita.

Excuse me, Tony, but there was *no ice storm that weekend.*

Oh.

Hmmm. What do I do with all this canned fruit?

You remember that storm, don't you? You remember the panic as weathermen assured us a "significant accumulation of ice" was on its way?

One-half inch of ice, they said, would snap trees in half. An inch would cause your roof to buckle. Two inches and your mail would have to be delivered by the Toronto Maple Leafs.

You know the technical term for three inches of ice?

The South Pole.

We were getting four inches.

You couldn't escape the glum predictions. They were on every TV channel. You'd be watching a football game, and you'd see these words crawling across the screen: "From the Eyewitness

News Storm Desk: We're gonna get it. We're not kidding. We are licensed meteorologists, dammit, and we've got Doppler! Snow is streaming in from the Midwest. Flakes as big as dogs. They've got hundred-car pileups in Ohio. AIIIEEEE!!!"

The storm's ETA was 4 P.M. Saturday. It would start as snow, change over to freezing rain and ice. And by Sunday morning we would all be dead.

That Friday night I did what any father would do: I brought my children together and told them the ice would bring down power lines all around town, leaving us without heat and electricity, that our neighbors' trees would come crashing down into our house. I told the kids to gather wood to burn in the fireplace to keep us warm until the Royal Canadian Mounties arrived in May.

Early Saturday morning I went to the supermarket to load up on provisions. Me and everyone else in the metropolitan area. The supermarket lot was filled. Streets around the supermarket were filled. I ended up parking so far away that my car was in a town that wouldn't even *get* snow!

Everybody had the same thing in their shopping carts: bottled water and toilet paper.

One woman had a cart filled with twelve jugs of water and eight six-packs of toilet paper. And I thought: Just how long does she expect to be snowed in? I mean, we're not in Finland. It'll be 45 degrees in two days.

Still, I shuffled dutifully around the aisles, trying to figure out what to buy. But by this time the shelves were mostly picked clean. I thought I'd wandered into the Stalingrad Safeway. In produce they were down to a few scrawny heads of lettuce, nine Brussels sprouts, a bruised plum left over from the *last* millennium. As I pondered whether to buy it, three people reached for it like it was the Hope Diamond.

Alas, there was no toilet paper left.

So I bought loose-leaf paper.

I saw people with cans of soup they'd have to eat cold when the power failed. Cold corn chowder. What could possibly be worse than that—maybe hot corn chowder?

My friend Nancy says that in this circumstance the only things to buy are "comfort foods," foods she describes as "we're locked in this house for four days with the kids food."

You mean like sweet, oven-baked cinnamon rolls with gooey white frosting? I asked.

"I mean like vodka," she said.

For some inexplicable reason I had a craving for Cream of Wheat, an item so unpopular that even in the face of imminent nuclear war it would still be on the shelves. So I picked up a box and went to see how long the checkout lines were. They were, uh, long. I would have needed a pitching wedge to get to the cashier.

Luckily, I ran into a woman I knew, who graciously offered to buy the Cream of Wheat for me and drop it off at my house when she was done shopping. It was then 10:15 A.M., and she was about to get on a checkout line.

"Um, you're not thinking about having it for breakfast *today,* are you?" she asked.

With my shopping out of the way and the storm of the century still a couple of hours away (This just in from the News 4 Ice Desk: "Oh, it's coming, baby!"), I went to the 1:30 showing of the movie *Shakespeare in Love.* When I came out I hooted at the morons waiting in line for the 4:30 showing. They'd be iced in! They'd have to live off the Jujyfruits stuck beneath their seats. Hahaha.

As I got in my car my heart swelled with joy as the first drops of freezing rain fell on my windshield. I went home to sit in my cold, dark, powerless home, like Ted Kaczynski.

Well, the afternoon passed, then the evening. I saw a few flurries of snow, but nothing as terrifying as, say, Carol Channing in bright light. There was some freezing rain that laid a thin coating on the sidewalks. The TV weather poodles kept insisting the apocalypse was at hand. Eventually, I went to sleep, assuming I'd wake up in a world of darkness, fear, and death. Sort of like Pat Buchanan's living room, only chillier.

Rapping on my window woke me at 5 A.M. I bolted out of bed thinking it was a flock of arctic scavenger birds pecking on the glass, coming to feed on my frozen flesh.

I walked to the window. Rain was washing down the street like a river. *Water.* No ice. But it was still dark, so I figured the streets were coated with black ice, which would surely kill us all within minutes.

I went downstairs and opened the front door. I gasped. The temperature was in the high forties. It felt like spring.

Good thing I loaded up on Cream of Wheat.

Eat My Dusting

Oh, sure, it's easy to be a weatherman now, when temperatures are mild and daffodils are blooming. No need to hide under the bed anymore like a scared Chihuahua. They're back on the set taking bows. A few sunny 65-degree days in March will do that.

But let's go back a few days—when THEY RUINED OUR LIVES!

A "*dusting*"?

That's what I heard from my smiling weatherman at 6 A.M., as he put the kibosh on concerns that a big snow was headed for us. "A dusting to an inch," he said dismissively, like maybe he'd call for a tee time.

A few hours later more than a million commuters had that word—*dusting*—boring a hole in their craniums as they ground up a hill in first gear, fishtailing in snow up to their grillwork.

Dust this, *pal,* is what they were thinking.

We don't ask much from the weatherman. There are maybe three days a year when we're truly in need of an accurate forecast. Will it snow? How deep? Tell us that and we'll even forgive that numskull chitchat with the anchor poodle about what the humidity does to your hair.

A dusting is what, one quarter-inch max? I got ten inches.

I got Norway in my backyard.

Do you have any sense of how much you missed by? It's like getting on a plane for New York and ending up in Kuala Lumpur. You expect a Knicks game at the Garden, and you get a rickshaw race in a dung heap. You couldn't have missed by any more if you forecast "a plague of toads dropping from the sky." If Mike

Mussina were this far off with his pitches, he'd hit the third-base umpire.

My favorite moment was watching the city's most celebrated weathercast in midmorning—home of the Thomas Edison of Washington Weather, the man who invented "humiture," a humidity and temperature index that he explains is "how it feels outside"; he particularly likes to talk about humiture in July, when we already know what it feels like outside. It feels like dying and decomposing. Anyway, this station's weatherman was preening in front of his Digital Doppler as he confidently predicted, "The snow is expected to start around noon."

At that moment flakes the size of human skulls were streaming down, and my car already looked like the mutant Sta-Puft Marshmallow Man in *Ghostbusters*. I started screaming at the TV set: "LOOK OUT THE WINDOW, YOU MORON!"

(I remember this moment very well, because I'd just read something in the paper that I'd found very funny. It was an article on Al Gore's presidential chances. Gore, who as you know invented the Internet, the automobile, movable type, and oak trees, was said to be in trouble with many voters who felt he "lacked charisma." Voters want charisma? My feeling is, Bill Clinton had so much "charisma" he needed to be blasted with a firehose.)

Let's be honest here: A baboon in a leisure suit could do as good a job with the weather as these guys. It's not like they've been spending hours reading instruments and laboring over charts. That's what the National Weather Service is for: Some guy in some office cubicle is most likely doing all the heavy lifting. These pretty boys are *reading* the weather, not predicting it. Being a TV weatherman takes one skill—pointing. You think you need Yale for that?

By the way, the next day, did any of them go on the set—that is, if they could get to work through the snow—and say they were sorry?

Nope.

Not one of them had the decency to say: "I am lower than pond scum. I am so loathsome, I make my own mother gag. *Please* let me make it up to you. Allow me to shovel your walk and sculpt the slushy leftovers into your likeness with my bare hands."

Instead they grinned and said, "Well, we got a bit more snow than we figured on." And they explained it with low-pressure ridges and jet streams and those little squiggly things on the map.

I don't care *why* it happened, isobar boy.

I care that it doesn't happen again.

A couple of days after the big snow I went to New York to watch the Lennox Lewis–Evander Holyfield fight. While I was there I turned on the Weather Channel and saw that another big snow was headed toward Washington. I was anxious to find out what the weathermen were saying, so I could alter my travel plans if necessary. I kept calling every twenty minutes to see if the snow would make me change my schedule.

This time the weathermen had dropped the grandstanding in front of the Digital Doppler. Twelve inches in Fairfax had crimped their style. They gave the forecast like deer at an NRA convention.

"We could get some accumulation," they said, "or no accumulation—or who knows?—maybe another Ice Age. It could start as snow or rain or sleet, and change to sleet or snow or rain. It could start tonight, or tomorrow, or next Lent. You should bring an umbrella—or maybe a bathing suit if global warming kicks in early. We'd like to be more definitive, but it's the weather, you know. It's sort of unpredictable."

Spare us your sackcloth and ashes. How much snow?

"Somewhere between a dusting and the Winter Olympics."

I Know Which Way
the Wind Blows

In my next life I want to come back as a weatherman.

That way I can be dead wrong 80 percent of the time and not get fired.

Excuse me, what happened to the snow?

The storm was supposed to get here last Sunday, and snow through Monday and Tuesday. Washington was going to be so white it would look like an Osmond family reunion.

Except by midday Monday the sun was out, the sky was blue, and whatever snow had fallen was gone. Tuesday I believe I wore shorts.

Not that I'm bitter. But I do have a question: Which local TV weather team is gonna reimburse me for the "Convenient 28-Pack" of toilet paper I bought?

This is the second time this winter our expert weathermen have predicted an apocalyptic amount of snow. They brayed it could be "the worst snowstorm in fifty years"—and we didn't get jack. You may remember a few years ago when "a dusting" was infamously predicted at dawn. By 9 A.M. we were on our way to eleven inches! It was like waking up inside an Eskimo Pie!

The same hairdos are still predicting the weather.

Apparently, this is like the Supreme Court. No matter what fool opinion you have, they can't get rid of you.

Who hands out jobs like this? Katherine Harris?

Last week they stood there with a straight face and said: You haven't seen this much snow since the final scene in *Scarface*. It will be so deep, by the time you dig your way through it you'll be underneath the Russian embassy.

They swept their arms to show you where the snow was going

to hit. They waved their hands around, up high with the clouds, down low with the approaching front. They're so agile. They're always putting things "in motion." It's like they're doing tai chi. Only tai chi is better at predicting the weather. So is Ty Cobb, whose only drawback is that he's dead.

Excuse me, Tony. Aren't you being a bit harsh? These are weather professionals. Members of the American Meteorological Society.

What did they do to join? Send in box tops? Wear a beanie with a windsock?

(Every time I say that, I get indignant mail from Channel 4's infallible Bob Ryan. Ryan's last letter accused me of "character assassination," because I said that, at the very moment I heard the forecast for "a dusting," Jean-Claude Killy was skiing down my block. Ryan took offense at my writing. "Look out the window, you moron!" Hahaha. Must I remind you, Bob? I am licensed to be sarcastic by the American Humorological Society.)

What a racket. These guys have all the bells and whistles, including the color-coded Digital Doppler radar. In the winter the colors are chilly white, blue, and purple. (Weather pros call a big blob of purple coming out of Canada a "Hello, you're dead" system.) The colors swirl and pulsate on the radar screen. It looks like a Lava lamp. For all the good it does, it may actually *be* a Lava lamp.

The day after blowing the forecast, the weathermen don't even do the honorable thing, which would be to go on the air, strip off their shirts, and beat themselves until they bleed. Instead, they rationalize. They say, "We were in the rain band, not the snow band."

No kidding, Sherlock. And I'm in the Nitty Gritty Dirt Band. WHERE'S THE SNOW?

You don't see weathermen in California predicting earthquakes, do you? Stick to what you do best. You're a meteorologist, dammit. Predict meteors.

I love when the anchor tosses it to "the storm center," and these guys come running onto the set holding the latest info in their hands, like Moses coming down from the mountain. Oh, please. Like any of them do anything but rip the forecast from the National Weather Service wire and feed it into the TelePrompTer. Here's all they really know about weather: It beats selling shoes.

I'm showing restraint, I feel, by not calling for public executions. But come on, you stand there smugly among your radar echoes and scare us to death. You send us scurrying for snow shovels and halite. (What's the deal? Do hardware stores call up and say, "We're up to our keisters in product here, and it's March. If we don't move these shovels soon, we're going Chapter 11. Could you maybe predict the Big One?") And *nothing* happens.

And without even a trace of irony, you blame *the weather*!

Oh I get it. You're saying: The weather, hey, it's unpredictable. Why didn't *I* think of that?

Do us a favor. Next time, read pig entrails.

My friend Tom says weathermen "ought to go around with electric-shock collars. And every time they're wrong, we turn up the juice a little bit. Eventually, even those stupid Pomeranians learn to stay in the yard."

I like that.

What I'd like more is if they replaced all our weather divas with chimps. That's right, chimpanzees. They're cute, they're cheap, they're low-maintenance. Everybody loves 'em.

Here's my friend Nancy's idea: The TV station lines up some props—say, a snow shovel, a pair of sunglasses, a raincoat, a parka, a straw hat, a pair of boots, and an umbrella. They turn the chimp loose. He picks one up, and there's your Accu-Weather forecast! If he picks the straw hat, you head for the beach; if he picks the snow shovel: Hello, you're dead.

Bad Weather Men

Once again we return to the fault line between men and women. Today's topic: the terrible summer thunderstorm.

Surely you have been in an office setting when a thunderstorm bears down. Women stay calm. They remain in their seats and continue working. They are nesters. What happens outside does not concern them—unless, of course, it is a sale on Manolo Blahnik strappy black stilettos.

Men salivate at barometric changes. We rush to the windows, pressing our snouts against them like basset hounds to see lightning. Scratch any man, and an inch down you find Al Roker.

I was at home Wednesday when the sky suddenly turned the color of road tar. The women in the house were oblivious. (Later, when I asked a woman about this, she said, "If I cared about what happened outside, I would live in a carport.")

Instinctively, I switched on the Weather Channel, where I learned we were under a Severe Weather Advisory. Yes! A violent thunderstorm with 70-mile-per-hour gusts and hail the size of eggplants was around the corner, and it would be here in ten seconds. I read the advisory aloud, like a World War II air-raid warden: "Stay inside and away from windows."

The women in the house did just that. I did what any man would do: I walked onto the porch and brought my faithful, albeit whimpering, dog with me.

"Stand by my side, Maggie, and together we will face the apocalypse," I declared.

"Are you crazy?" my wife called to me.

I turned to face her—a fortunate move, I must say, because at that very moment a gust of wind blew one of the hanging flower pots off its hook, and it hurtled past. It would have sheared off my head like a Randy Johnson fastball. That was enough for Maggie, who began scratching wildly at the door to go in.

"Judas," I hissed.

I stood in the fury—with my back resting on a plate-glass window, mind you, so a sudden blast of wind could shatter the glass and slice me like shaved ham—as the rain came down sideways and the thunder boomed and the wind snapped limbs off trees. I felt like Ahab lashed to the mast. I was alive!

What can I tell you? It started with the caveman, this primal urge to go out in a storm and become a human lightning rod. My friend Tracee grew up in Kansas, where tornadoes are common. "My dad always made my mom and me go to the storm cellar. Then he got in the van and started driving around," she shrugged. To this day during thunderstorms and tornadoes he drives his van downtown and sits in the bank parking lot on Main Street—underneath the cover of the drive-thru window so the hail won't damage the paint job, of course—and watches small animals blow by. My friend Monty, who's from North Carolina, said that in summer thunderstorms his dad enjoyed driving around and splashing through huge puddles. "He sounds like an Airedale," I said.

Men can sit for hours and watch video of a Force 5 hurricane, especially when it slashes into a beach-side house, crumbles it into toothpicks, and washes it away. Ha! Take that, Mister Rich Guy Summer Home! You know what else is great? Massive ice storms that cause cars to spin around wildly on the interstate and slam into other cars. Men also enjoy videos of animals eating other animals. I love it when they show a big snake swallowing a pig whole, and you can see the snake's body bulge out like an accordion where the pig is.

Ah, but I digress.

We were lucky. We never lost power in the storm last week.

The sudden loss of electrical power is another point on the fault line between men and women.

In a blackout, women turn totally shrewish about refrigeration.

They become Kelvinator harpies. They insist nobody open the refrigerator or freezer, for fear all the food will thaw and spoil—and this will mean the loss of thirty-five dollars' worth of lamb chops that were bought fresh two years ago and buried behind the TV dinners that were purchased in 1987.

What women don't realize is that men are *hoping* the meat defrosts. This gives men a chance to do what they love best: set fire to big hunks of animal flesh. It satisfies our need to incinerate things in a postwar world. In a power outage I open my refrigerator and freezer at least twenty times an hour to gauge how much time I have left until I can strip my freezer and begin a combination estate meat sale and charcoal orgy.

Much to women's chagrin, men also repeatedly open their refrigerators during power outages to check if their beverages are still cold. During a recent power failure, my friend Rich offered to drive and get ice for the house. His wife said, "We won't need ice if we keep the refrigerator door closed." Then she thanked him for being concerned for the family, not realizing his only motivation was to maintain ideal conditions for the stash of beer he keeps in a small refrigerator in the basement.

Every woman I know has the same reaction to the loss of electrical power: They want to go to an air-conditioned bar and drink martinis until power in their house is restored.

Women don't want to be dependent on candles. They don't like it when the dishwasher and the washing machine don't work. They don't like it when their kids are yammering because the cable doesn't work. Plus, women hate the junglelike heat and humidity, because it makes them sweaty and clammy.

Men see power outages as an opportunity to get lucky. The candles, the clamminess: There are fewer clothes to take off, fewer lights to dim, and you're already sweaty, so let's rock and roll. What else is there to do?

So maybe this explains the whole primal appeal of a raging thunderstorm. It plays to a man's strengths: seduction and the ability to barbecue spoiled meat.

The Shape I'm In

My loyal fan Vladimir M. Kabes sent me the following fax in praise of last week's hilarious column about John Glenn: "How can a respectable newspaper publish such disgusting, lowly and vulgar trash as Tony Kornheiser's 'Geezer' column? The abuse of an elderly, but trim and fit, man appears sorely misplaced from a fat slob."

How perceptive of you, Mr. Kabes, for noticing that I've become, as they say, a bit "thick around the middle." In fact, around my middle is a tire of flab so thick it appears that doctors have surgically implanted one of those circular floats that little kids take to the pool—only without the duckie head. I have recently taken to wearing vests to hide my belly. Soon, I fear, I will have to clothe myself in those billowing quilted things they hang on the walls of service elevators.

Mainly this is because I stopped going to the gym several months back, in June. It is now November, and thanks to the miracle of modern science, which allows potato chips to be packaged in four-ounce, eight-ounce, twelve-ounce, sixteen-ounce, and "trough" sizes, I've gained seventeen pounds! I now weigh 216. By USDA standards I'm eligible to be cut into steaks.

With the approach of the holidays, I fear for my life. I may keep eating until I grow so enormous that you will see me on *The Jerry Springer Show* being extricated from my house with a forklift. (Just imagine how Newt's gonna pork up now that he's no longer occupied with being speaker. By Thanksgiving, he'll look like the Bullwinkle float in the Macy's parade.)

I try to diet, but unfortunately I've come to the point in life where nearly everything disgusts or disappoints me except food. And so I eat all day long. If I had a family crest, at this point it would be a man with a chicken breast in one hand, a cheeseburger in the other, and a garland of sour-cream-and-onion potato chips around his head.

My friend Richard advised me to take a novel approach: Stop eating.

Astoundingly, this worked for him. He has lost twenty pounds in a year.

He says he visualizes a plate, and each day he gets to eat what's on that plate.

"Just one plate?" I ask.

He nods.

"How big is the plate?" I ask, imagining my one plate would be the size of Rosie O'Donnell.

My friend Nancy stays thin by eating meals that look as if they have come from the bottom of a hamster cage. She says she has had the same rule since she was twenty-five: "Never eat until you are about to pass out from starvation."

That's different from my rule, which is: "More cheese."

Everyone knows it gets harder to lose weight as you get older. My editor, a young man of forty-one, recently complained to me he was getting fatter despite his best efforts, which include the heavy lifting required to make my column publishable.

"Before I turned forty I had a thirty-two-inch waist," he said. "At forty-one it was thirty-four inches. By the time I'm forty-three, I'll have a thirty-eight-inch waist," he said, crestfallen.

I thought to myself: *A thirty-eight-inch waist. Man, those were the days.*

Imagine my dismay hearing that these punks can't keep weight off. What hope can I possibly have at fifty?

My boss George advised me to take an aerobic step course. He takes "step" with a bunch of women—a terrible mistake for a man. Men look like cows on ice skates as they try desperately to remember the steps and keep count with the music. Invariably they stumble over the step, twirl the wrong way, and smash into the women taking the class. Men who take step are menaces who should be forced to wear padding and running lights.

"How can you take step?" I asked George. "You're as graceful as a backhoe."

"It's a great workout. I get soaked," George replied.

"You wanna get soaked? Strap yourself to the conveyor belt and go through a car wash."

Here's my dilemma: I realize I won't stop eating unless I staple my lips together—and that would probably be bad for my radio career. So my only solution is to head back to the gym.

I signed up at a new gym last week. (Go back to my old gym? Are you kidding me? I have some pride, you know. I'm not going back there as long as I'm this fat.) I met with a trainer to craft a program for me. He was lean and in his early twenties. He greeted me with one of those smiles that said: I'm happy not to be working at McDonald's anymore.

I asked him to give me some exercises to lose weight.

He took me through some of the machines, working me out at ridiculously low weight levels. I've lifted seven-layer cakes that were heavier.

"How does this feel?" he asked more than once, as if he thought I might be in danger of a stroke.

I looked around the room to make sure he was talking to me, and not, say, Hume Cronyn.

I'd noticed that the free weights were all downstairs, where the serious lifters were.

I asked him if he might show me some exercises down there. "Oh, no," he said. "Let's keep you up here for a while so we can keep an eye on you."

I realized that he thought me old! I suspected he might even offer me some pudding.

My worst nightmare had come true. After years of calling myself fat, old, and bald, others were seeing me that way, too.

Devastated, dejected, and depressed, I sought comfort in the usual way.

Gimme a bacon cheeseburger—extra cheese—and a coupla bags of chips.

Don't Tread on Me

Lately I've been trying to lose weight (again!), so I've been going to a gym and running a couple of miles on a treadmill in the morning. I'm on the treadmill for forty minutes. I run at a very relaxed pace. If I ran any slower, I'd go backward in time.

The gym has two rows of treadmills. One row of seven machines faces the interior of the gym. There's a TV you can watch while running. But if you are on one of the outside treadmills, you have to crane your neck to see it, and you run the risk of flipping sideways off the treadmill. Is a glimpse of Matt Lauer really worth a ruptured spleen?

The other row faces out, onto Connecticut Avenue. There are eight treadmills in this row. This is where I prefer to run, because watching the commuter traffic provides a more pleasant distraction than watching a bunch of fat geezoids on StairMasters. (The gym I used to go to had the treadmills facing the aerobics studio, and you could watch young babes bounce around while taking step class. It was heaven. The day after they turned the treadmills to face the weight machines, I quit the gym.)

So the other morning, I'm in the gym jogging. I'm on the last treadmill on the right. That means there are seven treadmills to my left. And all of them are empty. Suddenly, a fat dope in a Hobart College sweatshirt gets on the treadmill RIGHT NEXT TO ME!

Talk about invading my space. In some cultures, that act would have meant we were engaged.

I looked down at my time. I had twenty-seven minutes to go, and now I had to spend it close enough to this yutz to exchange bodily fluids.

I was furious. I thought seriously of reaching over to the control panel on his treadmill and slamming down on his "Stop" button, so he would pitch forward and crash through the plate-glass window onto Connecticut Avenue.

That afternoon I related the story to my boss, George, screaming, "How dare this jerk get on the treadmill next to me when there were seven empty treadmills in the same row!"

George asked me if I'd have felt the same if the person next to me had been a supermodel in spandex. I conceded I might have been slightly mollified if it had been Wendy Rieger in that clingy leopard-skin blouse she wears on Channel 4. But the principle remained the same: You don't get on a treadmill next to someone when there are open treadmills down the row.

George told me I was an idiot and a baby, saying, "Tony, you're a self-absorbed egomaniac, and you refuse to accommodate yourself to anyone else."

"And your point is?" I responded.

George weakly theorized why this Hobart dolt got on the treadmill next to me.

1. "Maybe that's his favorite treadmill."

His favorite treadmill? Oh, please. I didn't know people built up emotional attachments to treadmills. Who is he taking to the Hobart prom, a Nautilus machine?

2. "Maybe he wanted to meet you."

Meet me? What is he, the Welcome Wagon? I'm up there shvitzing like a collie. What will he do next? Ask me to analyze the Redskins' offensive line while I'm soaping up in the shower?

Finally, George said, "Look, the guy pays the same amount of money as you do to belong to that gym, and he can run on any treadmill he wants. Get over it."

By this time, the ethical debate had spread throughout the department. Obviously, the smart people agreed with me that this was a clear violation of my space.

My friend Nancy told me that her hubby, David, was once running in a gym where the treadmill area was surrounded by mirrors. David glanced into the mirror to find a man on the treadmill in back of him looking into the mirror blowing David a kiss! Now there's a case of a guy wanting to *meet* someone.

My friend Tom was appalled by what the Hobart guy did. Tom equated it to violating "The Urinal Rule," which holds that you never, ever step up to a urinal next to someone if there is an open urinal somewhere else. That is just not done. Nor is there any talking at the urinal. Or any eye contact. Never. No way. You look straight ahead no matter what. Even if someone is being murdered two urinals down. Like in the movie *Witness*.

"Men don't stand there and chat?" my friend Nancy asked.

God, no!

"Women have conversations between the stalls," Nancy said. "Sometimes they say, 'Hold it, I've got to flush.'"

Chicks.

(This reminds me of the time in 1978, when I was a sportswriter in New York and I came to the old Capital Centre to cover the NBA finals between Washington and Seattle. During halftime I went to the rest room, and as luck would have it the only open urinal was next to Senator George McGovern, whom I recognized immediately. I was so excited I VIOLATED THE URINAL RULE! I actually began *talking* to him. I said, "Senator McGovern, I know this seems sort of awkward, but I just want you to know that I voted for you for president, and it's a great honor to, um, meet you, and I'd like to shake your hand, but I guess that would be rather inappropriate in this setting." But I digress.)

You'll recall that my boss George said I totally overreacted to the guy getting on the treadmill next to me.

So a few days later, George is on a treadmill in his gym in Virginia, and a woman ascends the treadmill next to him, even though there are open treadmills down the row. George notices this—but he can't say jack; he's trapped by his own self-righteousness. And in fact, he says to himself, "I can live with this. She has as much right to this health club as I do. She can run anywhere she wants."

Well, they're running together, side by side, for a few minutes when, in George's words, "the woman passes gas that would kill a moose." She cuts the cheese! It all but brings him to his knees.

Who says God doesn't have a sense of humor?

Suck It Up, Not Out

You'll forgive me if I seem a little down today. But my hopes, my dreams are dashed.

I don't ask much for out of life. I just want to fit into size 36 Dockers.

I was willing to do almost anything—except, you know, stop eating cheese fries.

Then along came liposuction, and I learned I could get the fat sucked out of my waist, no muss, no fuss. I've been dreaming about liposuction for ten years. I assumed I was a prime candidate in that I was: (1) fat, and (2) rich. What did that porpoise Kenny Rogers have that I didn't have?

But I read in *USA Today* that the death rate for liposuction is twenty to sixty times as high as the death rate for all operations—including those in which the patient pretty much *starts out* dead. Apparently, having liposuction is more dangerous than, say, being operated on for a gaping chest wound. You'd think that most people electing to have liposuction were relatively healthy. Come on, they're just fat. They're not in a coma. At least not going in. ·

Liposuction kills. Go figure.

Who'd ever have thought that if you wanted a couple of inches off your waist it might be safer to literally sit down in a frying pan and sizzle it off?

Really sick people, total goners, die at an average of 1 in every 100,000 to 1 in every 300,000 operations. In liposuction it's 1 in every 5,000. (And just our luck, Linda Tripp was holding number 4,999. Did you see all the stuff Tripp had done? A face-lift, an eye-lift, a nose job, a chin job, and a big load of fat sucked out of her neck. I've seen "fixer-uppers" that didn't need that much work.)

How is it possible so many people die from liposuction? What are the surgeons doing during the operation, playing Nintendo?

This is the worst medical news ever. I put my faith in medical science and this is what I get, a toe tag? Liposuction was my bailout. But I'll have to rethink whether it's worth dying to squeeze into corduroys.

I called Man About Town Chip Muldoon for advice.

"You didn't think you'd be playing Russian roulette with liposuction, did you?" he asked. "But, what the hell, roll the dice. Phyllis Diller always seems to dodge the bullet. Why not you?"

My friend Nancy wasn't so reassuring. "I always said I'd rather die than have a big, fat can," she said. "Now I see that's probably the case."

It still puzzled me why people should die after liposuction. So using my excellent medical training, obtained from close study of resuscitation techniques as practiced on *Baywatch,* I came up with a theory:

Okay, the liposuction patient has just been operated on. It's been, what, three, four hours since his last Grand Slam breakfast? Naturally, as soon as he comes to, he's lunging for the fried chicken or maybe a slice of cream pie. But he's so light, he just flies off the gurney and cracks his skull on the floor. Another statistic.

"Not bad," Chip said.

Chip's theory was based on a different school of medical thought: the hour-long drama as opposed to the half-hour eye candy. Chip said: "During operations on *Chicago Hope* they often drop a surgical tool inside the patient, and they can't find it. With liposuction, you're usually operating on someone the size of Louie Anderson. So you can lose an entire '57 Chevy in there, with no hope of fishing it back out. And that can be fatal, especially one of those models with tail fins."

This is terribly disturbing news because everybody my size wants liposuction. It gives you another chance at the buffet, doesn't it? You can take all those clothes you've been wearing lately—the oversize sweaters and the pants with the elastic waistband—and put them in mothballs. All the fat they can suck out of you in one hour, it'll take *years* to regain it. I was going to get liposuction and have my surgeon tattoo *Did Somebody Say McDonald's?* on my new shapely buttocks.

I imagined my first words upon awakening from surgery would be "More gravy."

(Liposuction is becoming nearly as popular as laser eye surgery, which is such a rage that Starbucks is now offering free laser eye surgery with ten purchases of "grande"-size coffees.)

The scariest news of all was the disclosure that any doctor can perform liposuction. One plastic surgeon was quoted as saying, "Even dentists have been doing it."

Dentists!

My doper friends in college became dentists because they couldn't get into medical school. I wouldn't let any of them sell me dental floss, much less open a hole in my body and suck out some flab. Who could possibly be below dentists on the surgical chain, optometrists?

According to the coeditor of *Plastic and Reconstructive Surgery,* any doctor can attend a seminar and "learn how to perform liposuction within a few hours."

I don't know about you, but I'd like to believe that learning how to perform a tricky surgical procedure would take somewhat longer than getting your prints back from MotoPhoto. So forget about liposuction. I need to find another strategy for dealing with my big behind. Oh, you're probably thinking: diet, exercise, willpower. Yeah, sure.

I'm thinking: size 42 Dockers.

Laughing Stock

After much deliberation I have finally decided to jump into the stock market. Even as the market climbed higher and higher, I resisted. Quite frankly, a man of my age has difficulty relating to anything that rises so high and so fast. But now I have decided to buy stocks.

I made my decision when my mailman drove past my house the other day in a Mercedes. He's been dabbling in the market. His initial portfolio apparently consisted of a single 29-cent stamp and he's been reinvesting his profits for a year.

It used to be that the mysterious intricate nuances of the stock market were unfathomable to idiots like me. Traditionally the men who scored big in the market had names like Chauncey Pickering Poockington IV, and the women who scored big had names like Mrs. Chauncey Pickering Poockington IV. But my friend Paul, who's a business writer, assures me that "now every idiot can make a killing."

So I think the time is ripe for me to get into the market—considering that the Dow has doubled since the time you began reading this. It is up so high that this time the folks throwing themselves off roofs are the ones who *don't* own stocks.

Be forewarned, though, if I go into the market, you may want to get out. I've tried this twice before. The first time was almost twenty-five years ago. A girl I had gone to high school with had become a stockbroker, and I went to her with my entire savings and told her I wanted to buy a stock that would make me rich. She told me to purchase a computer stock called Intel. This was before everybody had computers, so the stock was unknown. I bought five hundred shares at 16.

Day after day I followed Intel. It went up as high as 18, and down as low as 14. So it was pretty much becalmed. But every day I called my broker seeking reassurance. If I saw it going down one quarter of a point I'd say, "Do you think it's bottoming out? I have a bad feeling. I think we ought to sell before it crashes."

This went on for months. Finally she told me I was driving her crazy. "You're too needy," she said. "I'm a stockbroker, not a psychiatrist." She said that if owning Intel was too aggravating, I should sell it.

It was trading at 14 at the time. I sold it all.

That's me, Tony Kornheiser, Mr. Phlegm-for-Brains. To my knowledge nobody else in the history of the stock market ever took a loss on Intel.

It is now around 90. And that doesn't count all the times it has split. Intel has made so much money over the last twenty-five years that had I kept it, right now I could own Switzerland. The official Swiss currency would be the Kornheiser. It would be very strong against international markets. It would take only 12 Kornheisers to purchase a Lexus. But with 20, you could buy a Kornheiser Z-16F, a snazzy gull-wing racing car manufactured by Kornheiser Motor Works of Zurich.

But I didn't keep Intel. I sold it and bought a five-year CD at my bank, where it made 3 percent interest, which made me the laughingstock of everybody in my neighborhood, including many preschool children. I ran into my stockbroker friend a few months ago, and she reminded me about selling Intel at 14.

"You were a fool," she said.

"Yes, but at least my money was safe in the bank," I said.

"It would have been safe in the toilet too," she replied.

(By the way, she looked great; she'd had her nose done.)

Anyway, the next time I bought stock was in 1987. I remember it distinctly. I had saved up enough money to feel adventurous. And in the fall of 1987 I bought $10,000 worth of a variety of stocks. I remember the exact date, October 16, a Friday. The reason I remember was because on Monday, October 19, I got on a flight to Minneapolis to cover the World Series, and by the time the plane landed the stock market had crashed and my portfolio was suddenly worth $5,000. I lost half of my savings in two and a half hours. It's a good thing the World Series wasn't in L.A. That's a five-hour flight. I'd have been tapped out. I sold the rest of my stocks the next day, and I haven't been back since.

That relieved me of the responsibility of paying attention to Alan Greenspan, the saturnine chairman of the Federal Reserve Board. Isn't it great how Greenspan belches and the stock market panics? What power.

It's too bad he appears to have no zany sense of humor. Because if he did, he could call a press conference, stand at the lectern, clear his throat importantly, and say, "Ahem. Someone left the cake out in the rain. I don't think that I can take it, 'cause it took so long to bake it, and I'll never have that recipe again." And then just walk off.

Pillsbury stock would plummet! Thousands of Americans would lose their jobs! The president would urge calm! Julia Child would be appointed secretary of the interior! The dollar would sink against the yen! Wheat futures would skyrocket!

And then this bull market would turn into a bear market—right when I was set to jump in! Story of my life.

All the Stock Answers

You may recall that a few months ago I wrote a column about my bad luck with the stock market. I explained how I was the only person on Earth to have lost money on Intel, buying it at 16 and selling it at 14—about an hour before it started climbing like an F-15.

I'd like to thank the reader from Bethesda who, after figuring out all the splits of Intel after I sold it, informed me that had I held my original five hundred shares they'd now be worth $5 *million*. Thank you very much for pointing that out to me. Now die.

Though I had a savings-and-retirement strategy that some might have called "conservative"—I stashed half my money in gold bullion and the other half in my Uncle Boots's cremation urn—I decided it was time to be more adventurous. So I went into the market as the Dow was taking off like Gypsy Rose Lee.

Well, you saw what happened last Monday. The market plunged 554 points. I blame myself, of course. But experts said it all started because of uncertainty over the Thai economy. Are you kidding me? There's a Thai restaurant on every corner in my neighborhood. And why did the crash occur in the Hong Kong exchange? I thought its economy was booming since China took over. There's obviously full employment in China. Every eight-year-old is working eighteen hours a day in a fire-trap factory to make sure our kids get Christmas toys.

So, Tony, how much did you lose?

I probably lost tens of dollars. I thought about flinging myself out the window like folks did in the Great Depression—but since I hadn't put too much money into stocks yet, I just jumped off my porch.

When I came to work on Tuesday, everybody was calling his broker. I heard my editor Rich, a fretful Dow watcher, get on the phone and demand, "Get me [such-and-such]. It's the Big Kahuna!" I assumed Rich was buying a particular stock, although it's possible he was ordering lunch, and what he actually said was, "Give me a big tuna."

Anyway, Rich wanted reassurance from his broker. A broker, by the way, who once phoned Rich to say he had good news: One of his stocks had split two-for-one. "Let's see," the broker said, "you had twenty-five shares so . . . hold on, lemme check . . . give me a second, my computer's running slow. Okay, yes, you've now got fifty shares."

The day after the crash, Rich nervously asked his broker, "So, what do you advise?"

"Sit tight," the broker said.

Other brokers were giving equally sagacious advice.

"Think long term," said one.

"Think big picture," said another.

"Think about wearing a barrel and selling apples," said a third.

So I called my broker.

"I'm sorry, but he recently fled the country," his secretary told me.

No, I'm kidding. He put me on hold for a while, then said, "Tommy! Great to talk to you, pal. The crash? No big deal."

And as it turned out, it wasn't. By the end of the next day the market had come almost all the way back. And later in the week the Great and Powerful Greenspan, who simply by belching can cause blue chips to sway back and forth like the Wallenda family, said Monday's plunge of 554 points could prove to be a "salutary event." (I ought to introduce Greenspan to my cousin David. David used to consider a Category 5 hurricane to be a salutary event, because he had a glass and mirror business in Miami.)

The events of the week taught me I needed to pay more atten-tion to the market. I had a serious questions: How could this have happened? Could it happen again? And, most important, should I also order the tuna for lunch?

To be honest, I have no idea how the stock market works. I also have no idea how the Internet works, or how Doppler radar works, although I envision a stock market crash sweeping in from the Far East, El Niño–style—and we'll be able to see it coming through some kind of financial Doppler radar. It will glow with that deep red that indicates incredibly forceful winds, torrential rains, and cows flying through the air. And everybody's 401(k) will be sucked out the window. And the next morning I'll be working at Hecht's, selling bathrobes.

So I began to read the business section carefully. And the first thing I noticed was that every day you'd see the same photo of a group of Asians looking upward in terror. I'm assuming that the Asians pictured are watching the plunging Hong Kong stock ticker. But for all I know they're reading a message board that says, DISNEY PLANS REMAKE OF *FLOWER DRUM SONG*.

I also took careful note of the names of stock exchanges and indexes throughout the world. In England, for example, there is the "Footsie." In Hong Kong, there's the "Hang Seng." The currency in Thailand is the "baht." In Malaysia it's the "ringgit." Hahaha. That's so comical compared with the sophisticated names we have, like the "sawbuck" and the "finsky."

Finally, in desperation I went to my friend Paul, a business writer. I confessed that much of my anxiety was over the fact that the graphs in the newspaper charting the peaks and valleys of the market looked just like my EKG.

"Does anybody understand what happened in the stock market?" I asked him.

"Only after the fact," Paul said. "Those who claim to understand it really don't, because if they did, they'd be rich."

"Maybe they are rich," I said.

He thought about that for a second. "Hmmm," he said, "maybe they are."

Then he called his broker and ordered the tuna.

Investment Tanking

I love it when the stock market plunges 400 points and some financial analyst on TV says, "This is just a correction."

Four hundred points. Kaboom.

Seven hundred in two days.

You're now going to be eating soup until 2009, but this is just a correction.

Did you ever wonder what they mean by "just a correction"?

A *correction* is what they tell you so you'll stay in the stock market a month longer. Meanwhile, they're getting out before the *crash,* which will come tomorrow.

The flight of the stock market is dizzying. It's down 616 points one day, up 482 the next. The biggest loss in history could be followed by the biggest gain. The market has swings like my Uncle Sidney before Prozac. It's like betting on Oprah's dress size.

I wouldn't care EXCEPT IT'S MY RETIREMENT MONEY!

Either way, I'm going to end up in Florida. The difference is: If the market stays up, I'll be lying on a chaise by the pool at the Breakers Hotel in Palm Beach reading the *Daily Racing Form* while barely clad bar girls shuttle me frozen margaritas. But if the Nasdaq stays in the toilet, and flushes, I'll be the guy on the corner of Commercial Boulevard and University Avenue wearing a do-rag and carrying a coin changer on my belt, hawking the Fort Lauderdale *Sun-Sentinel* in the middle of traffic.

The Nasdaq, ha! Ever wonder what it stands for?

No Answers, So Don't Ask Questions.

People would be jumping out of open windows in downtown office buildings like in the '20s, except now they build the windows so you can't open them. So instead of committing suicide, they just fire their personal trainers.

I may have stayed in the Nasdaq too long. Internet stocks are melting down like Whitney Houston's career, which is currently a grilled cheese sandwich on Three Mile Island.

"Don't panic, it's just profit taking," the financial analysts calmly say.

Profit taking is what smart guys do when they bail out of a stock they believe has become overvalued. And how do the smart guys know when to begin profit taking? Usually, they program their laptops to buzz loudly the moment the name "Anthony I. Kornheiser" pops up on the list of investors.

The entire goal of investing is to not be standing when the music stops. I'm not only standing, God help me, I also appear to be dancing.

Analysts say, "Think long term," but at my age, long-term thinking is wondering what's on after *Friends*.

The sad thing is I have no idea what I'm doing. I don't even know which stocks I own. I don't know if I'm in high-tech, biotech, or Georgia Tech. There's a technical financial name for someone like me: "Moron." I thought the Nikkei was a concept car by Toyota.

I got into the stock market late. I was deep in my forties and I still had all my money in the bank, earning 2 percent, like it was low-fat milk. My friends laughed at me. Even the people at the bank laughed at me—they had all *their* money in the market.

So I gave my money to a financial adviser who promised me he would get me a greater return than the bank.

A baboon could do that, Tony.

Yes, but would a baboon give me steak knives?

I took a test to see how much investment risk I would accept. I was asked: "How would you describe yourself as an investor?"

   a. aggressive.

   b. moderate.

   c. cautious.

I wrote in: "victim."

I was asked: "If your portfolio lost 15 percent of its value over the course of one year, you would be . . ."

a. unconcerned.

b. slightly concerned.

c. anxious.

I wrote in: "Long dead, because when it lost 5 percent I would have leaped out the window."

So my guy told me he would be extremely cautious with my portfolio. He would buy only blue-chip stocks. I trusted his judgment. When the monthly statements of my holdings arrived in the mail, I didn't even read them. I took it on faith that my investments would make me rich. I practiced pronouncing the word *concierge*.

Then I got greedy.

I'm now taking stock tips from my radio producer, a twenty-nine-year-old college dropout who makes about fourteen cents an hour. He is heavily invested in Nasdaq tech stocks, which explains why last week he began to sell his furniture. He put me in "PPVI." I don't even know what it stands for. He said it was about to go through the roof. I bought it at 21. The other day, it was at 6½. But I'm sure that's just a correction.

My college friend Al is a day trader. A day trader is somebody who is so wired they won't let him through the Athens airport. About a year ago, Al told me to buy a tech stock he was sure would quadruple in no time. He went on and on about who was backing the stock, what its specs were, what its global prognosis was, blah-blah-blah. I bought it basically to get him to shut up. I bought it at 19¼.

After one day, I'd forgotten I owned it. Periodically, Al would call and tell me some gobbledygook about projected earnings or rumored takeovers, and caution me to hold on to the stock a little while longer—though in the fruit-fly universe of a day trader, "a little while longer" can mean "until the coffee percolates."

A few months went by with no word from Al. Then last week

the Nasdaq went blooey, and Al called, asking breathlessly, "Did you get out?"

Did I get out of what?

He rattled off a name that sounded like: mega-something.

I told him I didn't know what he was talking about.

"The stock I put you in! You don't remember it?" Al asked.

I said he was lucky I remembered *him*.

"I forgot all about the stock. Should I have gotten out?" I asked.

He told me it was now trading at 3. But he was still optimistic about its future.

"Did you get out?" I asked.

"Oh, yeah, sure. But I'm back in," Al said. "I'm calling to tell you it's a bargain now at 3. You know some morons bought it as high as 19."

Yeah, so I heard.

I'm Rich and You're Not

It's a pity you're not me, because I'm going to be extraordinarily rich soon.

In fact, I have *already won* the $31 million Publishers Clearing House sweepstakes. It's going to be announced on Super Bowl Sunday.

I may be a multimillionaire, but I am not inconsiderate. With my entry I included a note informing the Publishers Clearing House people that I'd be at my dad's condo in Florida that day. I advised the people on the Prize Squad to knock loudly and have patience. My dad is eighty-eight, and his hearing is shot. It may take him a while to get to the door. (I just hope the sirens and flashing lights don't make him think the paramedics are coming for his neighbor.)

I know I am going to win. It says right in the packet that "nobody has a better chance to win $31,000,000.00 than" I do. Here's the winning number, suckers: 00 5820 3289. Read it and weep.

I almost didn't enter three other sweepstakes that came in the mail. What do I need with them if I've already got $31 million?

American Family Publishers, for example, is giving away $11 million; they've got Ed McMahon's wizened puss on their envelope. That got me to reconsider: I'm pretty sick of Ed. I'm sure most Americans would be grateful if I used some of that money to put a hit out on him. The rest I could put toward helping promote world peace—or buying something really cool for myself, like a cruise missile.

American Express Publishing is giving away $1.67 million, which is chump change to me. I'll probably use it to buy hookers and a gold-plated, fifty-four-inch digital TV to put in my attic.

Mercedes-Benz is giving away a new sedan. (They're also giving away $2,500 in cash. But I'll probably just hand that out on the street in twenties or give it to my dog.)

I'm gonna be loaded.

Me, Tony Kornheiser.

Or, me, Ms. Toni Kornheiser. That's the name on some of my magazine subscriptions. Surely, you recall me writing a few months ago about the weird magazines I've been getting, like *Meat & Poultry, Fine Cooking,* and *People* in Spanish. Some gremlin has signed me up for all sorts of magazines under the name Toni Kornheiser. Magazine subscriptions are at the heart of all the sweepstakes. The only reason they're giving away a Mercedes-Benz is to get folks to subscribe to *Elle Decor.* I'd never heard of *Elle Decor*—I'd sooner subscribe to Ella Fitzgerald—but if there is a demographic *Elle Decor* is aiming at, I guarantee you I'm as far away from it as it's possible to be. The last two *Elle Decor* readers on Earth would be me and that fat guy in the Miller Lite commercial dancing with his Great Dane.

You don't think they'll withhold the money when Toni Kornheiser wins, do you?

I could shave my legs and put on a dress. For $31 million I'll wax my back, too.

It's a wonder I've never entered a sweepstakes before; they're so easy to win. I've never even played the lottery because I don't meet the minimum tattoo qualification at most of the stores that sell tickets. Plus, I don't have the rest of my life to spare waiting behind some fat doofus in a camouflage jacket hunched over forty lottery tickets, agonizing over which numbers to pick.

"Give me six, fourteen, eighteen, twenty-seven, ummm . . ."

"You did say fifteen?"

"No, fourteen. And give me, uh, three and eighteen. That's my Pick Six."

"Splendid. It is your wish then to select eighteen again?"

When I go to a convenience store, I'd rather see a guy with a pair of pantyhose over his head waving a sawed-off shotgun than some moron with a lottery form.

Have I mentioned how glad I am not to be a Canadian? You should see the fine print about Canadians in these entry forms. They must think Canadians are baboons. The Mercedes-Benz one specifies: "In order to win a prize, residents of Canada will be required to correctly answer a time-limited arithmetical skill-test question."

A Canadian gets thirty seconds to figure out: "What is the square root of eighteen, plus seventy-eight, times fourteen, minus six, plus the age of Wayne Gretzky's mother?" What is the problem they have with a Canadian winning a Mercedes-Benz? Do Mercedes do poorly in high-speed collisions with live moose? I mean, I'm sick of Céline Dion, but I wouldn't require her to recite *The Canterbury Tales* in order to win a Grammy.

At this point, my dilemma is how I ought to act when they give me the check. I don't want to pretend it's a surprise that I've won. Everyone can spot a phony.

So I'm thinking of coming to the door wearing a satin bathrobe, with a bottle of champagne in one hand and Charlize Theron on the other, then breaking the tension by saying something witty in Mandarin Chinese.

My friends have begun to ask me if I think having so much money will change me.

I can't tell you how much that question offends me, coming from my friends.

Of course, the money will change me. I intend to become insufferable. Okay, more insufferable.

I'm going to rub my money in everyone's face. There's a writer in town I hold a grudge against. I intend to buy his publication and, at the acquisition party, fire him and have his belongings thrown into the street. I'll hire Linda Tripp to shadow him everywhere, and tell everybody, "I'm his *best* friend!"

My friend Tracee's grandfather, who is ninety-four years old, has the sweepstakes bug bad. He goes to the post office in Lincoln, Kansas, every day to enter another one. He enters so many that his family got him a postage meter. I asked Tracee how much he'd won so far.

"Nothing yet," she said. "But he's convinced he's going to win the big one."

Not this year, gramps. It's mine.

Dealing with
a Lot of Frustration

There's road rage and air rage, and now here's garage rage:
I park in a lot where the cars outnumber the spaces. So when you can't find a space, you park in the aisle and give your key to an attendant.

This isn't rocket science. There's just one, simple, sacred rule: Give the attendant your key.

We pick up the story on a day when I have an appointment and my car is being blocked by another car parked in the aisle.

I go to the attendant and ask him to move the car so I can get to my appointment—nothing of great importance, really, just my one chance to receive a vital, life-saving organ transplant.

"I can't move the car," the attendant tells me. "I have no key."

"You have to have a key. Everyone leaves a key," I say. "That's the rule. Leave the key. The guy didn't leave you his key?"

"Not today," the attendant says.

Not *today*? What, is this guy on the "alternate day" plan? Is he going to wander by and drop off the key *tomorrow*? Which, you know, would be a little late for the transplant. But, hey, it's not like I had any big plans for the Fourth of July, anyway.

(This attendant is not exactly a parking lot savant. And believe me, there *are* parking lot savants. There used to be a vacant lot up the street where some guy parked cars on the dirt. Who knows if he had a license? Maybe he just opened a window of opportunity and hopped through. My friend Tom discovered it. "The first time I parked there," he said, "I thought I might be simply handing my car keys to a vagrant. The guy tossed them into one of those huge ten-gallon paint buckets that was filled with other keys. He gave me no tag, no receipt, nothing. I knew I'd never see those babies again. But ten hours later, when I was still fifty yards from the lot, this same 'attendant' who looked like he was homeless, this guy who'd seen me once in his life for a total of ten seconds—and even then didn't seem to even notice me—casually reached into the bucket and came up with my keys like he was shooting fish in a barrel. The man was a *genius*. And I'm thinking, *If this guy had gone into high finance, Alan Greenspan might be working with a squeegee outside the Holland Tunnel.*")

Meanwhile, the attendant in my lot couldn't find a key if he were Aerosmith's roadie.

"Is there some way to contact the guy and get him to move his car?" I asked, trying to maintain a certain level of calm, and by "a certain level" I mean something short of twitching and foaming at the mouth.

The attendant shrugged. He looked at the guy's sticker and tried to match the number to a master list. Not there.

"Do you know the guy?" I asked.

"Yes, he is a bald man."

"That's all we have to go on?"

Great. Michael Jordan is blocking my car.

The attendant called his supervisors. They showed up, took a look at the car, wrote some stuff down. And left. They waved pleasantly on their way out. I knew they'd get to it immediately. Maybe even right after lunch.

I began to stew. And by "stew" I mean "simmer at high temperature until done." I was the only car in the lot that was blocked—and there was nothing I could do about it but wait for the owner to be located. (And flayed like a flank steak.) Ten minutes went by. Then twenty. Then thirty, forty, and fifty. I looked at the car. It was a cheap piece of junk. I thought about getting into my car and plowing into this tiny tin can, knocking it over on its back like a turtle. Nah. Too genteel. As I pondered revenge strategies, I began to think . . .

WWTSD?

What Would Tony Soprano Do?

Would he, for example, take out a baseball bat and smash all the windows of this car? (He did that in one episode.)

Would he have four tough, brawny individuals with what Dr. Melfi might call "personality disorders" physically pick up the car, put it on a tow truck, tow it to a boat, take it out to sea, and turn it into a home for carp? (Tony did that to a person in one episode. But for laughs, he shot him first.)

Would he have Paulie Walnuts whack the guy?

Would Tony whack the guy himself?

Or would Tony show his sensitive side and simply knee the guy in the groin, then rip out his liver and feed it to a neighbor's pedigreed Pomeranians?

As I thought about how great it would be to actually be Tony Soprano—and we're both fat, bald guys named Tony with anger management issues, and our friends call us "T," so it's not that big a stretch, except for the fact that he is a fictional character, and as such, has much better dialogue than I have, not to mention a hot, psycho girlfriend—a bald man came toward the parking garage attendant.

"Whose car am I blocking?" he asked the attendant.

"Mine," I said.

The man walked right past me toward his car, a car key in his hand. He didn't acknowledge me in any way, except to mutter, "I'm an idiot."

He didn't say he was sorry.

He didn't tell me his name.

He got into his car, started it, and called to me, "I owe you big time." Then he called out a four-digit number that I assumed was his extension at work.

Like I should call him.

For what? So we could go to a karaoke bar?

I mean, he blocks me; he breaks the One Rule in the lot by not handing in his key; it's fifty minutes until he gets to his car to move it; I miss my organ transplant; he doesn't say he's sorry; he just tosses off a number that may or may not be his extension. Maybe it's some kind of slang, like "24/7," that has some secret meaning, like, oh, I don't know, "Up yours, pal." How would I know? I don't even know his name. And I didn't write down the number. What should I have written it down in, the blood that was pouring out of my eyeballs from waiting fifty minutes for this guy to move his car?

And now if I want to pursue this matter I should call him?

Like it's now my responsibility.

I should call *him*?

I should call Tony Soprano. Tony Soprano should call him. *Bada-bing!*

Down, Bob, Down

Someone has to say this, and it may as well be me.

I don't want to know any more about Bob Dole.

I want him to shut up.

It's bad enough to look at Dole now, after his face-lift—the new cheekbones they inserted are so preposterously high, and make him look so artificially chipper, it's like they injected a live squirrel into his face.

But what really gets to me is this TV spot Dole does about the problem of "erectile dysfunction"—which after the first reference he mercifully refers to as "ED."

Erectile dysfunction. Gaaaack. Bob, you ran for president. Why do you feel the need now to tell us that your executive resolve is wilting?

Have you no sense of shame?

He was big as a horse, of course, of course,
But a problem in bed led him to endorse
A pill that could save him from divorce.
And now once again he's a big stud horse.
Bob Dole, Mister ED.

How do you put erectile dysfunction back in the can? The next time Dole appears on *Meet the Press,* Tim Russert might say something like this:

"So, Bob, how are those erections coming? . . . I'm sorry, I meant those *elections!*"

This certainly doesn't make it any easier for Bob's wife, Liddy, to run for president. Now she'll be out there on the stump, as it were, and she'll have to answer questions about Bob's Big Boy.

The public discourse is being fouled by things that my friend Nancy refers to as Images We Wish Had Never Been Conjured Up. Certainly, Bob Dole waiting for the Viagra to kick in would qualify.

This coming week we have a two-hour dose of nightmare images: the Monica Lewinsky interview. *Two hours* of this cement-head blubbering with Barbara Walters. And if there's anyone we need to hear even less from than Monica, it's BaBa. Why she hasn't been put on a bus to the dog track by now is beyond me.

My point is that there are certain people who simply need to go away . . . now.

Take Dennis Rodman. And stuff him.

Is the word *unsightly* not in Rodman's vocabulary? (Hahaha. Did you read his "books"? The word *vocabulary* is not in his vocabulary.)

God help him if *he* ever has ED. You wouldn't be able to read the full inscriptions on all his tattoos. He has so many metal doo-dads stuck through his face, if there's ever another world war and we need scrap iron, we can just toss Rodman on top of the pile and go home.

Charlie Sheen. Christian Slater. Robert Downey Jr.

Please, don't speak.

Cher. You don't have a squirrel in your face, you have the National Zoo. What do you give as a home address now, Dow Chemical?

I don't want to accidentally come across *The Sonny and Cher Story* and find out that when you and Sonny were still married you told him to get out of your hotel room because you intended to sleep with "Bill" that night.

Bill who?

No, no, forget I said that. Let's not go there.

And Kathie Lee. I know so much more than I want to know

about Kathie Lee and her husband and her children and her clothing and her heartache when she found out that two thousand Indonesian children had gone blind sewing the beads on her bolero jackets. Isn't there something I can get that will take back all the stuff I already know about Kathie Lee? A Kathie Lee–ectomy?

I never want to hear the term "semen-stained" again.

(Unless it's a new shade of Duron paint.)

And Roseanne.

How did she get a talk show? Did she eat the previous host?

How much time has to be devoted to this load? We already know about her child abuse, her horrible marriages, her unmentionable tattoos, the pouches that were sewn into her stomach so she wouldn't eat anyone else.

My friend Nancy and I were talking about Roseanne the other day, and Nancy said, "She's so pathetic. They should put her out of her misery."

But she's not in misery.

We're in misery.

And Fergie, who has traded in getting her toes sucked for a 350-calorie stroganoff.

Is there no extradition treaty we can sign to keep her out of our lives?

I just saw her on the *Today* show—introduced as "Sarah, Duchess of York," and by now she's got as much pull in British royalty as "Colonel Sanders"—and she was talking about her fat behind and her new book, which is about her fat behind.

Katie Couric asked her why a duchess should be pushing low-fat jack cheese. And Fergie said, "So many say, 'What on earth is a duchess doing working?' 'Why is she talking about weight?' 'She should keep her private life private.' "

To which I would say: Amen.

Tragically, the batteries in my clicker were dead. But Fergie wasn't. She continued: "It doesn't matter whether you're a duchess, or who you are—whether you've got a title, or not a title—the fact is, if you've got a weight issue, you've got a weight issue."

Then she said to Couric that she wanted to have a career in television. So we'll be seeing more of Fergie and hearing more from Fergie and learning more about Fergie.

If I have a choice, give me erectile dysfunction.

Me, the Jury

I am being held hostage by the government.

All week long I have been on call for jury duty in the District of Columbia. But so far I have not been selected. I really want to serve on a jury, because (1) it is my patriotic duty as an American citizen and a participant in the democratic process, and (2) you don't go to work and they have to pay you anyway, hahaha.

I think it's really cool to be on a jury. Take the O.J. jury—the people on that jury got book deals, and they got on *Nightline,* and some of them even got to meet Greta Van Susteren! They were always being written about in the newspapers: "Juror No. 1, a thirty-six-year-old Caucasian male with a master's degree, who works for a high-tech corporation." Throw in a line about how "he likes to hunt and fish," and you've got *The Dating Game.*

I wonder what they'd write about me. "Juror No. 4, a fat, bald, old, whiny Caucasian man who dresses like a vagrant and has complained incessantly about the texture of the toilet paper in the jury lavatory."

Emergency update: A couple of weeks ago, I wrote about my friend Gino, whose roof fell in, dumping a ton of carpenter ants into his home. Well, I am happy to report that Gino got everything back together and repaired just in time for the big storm Thursday evening. A bolt of lightning struck in his backyard, toppling a tree, darting through the ground, up into his house's electrical system, making a bee-line for the room with the new roof, and roaring out and over his surge protector, frying his two computers, a fax machine, and a printer. I will continue updating this story as it develops. (Next week: locusts.)

Anyway, I have a vision of what I'd be like in the jury room, how I wouldn't have to say anything at all—it would be obvious how smart I was, so the others would naturally elect me foreman. The case would be murder one, a blockbuster. I would solve it secretly from the jury box, because of my Sherlockian savvy and a lifetime of judging human behavior as a journalist. During deliberations, I would bide my time, watching my poor clueless colleagues steamroll toward conviction, until I finally swayed them all to an acquittal by showing them the truth: how the defendant had obviously been railroaded by the Real Killer, his adoring but secretly faithless wife. Instead of merely delivering the verdict, I would point dramatically to her in the courtroom with an accusation, and she would fall to her knees, sobbing, and confess.

Of course, with my luck, I'll get a civil dispute over who owns a refrigerator.

But to use a court term, it is moot. I'll never get on a jury.

I'd be easy to bounce off a jury. Any lawyer could do it with a few questions. Humor columnists are in the business of writing outrageous, opinionated, totally indefensible things.

Lawyer: "So Mr. Kornheiser, you think you are without prejudice?"

Me: "Sure."

Lawyer: "Are you aware the defendant is an insurance agent?"

Me: "Sure."

Lawyer (*shuffling papers*): "May I direct you to a column you wrote in July of last year, where you said, and I quote: 'Insurance agents are just like big hairy water rats but not as cute, and if one of them is ever accused of a crime and I get on a jury he will fry like an egg?' "

Me: "Er."

Plus, what if they asked me typical jury-screening questions?

Lawyer: "So, Mr. Kornheiser, have you ever committed a crime?"

Me (*indignantly*): "No!"

Lawyer: "You mean you never *stole* anything? Ever?"

Me: "Um, do Dave Barry's jokes count?"

A few years ago I had jury duty, and I never got selected. I spent three full days sitting in a big room that smelled like disenfectant, along with about eighty other people waiting for my number to be called so I could be impaneled. But my number was never called. (I think I was the only one whose number wasn't called. A Fed Ex guy delivering a package got called, and I didn't.)

I spent the entire day, from 8:00 to 4:00, watching the one TV in the room, which was locked in on PBS. So you can ask me anything at all about the migratory habits of birds and flying insects in Oceania and I'll have an answer. Those were the most boring three days of my life. It felt like I had been chained to Dr. Art Ulene.

I suppose I should be grateful for not being on a jury. What if we were sequestered?

Being sequestered means that all of us on the jury have to do everything together. We eat together. We travel together. We watch specially selected movies that could not possibly prejudice us, so they cannot be about crime or courts or lawyers or injustice. Basically, it would be *Willy Wonka and the Chocolate Factory,* over and over again.

But what I'd really fear was if the other jurors found out I was a sportswriter. Because as soon as people find out I'm a sportswriter, they start peppering me with questions:

Who was better, Magic Johnson or Larry Bird? Joe Montana or Joe Namath? Yogi Berra or Secretariat?

Could Babe Ruth have won a gold medal in the giant slalom?

Can you get Michael Jordan to write me a recommendation for college?

Who would win if Joe DiMaggio played Ping-Pong against Martina Navratilova's cat?

It happens. It drives you crazy.

I'd sooner be on trial.

When the Sweat Hits the Fan

What's the greatest invention of all time?

Many would say it was the Wright brothers' airplane, Edison's electric lightbulb, or Gutenberg's printing press.

(Steve Guttenberg invented the printing press? The guy in *Police Academy*?)

But my feeling is, those are obvious. *Everybody* was working on those things. Even if the Wright brothers had taken the gas, somebody would have invented the airplane. What, you think 'N Sync would be going from city to city on their summer stadium tour by camel?

So we're all on the same page: We need to distinguish between an invention and a discovery. An invention is something that doesn't exist in nature—like Michael Jackson. But a discovery is already there; it's just waiting for someone to, um, discover it. Clearly, the top discovery of all time is boiled lobster. I mean, look at that bad boy. Who was the first guy who thought of *eating* that thing?

"Hey guys, listen to this. Tell 'em, Tommy boy."

"Okay, I know a lobster looks like a giant black spider from Mars. But I have this theory that if we drop it in a pot of boiling water, it will turn bright red, and we can crack it open with mallets and eat it."

"Sure, Tommy, sure. Whaddya think it would taste good with, *drawn butter*? Hahaha."

Eating lobster is a fascinating discovery. But I'm talking about inventions of epic proportion, inventions that have totally shaped our lives, inventions we could not live without. So we can eliminate Call Waiting and matching mother-daughter sailor suits.

I've narrowed the list to three.

Anesthesia, the TV clicker, and air conditioning.

My friend Nancy argued for flush toilets, but I asked, "Okay, which of the other three would you throw out?" That's a tough one, isn't it?

My dilemma was what order to rank them—which was solved for me on Monday night when my air conditioning went out.

I'm not so young that I don't remember the world without air conditioning. I remember well how my family got its first window unit when I was sixteen. Fifteen years I spent sleeping in a pool of sweat. (In retrospect, that may explain my lack of dates.)

Some people are nostalgic for the good old days. My feeling is: Let them ride horses to work, and when they get the flu, let them go to a doctor who will insist on bleeding them with leeches until they feel perky.

I want my room so cold in the summer that I can hang veal in the closet.

So when my air conditioning went out, I did not have a good night. I was shvitzing like an aardvark—even with the windows open and the fan set on Stockholm. I awakened several times feeling like I had been dipped in a marinade. I felt so clammy I thought maybe I'd been sleeping with Darva Conger.

Consequently, in the morning I wasn't full of high spirits. I believe my first words were: "If the air conditioning guy isn't here by nine-thirty, I will find him and hang him upside down from the shower rod like a roast duck."

Now I don't want to sound like a spoiled brat. I know there are plenty of people who don't have air conditioning, and I am no better than they. But normally I am colder. And that's how I want to keep it.

"What's the matter here?" I asked the repairman.

"Your compressor is broken," he told me.

"We have a service contract," I said gleefully.

I'm a big believer in service contracts. Over the years I must have paid $5,000 in service contracts on my air conditioner. I do

that precisely so that if the thing breaks in July, SWAT teams of refrigeration specialists will rush over with tanker trucks of Freon
and foam my entire house. In November, they can take their time.
In July, I want them crashing through the door before I hang up
the phone.

"Service contract won't do you any good," the repairman said.
"This box is twenty years old. We don't fix them that old. You need
a new one."

"Fine," I said. "When can we get a new one?"

"We can get a salesman over here tomorrow morning," he said.

"After I buy a new one, when will it be installed?" I asked.

There was an uncomfortable pause.

"We're pretty well booked up," he said.

Of course you're booked up. This is July! You know who's not
booked up? Nanook's House of Snowmobiles.

"Okay, how long?" I asked.

"Well, it won't be like a three-month wait," he said.

How reassuring. Two months would be, let's see, early September. By then, they'd need to come over here with a two-hundred-
pound Hoover just to suck me out of the carpet.

"I was hoping we could get it done sooner than that," I said.
"Because I just watched the Weather Channel, and you know how
the nineties are in orange? Well, there's a big fat band headed this
way the color of Strom Thurmond's hair. So I'm thinking tomorrow might be good."

He gave me his boss's number to call.

I called.

I got the answering machine. It said, "At [name of company]
we can assure you of a speedy response. We'll be there when you
need us . . ."

I need you.

". . . We pride ourselves in responding quickly . . ."

Good. I'm waiting.

". . . We apologize for the delay."

It took a few minutes, but I got a live body, and I explained the situation. He assured me that I could get a new air conditioner within one day.

"How much might this cost?" I asked.

"You don't want to know," he said.

He was right.

So now I am looking forward to being poor but refrigerated.

Lobster salad, anyone?

Where Have You Gone, Casey Jones?

It's bad enough I'm afraid to fly, and I have to take the train everywhere. Now the trains aren't safe. Now we have runaway trains! (How am I ever going to go anywhere from now on? I get my taxes done in New York. Will I have to get in bubble wrap and *ship* myself to my accountant?)

It turns out there was a two-man crew running this forty-seven-car train in Ohio, the conductor and the engineer. The conductor was already off the train. Then the engineer wanted to step off for a second, and instead of applying the brake, HE OPENED UP THE THROTTLE.

Lucy, you got some 'splaining to do!

Excuse me, you don't turn the engine *off* when you leave the train?

Okay, I'll guess: "Because you want to keep the AC going?" *Bzzzt!* I'm sorry. It's a train, dummy, not a Honda Civic parked in front of the Wawa with two kids and a dog in the backseat while you run in to get cigarettes.

I'm assuming the engineer got off to go to the loo. There's a sign in every train lavatory: DO NOT FLUSH TOILET WHILE TRAIN IS IN THE STATION.

So when he got back from the bathroom, then what?

a. "Dude, where's my train?"

b. "Hmmm, I could have sworn I left it right here. Oh, wow, this is the 'C' lot. Maybe I left it in 'E.' "

c. "Well, it'll turn up. I mean, it's not like I was so stupid that I left it in gear with the motor . . . Uh-oh!"

(At this point I believe it's Sandra Bullock's turn to say, "Ohmigod, I thought this was going to be a quiet vacation.")

Come on, this isn't a set of car keys we're talking about. It's a train, forty-seven freakin' cars long. Nobody's going to believe you've *misplaced* it. The only people who could misplace something that big and important are FBI agents.

Now add the fact it was carrying hazardous liquid, which turned out to be a concentrated form of stuff they put in mouthwash. If it's not diluted, it will "burn the skin on contact." Doesn't it make you feel good to know the active ingredient in Scope is some kind of flesh-eating chemical? By all means, swirl it around your mouth. ("Funny," my friend Nancy said, "but I thought it was hazardous if you *didn't* use mouthwash.")

So I guess I've taken my last train ride. I'll remember it fondly. It was on Sunday, from New York to Washington, and I came upon a piece in *The New York Times* about jargon specific to medical residents, a sort of "resident-speak."

I was shocked to discover that, when no civilians were around, doctors exhibited the same innate sensitivity to the suffering of others you'd find at a Soprano family outing.

It turns out doctors use terms like "beans," which are kidneys, as in, "Better watch that gentamicin level. You don't want to fry her beans." And "CTD": circling the drain—a description of a patient who's likely to die. To do a "wallet biopsy": Checking a patient's financial status before performing expensive procedures. And my personal favorite (because I am nothing if not a class act), "code brown," which laughingly refers to bowel incontinence that is obvious even to non-docs anywhere in a two-block radius.

Tony, this column is becoming one big bathroom joke. Stop it.

Let me then deftly switch gears. Remember last week when I wrote about that guy who didn't leave his key with the parking lot attendant, and as a result I had to wait fifty minutes to get my car off the lot? I don't want you to think that I'm stuck in a rut. But I had another "car rage" incident this week.

I was driving to work through Adams Morgan. Even with two lanes, rush-hour traffic crawls. So there are big signs along the curb: NO PARKING. NO STANDING. 7–9:30 A.M. Because if the curb lane is blocked, you can sit there long enough for the Wizards to three-peat.

Sometimes the curb lane is blocked by a garbage truck. You gotta live with that. And there are those beer trucks so huge that Rudy Giuliani, his wife, *and* his girlfriend could live in them and not get in each other's way. But beer trucks are doing God's work, so they get a pass, too.

Here's what doesn't get a pass: The other morning during rush hour there was an old gray Toyota parked in the curb lane, its flashers on. I counted four different light changes before I budged. To say I was fuming would be a serious understatement. You could have supplied California with energy for a decade by dunking my head in the Grand Coulee reservoir.

Then, out of the coffee joint on the corner, comes this fat babe, fortyish, carrying a cup of coffee. She heads lah-dee-dah for the Toyota (D.C. plates; I took the numbers and plan to base all future lottery purchases on them), opens the driver's side, starts the car, shuts off the flashers, and saunters off with the subtle nuance of, um, a forty-seven-car train.

This was far worse than that cluck who blocked my car in the parking lot last week. That wasn't intentional. Without intent, incivility is only a second-degree felony.

But this woman deliberately blocked a full lane of cars SO SHE COULD GET A CUP OF JOE! And it wasn't even truck stop joe, which you might be able to forgive her for. It was that yuppie half-caf mocha latte machupicchu four-bucks-a-cup crap. (My friend Tom said, "Wouldn't it be great if she went *back* because they didn't sprinkle cinnamon on it?") This babe hosed everybody on the street for ten minutes while she bought her designer coffee.

That truly stinks.

That's a code brown.

Alarming But True

My editor has cautioned me I shouldn't keep telling true stories about my life, because, in his words, "you're a fat, bald, old, whiny, white man, and you're not helping us get any younger readers with your boring geeze-bag stories." So to make this more accessible to young readers, whenever you see the pronoun "I," please substitute the young, hip name "Leonardo."

The other night, at 1:15 A.M., I was fast asleep (*Ed. Note: Younger readers should assume Leonardo wasn't asleep but getting ready to go out to a club*) when my home security alarm went off.

It sounded like eight thousand cats in a Fry Baby.

I flew out of bed, panicked. I knew I was supposed to remain calm, but my male instinct took over and I did what any guy would do: I bolted down the stairs half-naked, and for protection I grabbed the first sharp object I could find. (It was a slotted spoon off the drainboard, which I guess would have worked if the intruder were Julia Child, whom I could have ladled to death.) Then I desperately attempted to disable the alarm, failed, and ran into the front yard to escape the noise.

Let me interrupt here to say what you are no doubt thinking: *Tony, you imbecile. What do you mean you opened your door while your burglar alarm was blaring? You could have been killed by intruders—or perhaps bitten by the vengeful opossum that tripped the alarm. And if by some chance the burglars hadn't already gained entrance to your house, by opening the front door you were giving them access. You're a moron.*

Yeah, well.

Luckily, there was no burglar. But as the alarm clanged on I rocketed aimlessly through the house, by now completely deaf, trying to remember how to stop it. It had been installed five years ago, and I'd forgotten everything the installer told me. I'd even forgotten where the actual alarm was. Since the control panel was by the front door, I guessed the alarm was in the door—so I started kicking the door with my bare feet.

Fortunately, my wife remembered the emergency switch was in the attic, and she shut off the alarm.

"Hey, Bruce Lee, you can stop kicking now," she called down.

Then we waited for the response. Because that is what you pay thirty dollars a month for, right? The response. Some guy who looks like Bruce Willis, armed with an AK-47, screeching up to your door in a black 4Runner.

Nothing happened. Not even a phone call.

Angry, I called the security company at its Maryland number. The woman who answered had the IQ of kale. (Imagine my shock at not finding Einstein working the night shift for $5.60 an hour.)

"Our alarm went off," I told her. "Why didn't you respond?"

"Your alarm didn't go off here," she said.

"What do you mean it didn't go off there? Clinton could have heard it in Beijing. Frank Sinatra heard it."

"You must have disconnected it in time," she said. "If it rings for less than forty-five seconds, it doesn't register here."

"It rang at least two minutes. It lasted longer than *The Keenan Ivory Wayans Show*! (*Ed. Note: Leonardo liked that show.*) Look, there could have been a blood bath here—like that movie *Scream.* (*Leonardo thinks Neve Campbell is HOT!*)"

I demanded to talk to a supervisor.

So Ms. Marilyn vos Savant here put me on hold—for ten minutes.

I seethed. I lashed out impotently with my ladle.

Here's my state of mind. This tin-pot security company has taken my thirty dollars a month for five years, promising me security, and now when I need it, nobody shows up. This malfunctioning alarm has awakened all my neighbors, who already hate me for sending my son out late at night to stuff our extra garbage into their cans. So I want somebody's head on a stick. I want a SWAT team driving up to my house with guns drawn, and I want somebody dead on my property—even if it's a member of my own family.

I hung up and dialed the security company again.

This time I got Bob.

I told him the whole story, and asked why there was no response.

"I could have been killed here," I said.

"Yes, sir," he said.

"Shouldn't we be able to expect a response if we pay for your service, and you guarantee a response?" I asked.

"I would feel just the way you do," he said calmly.

I was beginning to like Bob.

"I wish I had spoken to you to begin with, Bob," I said. "By the way, I called a Maryland number. Where exactly are you?"

"Kansas City," Bob said cheerily.

"*Kansas City?* How on earth can you get here in a moment's notice if you're in Kansas City? A cruise missile from Kansas City can't get here fast enough to save me."

This is the modern world, you see. You pay for a home security quick response, and they route it through Kansas City or Omaha or Anchorage. And it doesn't matter how they route it—because they tell you your alarm isn't shrieking. You're standing in your front yard in your underwear at 1:30 A.M., listening to an alarm jackhammering into the night, and someone one thousand miles away tells you it didn't go off.

I hate technology. I hate this home security system. I'm turning it off, and tying paint cans to the top of my front door, like in *Home Alone*. Maybe a burglar will come in and kill me, but he'll be coated in periwinkle blue when he does it.

Ed. note: Younger readers should disregard this old-man ending. Leonardo loves technology. Leonardo has a cell phone and a beeper and accesses the World Wide Web from his car. Leonardo likes Puff Daddy, Natalie Imbruglia, and matchbox twenty. They're phat. The bomb! You'll love Leonardo's column every Sunday in Style.

Please Leave a Message

Lately, I've been having trouble reaching people on the phone. Nobody is ever in. If they are in, they're dodging calls with voice mail. All I get is a recording and a set of instructions. I'm trying to make a phone call here. How did I get inside a scavenger hunt?

Excuse me, Tony, but you're just discovering "voice jail"? This has been going on for years. And have you heard, the Beatles broke up?

Now my whole life on the phone consists of pressing numbers and leaving messages. I don't need a brain anymore—just an index finger and a tongue.

The truth is, people don't want to talk to other people. When my phone at work rings, I pick it up and hear the following:

"I'm looking for Tony Kornheiser's voice mail."

And I'll say, "This is Tony Kornheiser."

"Do you have voice mail?"

"Yes, but here I am."

"Oh, I wasn't expecting you. I was expecting your voice mail. I wanted to leave you a message."

"Well, you got me. I'm Tony Kornheiser. Talk to me."

Then there will be a pause. And the person on the other end will say: "Um, do you have e-mail?"

Obviously, it's safer to simply leave a message. Voice mail sanitizes a relationship. It's that thin paper collar they put over a toilet seat in a motel.

The worst part is to get trapped in the maze of options, never hearing one that fits your need. That's like sitting down and finding no toilet seat at all.

For example, the other day I had a rash spreading ugly red

blotches all over my chest. It looked like an octopus was sucking out my viscera.

I called the doctor.

"Hello. You have reached the Gildersleeve Medical Group. If you have a touch-tone phone, press 1 now.

"Hello. You have reached the Gildersleeve Medical Group's answering system. Your call is very important to us."

Yes, I feel the love. Recorded messages always make me feel wanted.

"If you are calling about a recent bill, press 1.

"If you are calling about making an appointment, press 2."

I have a rash. I want to speak to a doctor.

"If you have just been shot, stabbed, or have been in an automobile accident and you require medical attention immediately, press 3."

That's 3? They waited until 3?

"If you are interested in paging one of our doctors during one of his latest malpractice depositions, press 4.

"If you've seen any of our doctors driving cars you wish to know more about, press 5.

"If you think that new nurse we hired is pretty hot, press 6.

"If you need to speak to an operator, please stay on the line.

"Hello. Gildersleeve Medical Group."

"I have a rash. It appears that a fist-size alien is about to explode from my chest. In the absence of Sigourney Weaver, I'd like to speak to a doctor."

"I'll transfer you."

"You have reached the Gildersleeve Medical Group's directory. If you know the first name of the party you wish to speak to, press the numbers corresponding to the first four letters of that name, followed by the star key."

I don't know first names. All I ever call them is "Doctor."

"If you wish to hear a directory of first names in alphabetical order, press 2 now.

"For Alan, press 1.

"For Andrew, press 2."

How would I know if they're doctors? What if I press for Alan, and he turns out to be the guy who picks up the specimens?

"For Arthur Farberloin Cohen, press 3.

"For Arthur X. Cohen, press 4.

"For Artie Cohen, press 5.

"For physical descriptions of Arthur Farberloin Cohen, Arthur X. Cohen, and Artie Cohen, press 6."

I'll take Arthur X., Monty.

"Hello, this is Arthur X. Cohen. I am not in right now, but your call is very important to me. By the way, that music in the background—that's from Chuckie's piano recital last week. He was great. If you wish to leave a message for Mrs. Cohen regarding the Tibetan Freedom Concert, press 1 now. If you wish to leave a message for Chuckie, press 2 now. If you think I left a surgical sponge in you and you wish to fax me a lawsuit, press 3 now. Sorry, our au pair, Inga, no longer has voice mail privileges. If you wish to contact Inga, please leave a message at Hot Scandinavian Escorts. Have a wonderful day. Let's Go, Caps!"

I'm pressing zero now.

"Hello, Gildersleeve Medical Group."

A human voice. Thank God.

"Thanks for coming to my rescue. I have a rash indicating exposure to smallpox, and if my calculations are correct, we could all be dead by noon. You've seen *Outbreak,* haven't you? I need a physician dressed in a decontamination suit, stat."

"I'm sorry, sir. I am the receptionist. I'll transfer you."

"Hello. You have reached the Gildersleeve Medical Group. If you have a touch-tone phone, press 1 now."

I'm giving in, just in time for the millennium.

You have reached Tony Kornheiser's Sunday column. Your call is very important to me. I mean that. I would have given anything to have taken this call in person. But I am right now getting a hole drilled in my head. No, I'm kidding. I'm having a kidney transplant. Okay, the truth is I'm sitting here contemplating what I could possibly say to Anne Heche to, you know, turn her around. And I can't imagine anything you have to say that would be more important.

If you wish to hear about my bald head, press 1.

If you want to leave me some jokes for my annual New Year's joke column, press 2.

If you've got any good dish about Monica, press 3.

If my children, my geezer dad, or my dog, Maggie, reminds you of anybody in your family and you wish to tell me about it, press 4.

If you think Dave Barry is so damn funny, why don't you call him?

If not, stay on the line.

Mr. Computer Head

As far as I'm concerned, the computer I use at work is a type-writer that glows in the dark—a typewriter with its own party line. It is wired to other computers throughout the newspaper on a message system that allows anyone at the paper to contact anyone else electronically.

For example, with just a click of a key I can "message" my friend Gino with critically important work-related information that will help us win the Pulitzer Prize, such as: "FYI, I peed in the coffee machine again."

As with any new technology, though, there can be some "glitches"—an ancient Gaelic word meaning "stuff that can get you fired." For example, instead of sending the message only to Gino, I could click on the wrong thing and send it to everybody in the newsroom. Whoa! The next thing you know, I'd be taking orders at a drive-thru. Or as they say in Gaelic, "Would ye be wanting fries with that, laddie?"

That is why it is very important to have years of computer training given by competent professionals. The problem is, computer training appears toxic. I mean, will you LOOK at these people? They're like House Republicans, without the overwhelming charisma.

And they're relentless. My computer is constantly blipping with some indecipherable message: The CCI is down. And the CCI is up again. And the ACG is down. And the ACG is up again. I sit at my desk wondering if I'm working at a newspaper or a Viagra clinic.

(But seriously, I feel terrible, naturally, when the CCI is down. But I also felt terrible when Roy Rogers's horse, Trigger, died. And I got over it.)

Computer geeks divide people up into categories, including those who are eager to have the latest technology, called "early adapters," people like my friend Richard. He has programmed his state-of-the-art laptop computer so he can use it as a radio, a telephone, and a TV. He asked me if I wanted to do anything exotic with my computer. I thought briefly about rubbing mayonnaise on it.

"Actually, I just want to type on it," I told him.

So, unquestionably, I was the wrong person to receive the following message:

Please update your virus software! A new virus, worse than the Melissa virus of a few months ago, has surfaced. It can affect PCs with Windows 95, Windows 98, and Windows NT. 1. Make sure you are connected to the Internet; if you are on the Newsroom network, you are already connected to the Internet. If you usually dial into the Internet via modem (IBMnet, Compuserve, etc.), connect before starting the update. 2. Click on Start/Programs/Norton AntiVirus. 3. Look for the "Live Update" button. Click on it to begin the update. 4. You will be prompted "How do you want to connect to a Live Update server?" Click on the down arrow and choose "Internet." 5. Click on "Next" to complete the virus software update. As always, if you have any questions, please call Newsroom Technology.

Hello, I have a question.

What are you talking about?

You lost me at "Melissa."

When I read the words "Live Update server," all I can think of is Tom Brokaw.

Why are these people hounding me?

I still play ALBUMS. On a TURNTABLE. (Man, that Peter Frampton rocks!)

I mean, really, dot.com *this*.

Anyway, the systems people wanted to test "Y2K readiness," so they wanted everyone to shut off their computers.

So I messaged my friend Nancy: "I have to shut off my computer before I leave tonight?"

And she messaged back: "You have to shut it off in a certain way."

And I messaged: "What way? Do I press the two buttons?"

"Which two buttons?"

"Well, there's one on the bottom of the box where the screen is. And there's one on the thing the screen sits on; I guess it's called the 'table.' I've never touched those buttons, though. I've left my computer on, twenty-four hours a day, seven days a week, for years. I never turn it off at night. I just let it 'rest.' And in the morning I sign on, and I start typing these brilliant columns. It's a miracle, don't you think?"

She messaged back: "The 'table'?"

Then the computer people changed their minds. Or their microchips. DON'T TURN OFF YOUR COMPUTERS! they said in another urgent system-wide message: "Please remember to sign off and close out all of your applications. But leave the power on."

I messaged Nancy: "My *applications*? I've already been to college. [*Insert drug joke here.*]"

She messaged back: "Click on 'File.' Click on 'Sign Off.' DON'T PRESS THE BUTTONS!"

Within seconds I got a message from Don, the computer czar. The message said: "Don't press the buttons! I'll be right there."

(He must have been reading my messages. They can do that, you know. There is no privacy. In fact, they've been inserting suggestive lines in this column when I haven't been looking. Probably to get me fired.)

Get a load of the RAM on that cute new server! Wouldn't you like to download some of that, humma-humma!

Don showed up and looked at me like he was examining a Cro-Magnon Man.

"You don't use e-mail?" he asked.

"No."

"You don't use the Net? You don't link?"

"Not that I know of."

"You don't do *anything* with your monitor?"

"Um, I monit? . . . Look, for years I thought a hard drive was two hundred yards over water."

He told me to go home. Put on my eight-track. He'd take care of the Y2K test for me.

"Will my computer be on when I come back?" I asked. "Because I don't know how to rebeat it."

"That's reboot it," he said, sighing. "Yes, it will be on when you come back."

I smiled.

From what I understand the great Y2K fear is that we'll all go home on December 31, 1999, and when we come back to work on January 1, 2000, all the computers will have exploded.

I can't wait.

It's the Shame Old Songs

I have one word for you.

Just one word.

Karaoke.

Make it go away.

I know karaoke has been around for a while, but last Saturday was my first confrontation with it. I was at a birthday party for a couple of friends who were turning . . . hmmm, how can I say this delicately? Well, let's say they were turning a number that rhymes with "pixty," and by this time next year, I fully expect them to be dead.

Now I am no spring chicken myself. In fact, if I were a chicken, I wouldn't even taste like chicken—I would taste like mutton. But what is it about otherwise reasonable people that makes them think they can sing along to old rock songs? What makes a guy in his pixties think that because he can read the words off a prompter to "I'll Be Doggone," he will sound like Marvin Gaye? When in fact he sounds like the *Enola Gay*? Without oil!

Is it the margaritas?

Because believe me, they can't sing along.

They are blackboard-scratchingly bad. They sound like sheep being microwaved.

And the women always want to sing along to the Supremes. They always want to do "Stop! In the Name of Love," when all you're begging for them to do is: Stop! In the name of God!

Here is what karaoke does: It encourages people who have no musical talent to shriek into a microphone that amplifies the fact that they have no talent.

And once they get their hands on the microphone, they don't stop.

They do medleys! It's horrifying. It's like watching your grand-parents neck.

The last straw was a guy doing karaoke to the Eric Clapton song "Wonderful Tonight." I wondered how horrified Clapton would have felt if he had heard it. It would have probably driven him to take up the bagpipes. It's unthinkable that Clapton ever imagined that people at the age of pixty would be standing around a pool butchering his songs in the name of karaoke.

Karaoke must stop.

Excuse me, Tony, it has stopped. The only place it exists anymore is at birthday parties for pixty-year-olds. Nobody else would be caught dead doing it. It is self-indulgent to the point of nausea. Speaking of which, I know that you will be shocked—shocked!—to learn that Kelsey Grammer's MacBeth closed after just thirteen performances on Broadway. Kelsey Grammer's Macbeth. Who could resist that? "Out, out damned spot. You see, Niles, this is what happens when we let Dad buy a cheap Zinfandel, and Eddie knocks it over." What's next, Drew Carey's Richard III?

I understand the impulse to perform at a party. You figure: I'm among friends. How bad can I be?

Does the phrase "Neil Young in a hot skillet" mean anything to you?

Everybody wants to sing. Everybody knows someone who has gotten up at one of these karaoke things and, to the amazement of the crowd, has sung a classic Sinatra love song, like "In the Wee Small Hours of the Morning," in a tenor so warm and so perfect that the room grows still, except for the small, aching sound of tears being cried by the most beautiful women in the room. Every-body knows (and hates) a guy who can sing like that.

But it's not *you,* you dope.

When you sing "It Was a Very Good Year," you sound like a garbage disposal.

Some of us have the good sense to know that. My friend Nancy was at the party, and fearing that as the night went on she would grow bold enough to try karaoke, she said to her husband, "No matter what I say or do, no matter how I plead and beg, DON'T LET ME GO UP THERE AND SING!"

Nancy used to lip-synch to "Be My Baby" by the Ronettes. But, of course, that is not actually singing the song out loud. "My girlfriends and I could lip-synch every song from the girl groups of the '60s," Nancy said.

"So could I," I told her, then quickly added, "Well, what I mean is, I knew the girl groups as well as the guy groups. I, um, used to keep the radio on when I lifted weights and changed the oil in my car—and every once in a while there'd be a Shirelles song, and I'd make fun of it because it was just a bunch of stupid girls who didn't sing nearly as good as, you know, Johnny Cash."

My friend Tracee did more than lip-synch. "I used to play my sister's records and pick up my hairbrush like it was a microphone," Tracee said. "I did this whole show called *Tracee Sings*. I was great. I did ballads, then up-tempo songs, then some show tunes. I had choreography. I had stagings. Stagings! But I had the courtesy not to do it when any member of my family was home."

I, myself, have made the awful mistake of singing out loud. I do each year at Super Bowls. A group of sportswriters gathers around a piano played by Mitch Albom, who was doing this on Super Bowl Eves long before he committed his Tuesdays to Morrie. In fact, I am one of the stars, because I know the words to every song from the '60s. Yes, every song.

Example: In 1985, the Los Angeles Lakers won the NBA championship, and because they were led by Magic Johnson, one of the sportswriters thought it would be nice to quote from the 1965 Lovin' Spoonful song "Do You Believe in Magic?" But no one remembered the words. So my friend Mike Lupica of the *New York Daily News* called me at home and said, "Do You Believe in Magic?" and I rattled off: ". . . in a young girl's heart, how the music can free you whenever it starts." And I knew all the words up to "It's like trying to tell a stranger 'bout rock and roll."

And ninety guys had columns.

So because I know the words I get to sing. But my voice is awful. I have actually cleared the room. I am like Renuzit.

So when I am pixty there will be no karaoke.

There will be fondue!

Surviving Y2K

Can you believe those dopes who've spent the past six months preparing for the Y2K disaster—as if some stupid computer programming error is going to mean the world will be plunged back into the Stone Age? Give me a break. At the very worst, we'll go back to, what, 1969? I can live with that. There was that bad brown acid at Woodstock. Otherwise, it was a pretty good time. What I can remember of it.

So I did nothing about Y2K.

Then I looked at the calendar. Six days to go.

And it hit me: I'd done NOTHING!

I haven't bought a gun. I haven't learned how to gut and skin wild animals. And I haven't gotten enough cash back from my Discover card to purchase night-vision goggles. So now I'm panicked. Because all I can do is fill up the bathtubs with water—and I keep forgetting why I have to do that. What am I going to do with all that water, poach a whale?

It's probably too late to become a survivalist. All the really good tents are gone by now, and I look so dorky in overalls. (I asked Man About Town Chip Muldoon what he thought I would need to survive in the woods. Chip said, "A satellite dish, because they don't run cable out there. And one of those eternal-burning logs because it rains a lot and regular logs get too wet to burn.")

Just to do something, I bought five gallons of water and ten cans of tuna. And I went to the bank and got $500 in fifties.

"Why fifties?" my friend Nancy asked me.

"In case I need eggs," I said.

"I've got twenties," she said. "I'm sure I can get eggs for twenty dollars."

"Not if I'm offering fifty dollars," I said.

Nancy had panicked about Y2K long before I did. She's like Grizzly Adams. She loaded up on firewood, water, candles, batteries, gasoline, and propane for her outdoor grill.

She smiled triumphantly and said to me, "Your Ronco Rotisserie won't work if there's no power. You'll have four chickens sitting on a spit going nowhere."

Nancy also has "camping" food. She explained: "It comes in a brown paper bag, and it has a rip cord. You pull it, and the contents heat up before your eyes. You can have white bean soup in an envelope."

White bean soup? I wouldn't eat white bean soup in an envelope if it was the same envelope Abraham Lincoln wrote the Gettysburg Address on.

There appear to be two different Y2K panic scenarios.

In one, there is the fear of inconvenience. Everything that is run by computer will break down. There will be no power, no heat—perhaps even no pizza delivery. It'll feel like being trapped inside a Kevin Costner movie, except it probably won't last as long.

(I was particularly anxious about the impending loss of toilets until somebody said to me, "Do you really think there's a computer in your toilet?")

In the other scenario, the world ends through thermonuclear terrorist attack.

In which case you don't have to worry about the white bean soup.

Lately, to my great chagrin, I've come to think that perhaps there is some credence to the second scenario. It seems every day some nut job with a suitcase full of explosives is arrested at the U.S.-Canada border.

The border is thousands of miles long. Surely there have to be *a few* terrorists smart enough to cross over without going through an official checkpoint. It's wide open. You can walk across the border into North Dakota wearing spike heels and a thong, and the only thing you'll run into for hundreds of miles is a moose.

Either way, you don't think these terrorists are going to attack North Dakota, do you? No way. They're headed right here. We're the Big Enchilada, baby.

Washington, D.C. (official motto: "The Great Satan's Home Town!")

The State Department warns that whatever you do, avoid large groups of Americans. That's easy if you're in New Zealand. I'm going to be in a huge throng near the White House. Think there will be many Americans there? By midnight, I could be liquid.

I told this to Man About Town Chip Muldoon, and he said, "Make sure you stand near Regis Philbin. Regis is on a roll. It doesn't matter what happens apocalypse-wise, Regis doesn't go down."

(Not that I'm so sure I should listen to Chip, whose only concession to Y2K so far is that he bought "a couple of extra Reese's Peanut Butter Cups because they were ten for ninety-nine cents.")

I asked my friend Tom about his Y2K plans.

"Is that coming up already?" he said.

Hmm.

I worried that my late panic was insane. So I asked the most thorough, most conscientious, most methodical folks at *The Washington Post*—five top investigative reporters—what they had done about Y2K.

One had bought four gallons of water.

One had bought three gallons of water and a case of red wine.

One said her emergency plan was to buy seventy-five packages of ramen noodles.

One said she had to do her Christmas shopping first.

One politely asked me to go away or he would call security.

Everywhere I went, people seemed to be downplaying Y2K.

Take my boss, George, for example. He said all he's going to do is take out two hundred dollars in cash.

"In case everything breaks down, I can do Chinese takeout for a week," he said.

"If there's a catastrophe, why do you think Chinese restaurants will be open?" I asked.

"Because they're *always* open," he said.

So that's where I'll be. I hope they've stocked up on ramen noodles.

Whine 2K:
Onward and, Well, Onward

I don't like the new millennium.

I want the old millennium back.

This millennium stinks.

It's hard to put into words. But I have the sense the new millennium will be just like the last millennium—only more so.

But, Tony, it's only been a week.

Yeah, well, I've seen enough.

I'm still getting Harry and David catalogs. Ivana Trump is still here.

What's new about this new millennium? Maury Povich hosting *Twenty-One?* Please.

Sure, there are 40 billion TV channels now. But we somehow still run the risk of seeing Tori Spelling.

Everything interesting was already done in the old millennium.

Printing press. Done.

William the Conqueror. Done.

Bubonic plague. Done.

Sputnik. Done.

Regis. Done.

(My friend Mike is troubled by the glut of products spawned by the old millennium. He told me about an exhaustive record collection, "The 1,000 Greatest Songs of the Millennium." At No. 264 was Gustav Mahler's *Symphony No. 7,* edged out by 263, which was *Aqualung.*)

I'm looking for a breakout thing, something different in this millennium—the appearance of a new giant bird, for example, or a new continent; a brand-new number, say, between six and seven;

some lost episodes of *Seinfeld;* Elvis emerging from a pile of frozen catfish fillets in somebody's carport freezer.

My friend Nancy feels the same way. "The old millennium had edge," she said. "You never knew what to expect. In one century, you had the Dark Ages. In another, you had Same Day Blinds."

So far, it's all style and no substance.

(Tell the truth: When you were looking at the ball drop in Times Square, didn't you hope that just as it hit "2000," all of New York would go dark? *Bam!* Total blackout. I didn't think I was asking for much. I'd have settled for Peter Jennings falling off the roof. It was such a drag when nothing happened. Have you any idea how long it's going to take to get through all that tuna fish?)

The old millennium had great inventions.

Toast. Butter. How are they gonna top that?

Dandruff shampoo.

Air conditioning. I rest my case.

Man About Town Chip Muldoon thinks I am being too hasty in slamming the new millennium. He says, "Your prized invention of air conditioning came nine hundred thirty years in. It takes a while for the personality of the new millennium to establish itself. It'll look a lot different when Larry King's contract runs out."

But I don't buy it. Nothing will be invented in the new millennium. Things will just be "upgraded."

We'll spend our lives being retooled and rebooted, like Windows 95.

Nancy is already feeling crowded in the new millennium. "Too many people came into the new millennium with us," she said. "I thought some people would stay behind."

"Yes," I said. "Like Celine Dion and Kevin Costner."

That's why Russia's Boris Yeltsin should be everybody's hero for quitting on the last day before Y2K. Bo knows.

(Unless . . . maybe Bo *doesn't* know, or at least doesn't remember knowing. Maybe he woke up the next morning and said, "I *what*? The last thing I remember is doing a couple of Jell-O shooters with that hot little Miss Minsk.")

Remember how great the old millennium was? It had Beanie Babies *and* the Visigoths. This one has . . . well, it has virtually nothing. We're supposed to be excited by a dip in the Nasdaq? Unseasonally mild temperatures? We haven't even had a decent sex change operation in this millennium!

The last millennium had George Bush and Al Gore.

This one has George W. Bush and Al Gore Jr. It's so derivative.

Unless we dodge a bullet here, we're going to end up with a Bush-Dole ticket!

Speaking of political couples you don't need to hear from again until Y3K, I couldn't help but notice that the first lady has moved to New York. At first I wondered if the White House was undergoing renovation or if the British had burned it down like they did in 1814. But it turns out she simply moved away to seek employment.

I don't want to sound overly traditional, but in the old millennium the president and the first lady tended to live in the same house. I sort of liked that. I'm not saying every first couple got along; it wouldn't surprise me one bit if Zachary Taylor's wife took one look at his mutton chops and said, "Zack, bubbeleh, until you shave those bad boys off, you're sleeping on the couch." But it's disconcerting, having the president in Washington and the first lady in New York. It's a marriage, not a network news show.

The trouble with this millennium is it has no sense of history. Any schmo can go to court to contest a traffic ticket and declare it "The Trial of the Millennium."

The biggest problem with this millennium, though, is that none of us are getting out of it alive. Look to your left / Look to your right / We're all going toes up / In that long good night.

Yes, even Cher.

My
Peeps

There She Goes, Miss America

In light of the Paula Jones decision, I think I speak for all American men when I say:

I want to be president, too.

You can do anything! Hi, I'm the president, say hello to Mister Happy.

I'm no legal expert, but it seems to me Judge Susan Webber Wright's ruling pretty much says, "Let the big dog run."

Is this a great country, or what?

Clinton now can do pretty much as he pleases with whoever pleases him. It doesn't matter who comes out of the woodwork and says, "Bill Clinton nibbled my ear while I was reciting the Lord's Prayer to a visiting group of Belgian nuns." Everybody will believe it, and nobody will care.

It doesn't even matter if he's completely innocent of everything he's been accused of. It all just adds to the legend of his studliness.

Lincoln was called the Great Emancipator. Reagan was called the Great Communicator. Historians will look back on President Clinton as the Commander in Briefs.

Of course, like many Americans, I am deeply troubled about what has happened to the prestigious office of the presidency.

It's shameful that we have grown so accustomed to randy news stories, day after day, about our leader. We've become dismissive of genuine historic breakthroughs. I am not talking about the Paula Jones ruling, which was predictably splashed across the newspaper in type the same size as SEPTUPLETS BORN TO HICKS!

I am talking, instead, about the report last week that former Miss America Elizabeth Ward Gracen willingly, happily, and eagerly gave it up to Bill Clinton. Gracen was unhappy with folks saying Clinton pressured her to have sex. Au contraire, she said. She was hot to trot.

This was on page 12 of the newspaper.

Page 12! Behind some story about a skeleton being found near Spokane. Behind a story about the guano-infested Northern Mariana Islands.

Page 12! Thank you, Monica. Thank you, Gennifer. Thank you, Kathleen. You have ruined it for everyone. You have cheapened the notion of Bill Clinton's conquests.

The man bags Miss America, and it only rates A12?

Show some respect, people.

If I scored Miss America, I'd want that on A1, baby! I'd want it out there every day for a week, as a five-part series. Above the fold.

May I remind you: "There she is, Miss America/ Oh, there she is, your ideal . . ." If that only gets Clinton on 12, it makes you wonder who he has to sleep with to get on the front page.

Yeltsin?

Normally, we don't find out how overheated our presidents were until after they're dead. Sometimes it comes out in a biography or a John Travolta movie. Or maybe some former lover comes forward to tell her story, though by then she's a hag and nobody cares. But all these stories are about Clinton in his elected prime. The Miss America thing. The stewardess thing—the recent claim that on a campaign plane Clinton copped a feel while Hillary was snoring a few feet away. Does it never end?

I mean, you could lay these women end to end—oops, an unfortunate verb—you could *line* these women up, and the line would stretch from Washington to Arkansas. And their hair is so big it blocks out the sun.

And now back to Ms. Paula "My Heart Will Go On" Jones.

For those of you keeping score at home, here are some winners and losers:

Winner: You know him, you love him, you can't live without him . . . Slick Willie.

I'm sure you've heard that when Clinton got the news in Senegal, he celebrated by sucking on a cigar and banging an African bongo drum. How studly! Robert Bly, eat your heart out. In every picture I've seen, Clinton is so happy. (He looks like he just, well, crowned Miss America!)

Don't you wish Clinton would have called a news conference and said, "As I stand here at this lectern, I am reminded of a quote from . . . from . . . Oh, man I'm [expletive] psyched! Anybody want to party?"

Winner: Bob Bennett. Have another sirloin, counselor.

I hear Bennett's next client will be Wilt Chamberlain.

Winner: Monica the Harmonica. She can go in front of the grand jury now and say whatever she wants. That she went to the White House to have sex with the president, that she was only there to feed Buddy, that she was shopping for pantyhose when Ken Starr and a group of nihilists abducted her and forced her to go bowling. It doesn't matter anymore, except to people like . . . me.

Loser: Me. I'm going to miss the joys of the civil discovery process. They were hauling in every woman whose perfume Clinton had ever sniffed. Man, when did the guy have time to govern?

Now I'm going to have to start writing about more substantive issues, stuff I've never addressed before. Like my baldness.

Loser: Paula Jones. Thank you for coming, drive home safely.

I figure she can stay on the talk show circuit for about a month, and then if she's lucky it's, "I'll take Paula Jones to block."

Big Loser: Ken Starr.

You can stop singing hymns now, Ken. It's over. One man's "white lies" are another man's "alternative scenarios."

Will the last one out of the grand jury room please turn off the lights?

The Best Pictures
I Didn't See

I hate the Oscar column. You hate the Oscar column. Everybody hates the Oscar column.

But it's tradition. Last year I didn't write it, and I got hundreds of letters protesting its absence. Here's a typical letter: "Your Oscar column stinks. You never see more than two of the nominated movies, and you make stupid wisecracks about the Supporting Actress category, to wit: 'Act, shmact. Did you check out her casabas?' You're really an imbecile. But I'd rather read your odoriferous Oscar column than the slanderous crap you write about dedicated meteorologists. (Signed) Bob Ryan."

Bobby, sweetheart. It's not personal. It's Tradition!

Didn't see *Gladiator*. Why bother? It's old news. Management types unleash tigers to maul and kill labor. Loads of folks get their body parts sheared off. Heads are rolling like bowling balls on league night. Big deal. You see one head on a stick, you've seen 'em all. And the emperor wants to boink his sister. But, hey, it's only a movie so it's not really his sister—and did you check out her casabas?

Didn't see *Erin Brockovich*. Am I nuts, or did this flick come out in the Reagan administration? Seriously, this movie has been playing longer than Derek Jeter. What's the attraction—Julia Roberts in a push-up bra? *That's* worth eight bucks? Hey, I get NakedNews for free.

Didn't see *Chocolat*. It sounds like a girl movie. The plot is like: You eat chocolate, you feel amorous. Okay, fine. It's a small-town morality tale—without the morality; it's *Footloose* with hot fudge. Life is too short for me to see this.

Here's what life is too short for, Tony: the same stupid Oscar column again. What else you got?

Wait! I saw *Crouching Tiger, Hidden Dragon.* Loved it. An hour later I wanted to see it again. I loved *Traffic* even more.

Then do us a favor: Go play in it. Move on.

How's this?

News Item: "John Phillips, founder and creative force behind the spectacularly successful 1960s rock vocal group the Mamas and the Papas, died in Los Angeles. The Mamas and the Papas were best known for haunting, four-part harmony work on such songs as 'California Dreamin',' 'Monday Monday,' 'I Saw Her Again,' and the autobiographical 'Creeque Alley,' which told the story of the founding of the group."

Everybody who was anybody in the mid-'60s L.A. folk rock scene was in "Creeque Alley": John Phillips and his ethereally gorgeous California waif wife, Michelle; the other Mamas and Papas, Denny Doherty and tubby Cass Elliot; Roger McGuinn of the Byrds; John Sebastian and Zal Yanovsky of the Lovin' Spoonful; Barry McGuire, who wrote and, um, "sang" the quintessentially hideous "Eve of Destruction," which contained the line "My blood's so mad, feels like coagulating." (Cole Porter, eat your heart out.)

You recall "Creeque Alley," that autobiographical song the Mamas and the Papas released with the refrain "And no one's getting fat except Mama Cass"?

Most everyone listed is in his sixties now, except the lucky ones, who are dead. (You think I'm joking? Have you taken a close look at Bob Dylan and Keith Richards recently? Those guys look like they not only *felt* like coagulating—they did it.)

John Phillips was sixty-five when he died. *Sixty*-five! If he wrote "Creeque Alley" now, it'd be "Creak Alley."

John and Michy were getting kind of itchy
To leave assisted living behind.

Zal and Denny couldn't count to tenny
Took ginkgo pills to jump-start their minds
In a body cast Sebastian sat
He'd broken both his legs, slipping on the bath mat.
McGuinn and McGuire had long ago retired
To Lauderdale, you know where that's at
Everybody's at the early bird, except Mama Cass.

Why stop there? "California Dreamin' " could be just as valid an anthem for geezers as it was for restless youth:

All my hair is gone, or it's turned to gray
I slipped out for a walk, much to my nurse's dismay
Authorities were sum-moned
In fear I'd wandered away
Found me in the bushes, on such a winter's day.

(You know I really shouldn't do this, but I started thinking of how the Rolling Stones are probably going to keep touring no matter how old they get. I dread the day they come out and sing, "I can't get no satisfaction. I can't get no wheelchair traction. I might flip, I might slip, cut my lip, break my hip. I can't get no . . .")

I mentioned Bob Dylan before, and how he's a little weathered lately. He looks like a shrunken head inside a great leather coat. It won't be long now until he starts singing, "How does it feel to be fed oatmeal, to have your fruit all peeled, to lose your sense of feel, to use a safety seal?"

Once upon a time, I felt so fine
Wrote a real good rhyme in my prime, didn't I?
People call, say I'm bound to fall, end up in a crawl, in the nursing
*   home hall, my oh my.*
I used to be so amused, at Crosby, Stills, and Nash and the acid that
*   they used.*

I got osteoporosis now, my bones are fused.
Every five minutes I need a snooze.
I'm on Prozac now, I've got hostility to conceal.

Dylan's still a genius. He's up for an Oscar himself: Best Original Song for something he wrote for *Wonder Boys.* What if he wins, and someone asks him . . . "How does it feel?"

And he tells us! "How does it feel? To have your joints creak, to have a sagging physique, to wake up at three, and have to take a leak? Thank God Johnny's in the basement, mixing up my medicine."

Out with the Old, in with the Old

Longtime readers of this space will recognize this as the annual New Year's joke column in which I faithfully re-create a bunch of hilarious jokes culled from thousands of submissions.

Okay, hundreds.

Okay, dozens.

Okay, one day this week I asked my friend Nancy if she had any jokes that weren't filthy.

Everybody loves the joke column.

Readers love it because they can get big laughs by telling my jokes to people who haven't heard them yet—groups of Japanese tourists, perhaps.

I love it because the entire column takes twenty minutes to write. And I can duck out of work and go to the movies.

Sadly, jokes aren't what they used to be in Henny Youngman's day.

A man says to a psychiatrist, "You gotta help me, Doc. I think I'm a dog."

The psychiatrist replies, "Certainly, but until we're sure, stay off the couch."

Actually, jokes *are* what they were in Henny Youngman's day. Only now you don't have to wait until Sunday night when Henny goes on *Ed Sullivan* to hear them. You can get the entire Henny Youngman catalog by hitting a key on your computer.

Now, everybody knows *every joke*—because they're immediately circulated on the Internet.

Blond jokes. Totally Hair Barbie jokes. Klaus "Totally Herr" Barbie jokes!

There are more Web sites devoted just to spreading jokes than there are Web sites devoted to spreading something really important, like Cheez Whiz.

I have two jokes here. But I have no idea how many millions of people already know them.

Ray Saunders sent this: Little Timmy was working in the garden, filling a hole with dirt, when his neighbor peered over the fence and asked, "What are you up to there, Timmy?"

"My goldfish died," Timmy replied tearfully, without looking up. "I've just buried him."

The neighbor was concerned. "That's an awfully big hole for a goldfish, isn't it?"

Timmy patted down the last heap of earth and said, "That's because he's inside your damn cat!"

Bada-bing!

A seaman meets a pirate in a bar, and their conversation turns to their adventures at sea. The seaman notes that the pirate has a peg leg, a hook, and an eye patch.

"How'd you get the peg leg?"

"We were in a storm, and I was swept overboard into a school of sharks," the pirate said. "A shark bit my leg off."

"Wow. And the hook?"

"We were boarding an enemy ship, and their sailors had swords," the pirate said. "They cut my hand off."

"Oooh. And the eye patch?"

"A sea gull dropping fell into my eye," the pirate said.

"You lost your eye to a seagull dropping?" the seaman asked incredulously.

"Well . . . it was my first day with the hook."

Bada-boom!

Okay, no more. All the jokes I've got are either old or awful—or in these cases, both.

I'm scrapping the New Year's joke column. It's a new century, and I'm going to start a new annual tradition: a poetry column!

True story: Back in July, I got a letter from the famous conductor Leonard Slatkin asking me to take part in the National Symphony Orchestra's New Year's Eve concert. On the program was Camille Saint-Saens's *Carnival of the Animals,* which is frequently interspersed with Ogden Nash poems about a variety of animals: lions, elephants, etc. One of the animal groups included is "fossils."

Slatkin asked if I would write a poem on "fossils."

I said yes, I'd be happy to. (I say yes to everything. I have no intention of actually doing it. I'm just being nice. I mean, really, Leonard Slatkin? Like I care. The guy plays a tuba, right?)

Last week Slatkin's assistant called and asked where my poem was.

"What poem?" I said. Who do I look like, Angie Dickinson? (*That's Emily Dickinson, you idiot.*)

"The poem about fossils," she said.

"Oh, *that,*" I said. "Yes, I have it right here. Whoops, I must have left it at home.

"About fossils. Do me a favor: Refresh my memory. What about fossils?"

"How about using fossils as a metaphor for people in Washington?" she said.

Maestro, if you will:

If it's fossils you want, then it's fossils you'll get.
Stodgy. Decrepit. Embalmed.
They pad around Washington's Capitol Hill.
Carolinians, Jesse and Strom.
But Jesse and Strom are just two of so many,
Whose fossildom spreads far and wide.
There's Kennedy, Warner, Leahy, and Dodd.
Not to mention old coot Henry Hyde.
They win an election and squat here for life.
They think it's their God-given right.
Take a look at Joe Biden. After all his presidin'
Now even his hair plugs turned white!
Lautenberg, Lieberman, McGovern, Bill Roth,

Charles Rangel, John Dingell, Chuck Robb.
They're part of the landscape, like potholes and traffic.
Don't forget both Doles, Liddy and Bob.
I've been living in Washington twenty years now.
I am fossilized as a resultant.
My column's not funny. I'm stealing the money.
So just like everyone else in town . . . I guess I'll become a consultant.

Faces Made for Radio

Since the Starr Report came out I have been carefully monitoring the situation by watching all the talk shows, and as further proof of America's inevitable decline as a superpower I have noticed a horrifying trend on TV.

Print journalists.

I am talking about my colleagues from *The Washington Post, The New York Times, Newsweek, Time, The Wall Street Journal.* Every night they are on CNN, CNBC, and MSNBC, baying like the Hounds of Hell. Come on, fellas, do I have to mention names? These print guys are even more unsightly than the Beavis and Butt-Head of Impeachment—mousy, rumpled Lanny Davis and Joe diGenova, whose dapper little mustache and hair, which appears to be dyed the color of Rust-Oleum, make him look like a maître d' at the Olive Garden.

There's a reason print journalists work in print. It's because they look like bridge trolls.

They have bags under their eyes the size of hero sandwiches. They wear lounge-lizard suits and shiny ties spotted with marinara stains. They have eight-dollar haircuts, and foam flecks form at the corners of their mouths as they stare creepily into the camera. Their pallor suggests they've just climbed out of a sarcophagus. And these are the women! The men are unspeakable.

These people think *Clinton* should be ashamed of what he's done? Do they never look in the mirror?

The reason I don't go on these shows is because I *have* looked in the mirror recently. (I almost went on *Hardball* with Chris Matthews one night, but backed out when CNBC would not let me wear a bag over my head.)

My feeling has always been that if someone is going to tell me very bad news on television, I would prefer it were someone beautiful. My idea of a solid news anchor is Michelle Pfeiffer in a cocktail dress draped over a baby grand piano, sighing, "The Dow Jones Industrials fell 678 points today. Gosh, that's awful. [*Pause.*] How do you like my hair?"

The last thing I want to see on television is a horse-faced blond federal prosecutor or a hunchbacked homunculus of a newspaper scribe. You can't lightly apply makeup to these folks, you have to spackle them.

My fellow print journalists, I have one word for you: *radio*.

It's amazing the specimens Larry King has as guests. They make Larry look like Brad Pitt. Where does he find them? I saw this one congressman from the House Judiciary Committee whose eyebrows were the size of badgers. Far be it from me to criticize somebody else's hairdo, but this guy had a hair transplant that looked like it had been done by a backhoe. I tell you, this guy even looks ugly in Braille.

Just in this past week on TV I saw people I hadn't seen in years—and in many cases people I'd hoped never to see again—crawling out of the dustbin of history to comment on President Clinton.

It was like watching *Meet the Press* morphing into *The Hollywood Squares.*

Imagine this: Along the top row you have the Watergate Crawlbacks: John Dean, Chuck Colson, and Robert Bork, all of whom are currently on the cable circuit. After twenty-five years Dean looks as pale and skeletal as the Grim Reaper, but Bork still has that babe-magnet beard. On the bottom corners you have publicity hound lawyers. There's Alan Dershowitz, who debated Jerry Falwell on CNBC a few days ago about what the American people really want now, when what the American people want is for both these windbags to sail over a cliff in a Hyundai. There's Roy Black, whose hair suddenly went gray in the year since he defended Marv Albert, as if Marv was the Amityville Horror. In the middle of the row sits perennial frat boy Dan Quayle, eagerly slamming Clinton's character, but praying that nobody asks him to spell "Altoid."

And in the secret square: Michael Dukakis!

Yes, Dukakis was on *Larry King* last week—surprising some of us who thought he was dead. It was eerie to see him because he's now the spitting image of Rod Serling.

And talk about *The Twilight Zone,* amid all the Sturm und Drang about whether Clinton should be impeached, tried in a civil court for perjury, or simply stretched on a rack until his organs pop out, the man is making a huge comeback. Even prominent women are speaking in Clinton's behalf, and apparently not simply paying him, um, lip service.

After Clinton's grand jury testimony was aired, you could feel the momentum shifting toward him. More and more women looked at Clinton closely, and as they watched him bite his lip and put on his glasses to read that statement where he admitted he was a garden slug, they were overwhelmed with hormonal feelings:

"He's hounded. He's wounded. And he's really kinda cute. I could maybe date him."

Clinton got a standing ovation at the United Nations the other day. Which may be because so many of the world's leaders are alpha men who think this dalliance with Monica Lewinsky is overblown—considering in their own countries they do it with llamas.

It's beginning to look more and more like Clinton's going to skate for this, that he'll be able to parlay an admission of lying into a censure and then . . . a victory cigar.

If you've got 'em, smoke 'em—or whatever.

Someone Save
My Life Tonight

Forgive me. I've got sex on my mind. I know this isn't the season for sex. Around Christmas we're all supposed to be concentrating on more spiritual matters. But this is the season of miracles—and for most men, finding somebody willing to have sex with you is a miracle.

Sex is on my mind because of a new medical study in Wales suggesting that frequent hoo-hah can save lives. Welsh men who, in the local vernacular, "shag" at least twice a week have a 50 percent lower risk of dying than men who don't. (And those who do die are often grinning.)

This report is bound to put a strain on women, since it encourages them to have sex with men in order to save lives. (Would Florence Nightingale have gone into nursing if she knew *this*? Florence Henderson, maybe.) Women are already in a frenzy during the holidays, baking stuff, making sure the cards and packages are sent out on time, getting their kids' hair cut, and buying them fancy clothes. The last thing they want to do is have sex with some guy sitting on the couch in his underpants watching bowl games.

True story: The male reporter who brought me the news of this study said he encountered a group of female reporters who said to him plaintively, "We're not going to run this story, are we?"

Conversely, this report is great news for men, as we now have the moral, ethical, and perhaps legal high ground in every airport bar and aerobics class worldwide. Me, personally, I'm thinking of filing a criminal negligence suit against Heather Locklear and Courteney Cox for conspiring to commit murder by failing to have sex with me.

For a decade, researchers studied nearly a thousand Welshmen in a town called Caerphilly (pronounced as in "Oooh—*carefully, luv*"). The men, ages forty-five to forty-nine, were separated into three categories:

1. Those who rutted with the frequency of barn animals.

2. Those who said they had sex less than once a month.

3. Members of the clergy, shepherds, and all the schmoes in between.

Now let's understand one fact: All men exaggerate about how much sack time they're getting. If a researcher walks up to a man and asks him, "When was the last time you had sex?" the man will say, "You mean the last time *today?*"

I'm between forty-five and forty-nine and the truth is that men my age, especially the married ones, can't even *remember* the last time they had sex. We'd have a better chance pinpointing the last time we took a chain saw and cut off the legs of the dining room table.

My guess is that all those Welshmen who claimed to have sex at least twice a week—referred to in the study as "high orgasmic frequency"—were lying like Pinocchio. It's a bit fuzzy, based on what I've read, whether orgasmic frequency refers to sex with a partner or sex with one's own bad self. Either way, the Big O is good for what ails ya. (As for the Welshmen who volunteered they were having sex less than once a month, I'm surprised they lived long enough to fill out the survey.)

Former No. 1 song lyric in Wales: "What's new, pussycat? Whoa-oh-whoa."

Current No. 1 song lyric in Wales: "Uh-uh-uh-uh, stayin' alive."

I'm convinced men devised this study from top to, uh, bottom, because it offers no conclusion whatsoever whether boinking is good for women, too. This is such a guy thing. It's like the old joke: Two men are walking together, and one asks incredulously, "Do you know how many orgasms women can have?" And the other says, "Who cares?"

Another reason I'm so obsessed with sex today is because I've been reading about the new catch-22 hair-growing drug, Propecia. Taking one pill a day might give me enough moss to snag babes. But in some men it causes impotence. When you stop taking the pill, your sex drive will return—but whatever new hair you've grown will begin to fall out. So timing is of the essence.

The worst news about this drug is that you can't load up on it. Taking more than one pill a day won't work. I'd hoped to take a whole bottle at once and start sprouting hair like a werewolf—then run to Hooters and try to persuade someone named Tiffany to save my life. I tried that with Rogaine. You're supposed to squeeze an eyedropperful on your scalp each morning and night. I poured it on like I was basting a turkey. Sadly, I'd have more luck growing mangoes on the polar ice cap.

To this day, though, I keep smearing on Rogaine, hoping for a miracle.

Which brings us back to Christmas, doesn't it? And toys. (No, not sex toys—unless you happen to live in Caerphilly.)

This year's big toy was supposed to be Sing & Snore Ernie—in the tradition of Tickle Me Elmo and, a few years back, Bite Me Saddam. I'm happy to report that Sing & Snore Ernie is a colossal failure. Speculators bought them up, hoping for a huge score. Now you can find dozens of ads in this newspaper trying to unload Ernie for "$200 or best offer" or "$150 or best offer" or "Wedge of Gouda cheese or best offer." Pay attention to the words "best offer." They're slang for: "I'm taking the gas pipe with this dead lox of a doll. SAVE MY LIFE!"

Hey, pal, there's a better way to do that.

A Pill with Potential

For all you people learning to speak English, it is critical that you know the difference between *important* and *impotent*.

They may sound alike. But believe me, they are not.

One suggests you are a big man. And the other . . . ah, the other does not.

I bring this up because of the arrival of Viagra, the ten-dollar pill that treats impotence.

You heard right: only ten dollars and you can perform well enough to earn a spot in the Clarence Thomas Video Collection.

On a personal level, I'm thrilled about this medical breakthrough. Not that I've ever had a problem like that. Me? Oh no. Never. I don't care what you heard about New Year's Eve. I had four glasses of wine. I was tired. It was the wine. Honest.

Isn't science wonderful? Last year they came out with a pill, Propecia, that grows hair. The drawback: It can take away your sex drive. But now I can pop a bald pill, then take the impotence pill. I just have to be very careful to take the pills in the right sequence.

I wouldn't want to reach for my comb and find an oar in my pocket instead.

As you might imagine, the demand for Viagra has been overwhelming. At a Georgetown University clinic the phone system had to be adjusted to handle a flood of inquiries. Callers were instructed to "Press 3 for Viagra."

Wow, if you get potency on 3, whaddya get if you press 1 or 2? "This is Heidi Fleiss. And how may I help you?"

Impotence is an embarrassing circumstance, a heartbreaking failure. People who make jokes about it are cruel and insensitive; impotence isn't funny. It affects 30 million men—most of whom have heard lines like, "Really, it's okay, honey, I understand. I didn't even notice. Oh, and how's little Johnny Spaghetti today?"

Scientists say the pill works by relaxing certain tissues, allowing blood to flow in. This creates a condition that medical professionals refer to as Lorena's Wild Ride.

You must be forewarned, though, that Viagra has a limited window of opportunity. It works within an hour of taking it. Once that hour is up—you're not. The clock is ticking. You can't afford to have a spat with your squeeze. Boy, has she got you over a barrel. What if you've only got ten minutes left and she says the magic words, "Tiffany and Co."?

It occurs to me that the rising potency tide should float all boats, if you know what I mean. If this pill helps impotent men, think of the jump-start it can give the rest of us virile and studly hunks. I envision a horde of men pogo-sticking their way across this great land—and women everywhere locking themselves in storm cellars, waiting for the Viagra Hour to pass.

Of course, the pill carries the proviso that it won't work if a man isn't sexually aroused.

Hahaha.

Like it's difficult to sexually arouse most men. Anything in bare legs walking by—even Prince Charles in a kilt—would work. Betty Rubble would work.

Here's a great practical joke: Slip President Clinton a potency pill.

But, you ask, what if he isn't feeling frisky within the hour?

I'll wait for the laughter to die down.

(Along this line, my friend Rich's father-in-law suggests that the Democratic candidate's campaign slogan in 2000 should be: "Win One for the Groper.")

Last week men were flocking to the Internet to obtain Viagra prescriptions. One Web site was actually called www.penispill. com. Presumably you could access it with most software.

The pill's reported side effects include indigestion and headaches, though the phrase "Not tonight, dear, I've got a headache" has yet to be uttered by any Viagra users. Curiously, some patients have noticed a temporary blue tinge to their vision.

It had to be blue, didn't it? (*It had to be blue. I wandered around, and finally found somebody who would make me see blue.*) Viagra gives new meaning to the song "Blue Moon" and to the phrase "Ol' Blue Eyes is back."

Sadly, there is already a fight over who will pay for Viagra prescriptions, the patient or the insurance carrier. Insurance companies do not want to be scammed by nonimpotent men who are just being greedy. So users face the horrifying prospect of being asked to show documentation of impotence in order to purchase Viagra. What are you supposed to do, whip out a card that says "Certified Flaccid" or "Help, I've Fallen and I Can't Get Up"?

Gentlemen, we can agree that this is a great pill. Although, I must admit, perhaps not quite as great as a pill that would make a woman desire you with the overwhelming passion they'd lavish on Yanni all day, every day.

Men would pay way more than ten dollars for that pill.

Some would go as high as twelve-fifty.

Unsafe Way?

As a Safeway shopper, I noticed recently that the clerks were behaving very seductively. They'd make deliberate eye contact with me, hold my gaze, then smile and ask if there was anything they could do to make my shopping experience more satisfying—anything. "Oh, Mr. Kornheiser," somebody would purr near the vegetable bin, "could I help you select a particularly succulent portobello mushroom, worthy of your strong hands, your sensitive soul, your musky scent?"

I was stunned—considering I just went in there to get Beano.

Having heard of the legendary "Social Safeway" in Georgetown, where the well-heeled troll for pickups, I thought maybe I had wandered into the "Porno Safeway," and any moment now the checkout clerk might rip off her smock and ravish me right on the conveyor belt. As everyone knows, supermarkets are hotbeds of repressed sexual activity, with all those folks stroking zucchini and sniffing melons.

So imagine my chagrin at finding out the Safeway babes didn't actually consider me drop-dead studly—they were just following company policy. According to a recent story in the *San Francisco Chronicle*, Safeway's "superior customer service" policy includes instructions for employees to make eye contact with shoppers for at least three seconds.

My writer friend Tracy was astonished at this. "Three seconds of eye contact with each customer?" she said. "I can't even look a *lover* in the eye for three seconds without starting to laugh."

Personally, I can't wait for Giant to take "superior customer service" a step further—interns in every aisle!

After learning of the Safeway policy, I was thinking of asking

Bill Clinton to come shopping with me, since the clerks there might be the only women left in the country who would still smile at him. They could put him to work. He'd show them superior customer service. I could see him in a little apron, standing over one of those skillets they use to cook free samples, asking, "Ma'am, would you like to try this sausage?" (And now that he's begun apologizing like a windup toy, think of the catharsis he could have in a supermarket, issuing *mea culpas* to customers because the store ran out of sale Depends.)

The *Chronicle* story involved a complaint from some Safeway clerks who said the customer-friendly policy resulted in unwanted advances by patrons who'd misread the intent of the smiles and greetings, and started propositioning the workers. A produce clerk said she was sexually harassed by a doctor, a minister's son, and several elderly customers who'd never behaved offensively before the policy was introduced. (Another new Safeway task for Clinton: Imagine the irony of him standing in the aisle advising solemnly, like Mr. Whipple, "Please don't squeeze the help.")

Of course, sometimes this attention isn't completely unwanted. A married mother of three told me she once worked at a Florida supermarket where employees had to wear pins that said "TIE," for Total Involvement Everyone: she felt it stood for Total Idiots Everywhere. She said teenage girls sought checkout jobs strictly to meet cute guys. I asked her if she had ever been hit on by a minister's son.

"No," she said. "But I wish I had."

While Safeway officials deny there is any such "three-second" rule, they admit they tell employees to smile and greet customers, and maybe chat them up a little.

How are you? How do you like this weather?

(Is your divorce final yet? You like me in this tube top?)

That's nice, I guess. But if I'm running in for milk and bread, I don't feel the need to share my life story with some guy with a Mr. Natural tattoo scaling salmon. The last thing I want is somebody looking up from a bucket of sliced beets and saying to me, "That thing on your face, maybe you ought to get that looked at."

What am I going to see next, a guy doing stand-up in the produce section?

"And I wanna tell you, we've got eggplants so fresh, I had to wash their mouths out with soap. . . . Is that a banana in your pocket, or are you just happy to be in Safeway? . . . Hey, I'll be here all day!"

I think you can carry touchy-feely too far. The last thing you want in a supermarket is a poetry reading by lustful Montgomery County State's Attorney Robert "Rod McKuen" Dean. ("I am empty. Come again," he wrote, referring perhaps to the run on potato salad at the deli counter.)

Where I grew up, in New York, nobody ever spoke to you in a supermarket. Except maybe to say, "Hey, what are *you* looking at?"

The first time I shopped in a Washington supermarket the guy doing the checkout asked me, pleasantly, "How are you today?"

I responded in typical New York fashion, "What's it to ya? You writing a book?"

I'm probably hopelessly old-fashioned, but I go to a supermarket to buy stuff. Is it so hard to understand that if my main purpose in pushing this dopey shopping cart around was to seek conviviality, I wouldn't be carrying a 25-cents-off coupon for Sani-Flush? If you want to know my position on the medical and athletic ethics of a power hitter's use of androstenedione to build muscle mass and create an advantage that enables him to slug balls farther and harder than anybody in history, call me. But as long as I'm on the checkout line, do me a favor and get me out of the store before my Chubby Hubby ice cream melts, okay?

A Sorry Situation

I am feeling very positive right now, very upbeat. The week didn't start out so joyously. Oh, no. The spy plane thing was very ominous. We couldn't make any progress with China. They insisted that we apologize for spying on them, and we insisted that we never apologize—and as proof we cited NBC continuing to show XFL games on prime time.

But things are much better now. We've gotten our people back. (And we didn't have to tie the pandas to a tree and threaten to turn them into "the other, other white meat" to do it.) We wrote a letter to China that smoothed everything over.

The trick was to convince the Chinese we were sorry without actually using the words "We apologize." We solved this semantic dilemma by using "the Eskimo analogy." In native Eskimo dialects there are nine hundred words for "snow." Each distinct. Each with a different nuance. To solve the China crisis, we needed to come up with a word that in translation would convey our apologies to China, without explicitly sounding in English like "We apologize." Our linguists were able to come up with an exact match: "Boo-yah!" So every time we wanted the Chinese to believe we apologized, we wrote, "Boo-yah!" This made the Chinese very happy. When the letter was read aloud on American television, it sounded like another edition of *Sports Center*—and won the time slot among the target demo of males eighteen to twenty-five:

"We're truly sorry. We have profound Boo-yah! We feel awful. Honestly, we couldn't feel worse. We are beside ourselves with Boo-yah! Can we get you something? Some tea? A cookie? We feel positively miserable. C'mon, eat something. Moo shu pork?

"We weren't spying on you. It was a surveillance plane. We were surveilling you. You know, like they do on the ground when one guy stands in the middle of the road and looks through a small telescope mounted on a tripod, and three other guys hold up traffic in both directions for three hours. Surveilling, surveying—whatever. It was like that. Except in the air, with twenty-four people running a billion dollars' worth of ultrasensitive electronic equipment aimed at getting high-resolution magnetic imaging of all your military equipment. But, no, it wasn't spying. Why would we spy on you guys? We like you. We think of you as just like us, except with bad haircuts.

"Can we have our plane back now?

"What could you possibly want with it? It has no speed at all. It has *propellers,* for crying out loud. It can't outrun the Goodyear blimp! (Tell the truth: The reason you like it so much is because it looks like something Mao flew in, right?)

"Did we say we were Boo-yah?

"Terribly sorry. We're so sorry, Uncle Albert. We're so sorry if we've caused you any pain. We're Boo-yah for what happened to your pilot. We're Boo-yah for landing on your soil without getting verbal permission. (Though it's not like we had a lot of options. We were in a plane that was flying without a nose cone, thanks to your guy, Wang Wei Corrigan. Where'd he learn to fly, Home Depot?) We're unbelievably sorry. We're sorry for Chun King frozen dinners. We're sorry for Jackie Chan movies. We're sorry for that whole David Carradine kung fu thing; that was lame. Me, personally, I regret watching Lucy Liu on *Ally McBeal.*"

So the spy thing is settled. But as good as that is, that's not the best news. The best news was the front-page story on how human fat cells can be transformed into muscle cells and other kinds of useful cells. Researchers found that greasy, yellow gobs of fat extracted during liposuction could be turned into healthy, productive cartilage, muscle, and bone. I think the headline was something like HEY, CARNIE, YOUR SHIP JUST CAME IN.

(This was reported in the current issue of the journal *Tissue Engineering*. I hate myself for letting my subscription lapse. I'm such a dope; I signed up for *Modern Capillaries*.)

If I understand this correctly, it means: The fatter you are, the more you can serve your fellow man. Well, I got a 39 waist. I got fat up the gazoo. You're looking at Albert Freakin' Schweitzer here. I could get the Nobel prize in liposuction. Plug in the hose and Hoover me, baby.

Since the surgery is charitable in nature, I figure it should not only be deductible, I'm thinking *The Washington Post* might give me matching funds!

Wait, it gets better. The story says that if fat cells live up to their potential, "their first application will probably be for space-filling jobs, such as plumping up wrinkles, or *enlarging breasts*."

I can help Britney Spears!

Is this a great country, or what?

This is so mind-blowing. To think all those Double Cheese-burgers I've eaten would make me, in essence, a philanthropist; to think that saying, ". . . and super-size it!" would be a far, far better thing I do than I have ever done. I mean, who knew?

I feel like Mother Teresa.

Excuse me for a second. "Hey, somebody bring me some more Häagen-Dazs. I've got the Lord's work to do here."

From now on, there'll be no hesitation. I'll say it proudly: "Extra cheese."

The one thing I don't understand is: If they can take the fat out of your body and turn it into muscle somewhere else, why can't they just give you a shot of something and turn the fat inside your body into muscle right there? Like—poof!—one minute you're scarfing down a hot fudge sundae, and the next minute you've got rock-hard abs. It's science at its best.

Denise Austin, you're toast. Speaking of which, make mine with butter.

Love at First Buck

Forget Neil Armstrong walking on the moon. We've just seen an even greater moment on TV.

It came near the end of *Who Wants to Marry a Multi-Millionaire?*, the megahit where a rich dork got to choose his bride from among fifty hopeful contestants who paraded before him in bathing suits—and basically guaranteed to boink his brains out at the end of the show if he picked them.

But, Tony, none of the women KNEW him. They didn't even SEE him until the end of the show.

And your point is?

Anyway, the moment I loved was right before the multimillionaire made his selection—when the field had been winnowed to five—and each woman was given a chance to make a final appeal to become his arm-candy missus. And one said, "I think people have been overemphasizing the monetary aspect here. This is not about money. It's about the search for a meaningful relationship."

Excuse me???

Wait. Let me list everything these women knew about this man.

1. He had oodles of money.

2. See No. 1.

Our multimillionaire picked a blonde with washboard abs, who promised, "I'll be your friend, your lover, your partner. You'll never be bored."

I suspect she had him at "lover."

We saw their entire courtship, all thirty seconds of it. The only thing we missed was when she signed the prenup. Oh, grow up! Of course she did. I assume it was during a commercial.

They were married on the set by some judge from Las Vegas. (You were expecting an emissary from the Vatican?) As the bride and groom exchanged rings, the judge said, "The rings represent your love . . . they show your commitment."

Commitment? They didn't even know each other's last names! They didn't have time for love at first sight. They could only squeeze in love at first si—

Hello? You're getting married here, not changing long-distance carriers.

I give this marriage a real good chance.

It should last at least until tomorrow afternoon at 2:00 (1:00 Central).

Who Wants to Marry a Multi-Millionaire? is the most grotesque, degrading show I have ever seen—worse than anything Geraldo Rivera could come up with even with full cooperation from the cast of *Baywatch*. I can't stress enough the baseness of this show. It is humiliating to both men and women. (Have I left anyone out? Shamu, perhaps?) It's scabby even for Fox, if that's possible.

And it is brilliant.

Like everyone else watching *Who Wants to Be a Millionaire,* I missed the first hour of *Multi*. I tuned in to see a parade of babes in bikinis and a guy looking through a peephole as though it were some "live sex" joint on Forty-second Street. I knew *this* was the kind of quality family entertainment I'd been crying out for!

Inevitably, the women answered dopey questions about themselves and their hopes for this "marriage." I was praying just one woman would be honest enough to say, "I hope to file for divorce as quickly as the law allows, and soak this slob for half." Alas . . . Not only was Diamond Jim judging their answers, but his friends and family were actually *scoring* them, as though it were round-by-round at a prizefight.

The only woman I would have given a perfect 10 to was the one who ad-libbed, "You know where I'll be." I figured, yeaaahhh, baby, in the Ballroom, with the Lead Pipe.

The host, Jay "Will It Happen for Me Like It Happened for

Regis?" Thomas, was assisted by a woman with runaway breasts who looked as if she had accidentally yanked the "inflate" cartridge on her flotation vest. This turned out to be Miss America 1993, Leanza Cornett, who appears not to have missed many meals in the ensuing years.

I listened to these women pooh-pooh the idea of marrying for money. (One woman said, "We're all just people here," and I felt like saying, "Okay, honey, marry a cab driver.") The woman who eventually won was asked to picture their life together and she said with a straight face: "Quiet time by the fire. Me reading. Him doing what he wants."

What if what he *wants* to do is burn the money? How much would she enjoy spending quiet time on a subway grate?

When it came time to meet Mister Multi, they showed a film and photograph montage that resembled a Viagra ad. He was described glowingly as a graduate of Penn State, a hockey player, a real estate mogul, and a motivational speaker, with homes in San Diego and Vancouver. In the flesh, he turned out to be a stocky, dweeby guy, the kind you knew ate paste as a boy. He actually said, "I feel really comfortable here. I know I've found my love tonight." I found myself silently mouthing the phrase: tragic honeymoon accident.

Tell me you're not hoping to find out that Darva—that's her name, Darva; it's Hindu for "I Hit the Jackpot!"—has been married seven times before, and in each case her husband mysteriously died. Tell me you're not hoping that Rick is a flimflam man with outstanding warrants in twenty-seven states. And gay.

My kids asked me if I thought Darva might back out once she saw Rick.

"What if he has bad breath?" my son asked.

"You'd be amazed at how much mouthwash a million dollars can buy," I said.

"What if he's *really* ugly?" my daughter asked.

"Honey, not even Abe Vigoda in a cocktail dress is gonna scare Darva off."

Then Rick and Darva kissed, and I don't know about you, but I could feel something in my loins. In my case, I was sitting on the clicker.

I was moved by their sincerity—especially when Rick said, "The person I ask to marry me has my total commitment. Er, what's your name again?"

I'm sure it's going to work.

No, not the marriage. The show, stupid.

A Saga with Staying Power

It's fifteen years from now. Elián "El Duque" González, now twenty-one years old, is getting ready to graduate from the University of Maryland, with a major in English.

Yes, he's still here.

They're *ALL* still here.

The father, the father's wife, the other son (now at St. Albans). Great-Uncle Lazaro, now a snowbird with condos in Opa-Locka and Scaggsville. Lazaro's daughter, the bombshell Marisleysis—who is now calling herself "Skye" on Channel 7's *Eyewitness News,* where she's in the chopper doing traffic.

Even the fisherman is still here. (Don't ask.)

It's like the Partridge Family.

Other Miami relatives drifted up over the years. They opened up a Cuban-Israeli restaurant in Bethesda called Havana-Gila.

In Miami, the extended family owns and operates Elián's World, a theme park built on a former toxic waste dump at the Dade-Broward line. The most popular attraction there is Janet Reno Land, home of the killer coaster Elián's Wild Ride—a stomach-churning trip in the government van that whisked the boy away at the crack of dawn. At the end, you can pose for a souvenir photo with an animatronic Border Patrol agent threatening you at gunpoint. And don't forget to visit the Dunk Janet booth at the Funhouse.

Elián's schoolmates from Cuba are still here, too. They came up to replicate his bucolic Cárdenas classroom and provide a bridge back to Cuban culture. Except nobody set foot on that bridge. One visit to Kings Dominion and they all applied for asylum.

Everybody's here.

Even Fidel is here. The other day I saw him at the Connecticut Avenue Safeway poking through the kiwi fruit.

Auntie Janet Reno wanted Elián to spend "quiet time" here. But it looks like Elián's going to spend "till the end of time" here.

You don't really think Elián's going back to Cuba, do you?

Grow up.

Why would his father take him back? Juan Miguel just won the lottery. He's livin' large at the Wye Plantation. True, he's been on plenty of plantations before—only this time, he's not chopping sugar cane.

Whaddaya wanna do today, Juan Miguel, lounge by the pool or play thirty-six holes of golf?

Sure, if he went back he'd get a hero's welcome from Fidel. And then what? Pluck chickens? He can do that on the Delmarva and *keep* the SUV.

Anyway, Elián has to remain here until an appeals court in Atlanta reaches a decision on the asylum claims filed on his behalf by his relatives. By the time it's ready to render a decision Elián might be old enough to actually understand what "asylum" means.

In the meantime he's the hottest Cuban kid since Little Ricky Ricardo!

There'll be books, movies, CD-ROM games, TV deals, the Elián Collection at Target. He'll become America's Child. He'll be sort of like ALF.

At least at that point Elián will be earning his own money, and picking up the tab for his entourage. Because here's what everyone wants to know now: WHO'S PAYING FOR THESE PEOPLE?

Elián gets whisked out of Miami to Washington, and within hours his Miami relatives (plus the fisherman!) show up at the main gate at Andrews Air Force Base carrying Easter baskets. They stay in a Georgetown hotel. And every day the gossip columns report where they ate the night before and what kind of tip they left. They have to have racked up huge bills: airfare, hotels, meals; nets and lures for the fisherman. (Seriously, what is the deal with the fisherman? Okay, he saved the kid's life. But what's he doing in the closet? Is this some sort of ancient Cuban custom, that if someone pulls your nephew from the sea, he gets to live rent-free in your house? Now the fisherman—he's really a guy who cleans houses, but "the Mopman" doesn't resonate—the fisherman says he's thinking about running for political office. Who does he think he is, Donald Trump?)

And what's the deal with Marisleysis? She's on TV shrieking so much, I thought she was the Nanny! If I were Elián, I'd *pay* the INS to haul me away from her.

We've all been subjected to Marisleysis's conspiracy theory about how the sweet photos of Elián and Juan Miguel had to be "doctored," because Elián's hair in the picture was too long. Then, Marisleysis "demanded" a face-to-face meeting with Bill Clinton and Janet Reno. I mean, really, who died and made her Eleanor Roosevelt? Now she's screaming that Elián is being brainwashed: "They've taken his mind! No one can tell me that Elián wants to leave America! No one!"

Many of you may be thinking the same thing at this point: And they're *still* not selling Valium over the counter?

Elián González has turned our political system upside down. Republicans, who normally are the party of guns, are decrying the show of firepower used to pry Elián away from his lawbreaking relatives. While Democrats, who are normally the party of care and compassion, are defending the decision to send in an armed SWAT team to break down the doors at 5 A.M. on Easter weekend. Deliver me from that fat camera-hog senator from New Hampshire, Bob Smith, who squired Marisleysis, Lazaro, and the fisherman around Capitol Hill like prize poodles. Deliver me, too, from the mayor of New York calling the INS raid "storm-trooper tactics." This from the guy whose crackerjack police force emptied their clips at an un-armed man after they confused his wallet for a gun. (I make that mistake all the time. When I go to pay my bill in a restaurant I often reach for my wallet—and shoot the waiter instead.)

The truth is this whole thing has become less and less about little Elián, and more and more about big Janet Reno. She's the lightning rod for all the debate. Right now Janet Reno is the most talked-about woman in the country.

And, boy, is Darva jealous.

Just Me and U-235

Understandably, the U.S. government is upset about recent disclosures concerning lack of security at our nuclear research facilities, where our precious atomic secrets are leaking like duck sauce from a takeout container. Just last week, for instance, when the techs at Los Alamos had barely enough cash to cover the Domino's special with mushrooms and extra cheese, they tipped the delivery guy about four pounds of plutonium in a silver suitcase.

In the hysteria that has followed such revelations, U.S. officials have scrambled to institute tighter security measures. But it turns out that the weapons they're most concerned about aren't necessarily nuclear.

Forget about Wen Ho Lee. The apparent, um, root of the security lapse in the eyes of the national security establishment is . . . Mister Winky!

Spurred by the fear of a Mata Hari scenario, a new Department of Energy policy requires our nuclear scientists to report their amorous contact with foreigners from any of the twenty-five nations we have designated as "sensitive" because they don't meet our standards of democracy, human rights, and Starbucks concentration. (The list of "sensitive" nations includes China, Russia, Israel, India, and Pakistan. But not Canada, so if you can get Shania Twain in the sack, go for it!)

Thank God, though, the American government has shown maturity, sobriety, and self-restraint by limiting this xenophobic overreaction to "repeated sexual contact." In a landmark victory for every man in every bar in every American town at 2 A.M., the Department of Energy's "Kiss and Tell" policy has specifically exempted the one-night stand. (Note to feminists: Yes, there MAY be some women scientists who are also cheering this decision, and if there are, would you please tell them to call 334-7350 and ask for Antonio, Lord of Last Call.)

To review then what our government stands for:

1. Repeated sex with foreigners may constitute a security breach, and it must be reported. (When asked if scientists would be required to report repeated sex with the rock band Foreigner, DOE officials admitted that was still a "gray area.")

2. One-night stands! Yeah, boyyy!

So come over here, my little sparerib, and let's get it on!

Of course the policy presumes (a) that the "sensitive" countries aren't smart enough to get foreigners from a country not on the "sensitive" list to entrap the scientists, and (b) that a really hot babe couldn't get a man to spill his guts in one night (a virtual eternity, in guy time). Speaking as a patriot, I would sell my country out in an Islamabad minute for one hour with Benazir Bhutto.

I think the greater issue here, though, is the revelation that U.S. nuclear scientists are actually having sex with foreigners—and not just with themselves!

Nuclear scientist is hardly one of the traditional sex-magnet occupations, like athlete, U.S. president, millionaire, and ombudsman. Do you realize what this will do for enrollment at MIT and Cal Poly? Exponential!

But despite the enlightened move regarding one-nighters, the agency draws the line if said sensitive foreigner shows up for a return engagement. The rule requiring scientists to report sex they've had with a foreigner "on more than one occasion" states: "Such contact must be reported regardless of whether the foreign national's full name and other biographic data are known or unknown."

Unknown? These are rocket scientists! And if after multiple sexual encounters they're not even on a full-name basis, when would "country of origin" come up? (Are we hoping for a tattoo of a world map with an arrow that says YOU ARE HERE?)

And where do naturalized citizens fall in this rule? Let's say I suddenly got nuclear security clearance; could I freely boink Charo?

What keeps me up at night is imagining the meeting in which a room full of highly classified government employees is about to declare sex with sensitive foreigners off-limits when some, um, rump group pipes up with, "Come on, guys! Not one-night stands? I mean, can't we even do it just *once*? You make this rule, nobody will become a nuclear scientist anymore. They'll gravitate to professions where it's okay to have sex with foreigners—like the Peace Corps! I beg you, don't force us to choose between cold fusion and hot blood."

And what pol went for that argument, anyway?

Senator *Blutarsky?*

The crux of the problem the policy makers faced was defining "close and continuing contacts." To appreciate the difficulty, remember how the president answered the question "What is a sexual relationship?" by saying, "It depends what you mean by 'is.'" (Actually, it's a good thing nobody asked Bill Clinton for his definition of "close and continuing contact," because he probably would have said: "Having Paula Jones soldered to your leg.")

Of course these are highly technical issues, too complex for us to expect nuclear scientists—preoccupied with highly classified weapons systems—to remember in the heat of action. So I am making my own contribution to national security—an easy mnemonic device to help our brave scientists remember what situations are "go for liftoff!"

In the form of the following limerick:

I once bagged a spy from the Knesset.
Can't recall any night that would best it.
Though she probed about nukes,
Sought a list of our spooks,
I'm not even obliged to confess it.

A Truly Gifted Man

Like most men I want no part of buying holiday gifts. At the last possible moment I trudge to a department store and I scan the floor for a saleswoman around my age, who will take pity on me. I approach her with a soft smile and a shrug. "I have to buy gifts," I say, pleadingly, "and I have no clue what to get. Left to my own devices I'll end up with Oil of Olay and stool softeners. Could you please help me?" Two hours later I've got all the gifts I need.

My late friend Pete, a sportswriter, also had a foolproof plan for buying Christmas gifts. Pete had a friend who you might say carried the floral-arrangement gene. Every year at Christmas, Pete would summon the guy to Runyon's, the New York bar where Pete hung out, hand him a thousand dollars, and say, "I need nice gifts for ten women. Keep the change."

How I admired that. Pete did his shopping and never left the bar.

Here is what women need to know about men: We're only buying gifts because you expect them. If it were up to us, we'd just as soon hand you some cash and go back to watching the Pamela and Tommy Lee honeymoon tape.

The best thing you can do is tell us exactly what you want. I mean, exactly.

Men like a woman who'll say, "I'm out of this body lotion. Lancôme Trésor. The eight-ounce size. You can find it at Lord & Taylor in Chevy Chase. Second floor. They're open until nine."

We can handle this. And we'll gladly get a decorative gift bag to put the lotion in.

(Those fancy bags are a godsend. For years I have tried to wrap presents by myself. I tear off a piece of wrapping paper that should easily be sufficient to wrap the Great Wall of China. I fold the paper, snip it with scissors, and tape it to the box—yet invariably part of the package is showing. I try to disguise this with another sheet of wrap that clearly does not match the pattern of the first sheet. And by now I'm usually totally out of paper, so I have to use a piece of a grocery bag. My gifts look like they've been wrapped by Ted Kaczynski.)

My friend Nancy says, "I prefer a man who admits that he knows nothing about gift-giving and will try to buy his way into your heart, rather than a man who is arrogant enough to think he knows what a woman wants. To those men, it's never about what she wants, it's about what *he* wants."

She related the story of the first gifts the man who would later become her husband gave her: "A book on whitewater canoeing and a can of bug spray."

(By the way, when she opened the package, she wept.)

I understand that gift. Last year I gave my wife an electric can opener.

I've never been good at buying gifts for women. As a young man my imagination was limited—as was my objective—and I always bought women the same thing. Nightgowns.

I probably bought my wife fifteen nightgowns—usually the kind you'd see in a Larry Flynt magazine, next to pictures of women who had sex with various Republican congressmen (upcoming pictorial: "Women of the Junior League").

She wore them once, to please me, then ran them through the disposal.

"Of course she hated them," my friend Liz said. "You were buying what *you* wanted her to wear—things with snaps and leather trim. Don't you know those sheer fabrics create all kinds of static electricity? You can be asleep and suddenly there's spontaneous combustion and you're on fire!"

A chick so hot she's on fire! Man, that turns me on!

Liz sighed. What women really want, she said, is sweatpants. "When flannel can be made sexy, then the world will be a better place."

Men have no problems buying presents for other men. (Except for the awkwardness in giving a present to another man, which has to be accompanied with manly clasps on the shoulders and the promise of skinning a moose in the morning.) All you have to do is find something you'd want for yourself. And buy two of them.

The other day my young friend Michael told me he was visiting his girlfriend's parents for the holidays, and he had to bring them a gift.

He intended to buy gifts that any twenty-three-year-old man would buy: CDs and video games.

"I don't think in terms of what people need," he explained. "I think in terms of what I like. Hopefully they'll like CDs and video games, too. And if not, the hell with them."

Spoken like a man.

Sadly, Michael's girlfriend said that video games wouldn't do, and he should think more in terms of what her family needs. Lamps, for example.

"Don't they already have lamps?" Michael stammered.

"Yes, but they're old," his girlfriend said.

Michael had no idea where to buy lamps. Men don't know from lamps.

Do you know how far down the gift list I would have to go before I got to lamps? It would be under "live eels" and "autographed photo of Tarik Aziz."

Men like overhead lights. A man wants to flip a switch and get light all over the room, not in some small corner. Table lamps are too prissy. And stand-up lamps get in the way when you want to play Wiffle ball in the living room.

Men are happy with bare lightbulbs. I have one of those bathroom light fixtures with six frosted decorative globes arranged horizontally above the mirror. One by one the globes went out, and I didn't notice. One day the last bulb went out, and I looked up and realized I was shaving in the dark. I went outside, un-screwed a sixty-watt bulb from the porch light, put it in my bath-room, and I've been happy ever since. Now my bathroom looks like a man's bathroom should—like it belongs in a bus station.

So if anybody wants to buy me a lamp or frosted decorative globe for the holidays, I'm not interested.

But a new bulb for the front porch I could use.

Out, Damp Spot

My friend Gino was looking forlorn, like a basset hound at a funeral. I asked what was wrong.

"The roof fell in," he said.

"You mean, like, you're swamped with work?"

"No," he said.

"You mean, like, all sorts of things went wrong at once?"

"No," he said. "I mean, like, the *roof* fell in."

What follows is a story with many important lessons for the American homeowner, such as the need for maintaining sound structural integrity, and the value of having adequate insurance, and the wisdom of not letting male humans own homes, on account of they are idiots.

The story began a week before, when Gino was in his den and noticed a steady *drip, drip, drip* from the window beside him. The water was falling from the top of the window onto the sill, inside the house.

This struck him as odd. It wasn't raining. It hadn't rained for days.

Now, Gino was not born yesterday. He knew something had to be done. So he did what any man would do. He got up and made himself a sandwich.

When he got back, the dripping had stopped. Another homeowner problem solved!

(This is typical guy behavior. My friend Nancy recently smelled something burning in her house, but she couldn't find anything wrong. She was afraid that it was an electrical fire, so she asked her husband to do something. He did what any man would do: He opened the windows to get the smell out, and went back to watching the ball game.)

Anyway, a couple of days after the dripping incident, Gino was back in that same room, typing, when suddenly the computer started fizzing.

Gino does not know much about computers, but he knows they seldom fizz.

He looked up. Water was dripping into it from a pinhole leak in the ceiling. Again, it was not raining outside.

Gino did exactly what I would have done in that circumstance: He moved the computer.

Then he resumed happily banging away on the keyboard, until he noted the sound of his daughter screaming. He looked up. The pinhole was widening. It was the size of a marble. Then, a second later, it was the size of a football.

Something was clearly wrong—finally, this hit him, like a dash of cold water in the face. In fact, it hit him *exactly* like a dash of cold water in the face.

"It was like someone was in the attic, tipping over a bathtub," he says.

You can tell a lot about a person by how he reacts in a crisis. Here is the canny homeowner strategy Gino came up with: He put a pot on the floor and waited until morning.

By morning, he had it all figured out. In a slap-to-the-forehead revelation, he remembered there was an air conditioning unit up there in the crawl space above the room. So he phoned the air conditioning guy.

The air conditioning guy climbed up to the crawl space and said, yes indeedy, the unit had malfunctioned and spewed water all over. He fixed the leak. As he was leaving he said, "By the way, it's crawling with termites up there."

"Termites?"

"Yeah," said the air conditioning man, disapprovingly. "It's really creepy. It made me wanna puke."

So Gino called the exterminator.

The exterminator went up into the crawl space. Then he came down.

"You don't have termites," he said.

"Whew," Gino said.

"You've got carpenter ants."

"That's better, right?"

"Not really," said the exterminator. "Why do you think they call 'em carpenter ants?"

"Because they are skilled at basic home repair?" Gino said, hopefully.

"Good thing you called me, though," said the exterminator. He had a manly hitch in his voice, like Marshal Dillon after running the bad guys out of town. "I put some powder down. It'll kill them." And he left.

What happened a few seconds later can only be described as mystical.

Gino's two dogs began acting strangely. They were obeying some timeless imperative, some instinct born in the wild that gives dogs an ability to sense danger and react in a manner that features random moronic drooling and yowling and aimless galloping in circles.

"What's wrong, boy?" Gino asked his Labrador retriever, Harry S Truman.

Before Mr. Truman could explain, the house shook with a terrific crash. Gino ran to his den and opened the door. For a moment he just stared, slack-jawed. Then he slammed the door, turned around, and said in a very, very loud voice a very, very bad word, which caused the dogs to madly suck up and apologize for whatever they had done.

Then Gino opened the door again. This is what he saw:

Under the weight of standing water, the ceiling had collapsed. Water was cascading into the room, along with ten thousand ants.

Ants. Gigantic black ants were raining down from the roof,

writing in agony. They were dying from the poison. The dogs were wolfing down poisoned ants as fast as they could. Gino was stomping ants and yelling at the dogs to stop.

The phone was ringing. Help was at hand!

It was someone selling commodities options.

This all happened last Monday. I am pleased to report that everything is back to normal. The dogs are okay. The air conditioner is working fine. Gino's house is no longer infested with ants. Now it's infested with contractors.

Pranks for the Memories

There are college pranks, and there are college pranks. But you can stop calling now. I think we've got a winner.

This guy put a *cow* on the dome of the historic Rotunda at the University of Virginia!

It happened thirty-two years ago, and for all that time the identity of the perpetrator remained a secret. For thirty-two years the poor county sheriff had this unsolved "Bovine B&E" on the books. It turns out the man responsible is now president of Nasdaq. His confession was front-page news last week.

(Apparently, one of his friends cowed him into it. Now I'm milking the story. I'd butter stop with the puns before I look like an udder fool.)

The perp's name is Alfred R. Berkeley III.

Make that "Bossy" Berkeley.

He put the cow fifty feet above the ground, on the dome Thomas Jefferson designed. The president of a multibillion-dollar stock market. Oh, man, I wanna party with you, Alf.

Got any hot stock tips? Anything about to moooooove up?

(And get this: The reason Alf put the cow on the roof was to outdo his dad, who once hung stuffed animals on the tree outside the U-Va. president's office. I shudder to think what Alf would have done if his dad had hung U.N. inspectors from trees, like Saddam Hussein.)

All right, class, let's compare and contrast: The president of Nasdaq puts a cow on a roof. The president of the country says that, in college, "Yeah, I took a toke on a joint—but I didn't inhale."

What does that tell you about hands-on, take-charge leadership?

The Nasdaq guy ought to be president of the United States. Here's his slogan: "Make Cud, Not War."

The only disappointing thing in an otherwise totally uplifting story is that Mr. Berkeley has expressed regret at dragging the cow up about a hundred steps and coaxing it onto the dome. "I have a lot more of an adult view at age fifty-three than I did at twenty," he said.

Nobody's buying that, Alf. You put a cow on a roof. You're a legend. You can run that maturity jive in public, but here's what you're saying in private: "High five, baby!"

(Livestock are part of a hallowed prank tradition. Remember the horse in *Animal House*? Dorfman was supposed to shoot the horse, and he didn't know the gun was loaded with blanks. So he shot into the air—and the stallion dropped dead of a heart attack. After being sedated and hauled from the dome, Mr. Nasdaq's cow died of Valium-related causes. Sadly, it's always the hoofed animals who suffer.)

After I read about the cow, I went around the newsroom asking people what college pranks they wanted to confess to. And there's actually another local cow heist to report:

Two guys at the University of Maryland got the idea of "borrowing" a cow from the veterinary barn and depositing her in a women's dorm. An accomplice I'll call Elsie helped by opening the door to the dorm.

"They led her to the elevator, and the floors were linoleum tile," she recalled. "So the poor cow kept sliding. The sliding made her nervous. The more nervous she got, the more cow pies she deposited along the way. Anyway, they put her in the elevator, and pressed 8."

And then what happened?

"The door opened. She got off."

And then?

"She enrolled, didn't she?" my friend Liz asked. "Didn't they give her a football scholarship?"

Liz went to Yale, so everything about Maryland sounds funny. Liz couldn't recall any pranks at Yale. The students were probably too busy reading Sir Isaiah Berlin and voting stock proxies.

"The only thing they had when I went there was streaking," Liz said. "That's why I went to Yale. It was idyllic. I saw naked men all over campus. I said, 'That's for me!' "

Actually, there was a famous prank at Yale in the mid-'70s. Some Yalies persuaded a grad student in chemistry to brew them up a chemical that smelled just like human vomit. They poured it down a ventilator shaft in the dining hall, and the smell was so gross that the dining hall had to be closed for months. The ringleader ended up, years later, being a speech writer for George Bush—who later famously blew lunch in Japan, but we won't get into that.

Many people at *The Washington Post*—too many—went to Harvard and Yale. Their livestock pranks typically involve cyclotrons, cloning, and transplanting the head of a cow onto the secretary of state. I prefer the good old days of panty raids. Now, with coed dorms and political correctness, boys are going on panty raids to find something clean to *wear*. (Hey, here's a campus prank: How about slipping some Pergonal into the dean's wife's punch and waiting for her to give birth to septuplets!)

Okay, my turn. Thirty years ago at Harpur College (the Harvard of Route 17) there was this party off campus. And at this party there was a bowl of mints. And people were really hungry, they would eat anything, because they had what was commonly referred to at the time as the "blind munchies." (I won't go into why, because I'm up for an ambassadorship.) And a friend of mine had the bright idea to stir the mints with his . . . well, not with his hand.

And I know who ate the mints. But I'm not talking until they make me president of Nasdaq.

The Boxer Rebellion

I was listening to the radio the other day when I heard a couple of guys talking about how they could tell it was getting closer to winter. They felt chilled in the morning when they went outside to pick up the newspaper in their underpants.

That's how guys walk outside to get the paper.

Mostly naked. ("If the paper is right on the step, I'll lean out fully naked," the stylish Michael Wilbon reports.)

And why not? Who do you think you're going to run into at six in the morning on your front lawn, Greta Van Susteren?

To get my paper I have to walk about twenty feet into the yard. It's my yard, right? So what's it to you what I wear? I'm out there in the pair of ratty boxers that I sleep in, with my fat stomach lapping over the elastic waistband like the beginning of an avalanche.

Shoes?

Are you kidding me?

No real guy puts on shoes to get the paper. Even in snow or sleet you just go out in your bare feet—and hop around gingerly in the cold like you're stepping on Legos. Most guys can hit the first patch of snow, pounce on the paper, and scuttle back to the porch before all of their toes turn blue.

I know what you're thinking: *What if somebody sees you? Won't you be embarrassed?*

Absolutely not.

Regularly, I'll be out there in my underpants, and I'll spot a neighbor in his drawers collecting his paper. It's such a common thing for guys to be outside in their underpants that we might even have a conversation—albeit a brief one. (Brief, get it? Hahaha.)

Of course, every once in a while some stranger will saunter by and stare at me, like I'm some sort of suburban performance artist. And I'll say, "Hey, pal, what are *you* looking at?"

You're lucky I don't go out there buck-naked.

(Well, at this point *I'm* lucky, too. People reach an age when they should never be naked, not even in the shower, because it's just too unsightly. I made the horrifying mistake of glancing at myself in the bathroom mirror one day three years ago, and I have never taken off all my clothing since.)

Women, though—even lingerie freaks, women who appear in Coolio videos—would never *think* of picking up the paper in their underwear.

My friend Liz says, "Women can't be seen in their undies, because they will be accused of Asking For It. No man in his underpants is ever Asking For It—he's just pathetic."

"I'm afraid to walk around on the ground floor of my house scantily clad," my friend Helen told me. "I did once, and wouldn't you know that a neighbor knocked on the door, and I cowered in the corner until he went away."

(This conversation led me to the realization that women are not only genetically more modest but also that "scantily clad" is a uniquely female phrase. A man would never call a woman "scantily clad." A man would say, "So I knock on the door, and I see this babe hiding in the corner, totally hot to trot, right out of the Victoria's Secret catalog!")

When women go out early to pick up the paper, at the very least they're swaddled in robing. And they are hugging their clothing tightly to their bodies, as if they were refugees from a slave-labor nudist colony. Of course, they appear to be embarrassed when you see them like this. Unlike men, who will wave at you—then grab their crotch.

More often, though, women don't go out to get the paper until they are fully dressed, and fully made-up, as if a fresh coat of lipstick will make the news from the Asian markets any better. Women often pick up the paper and take it directly to work with them—defeating the purpose of having it delivered to their home at 6:00 in the morning. In fact, I know one woman who says there are just two reasons for a woman to have a man in her life: One is to take the car to the mechanic. The other is to pick up the paper in the morning.

The reason that men and women behave so differently about getting the paper is because, as Mr. Henry, America's best-loved feature writer, points out, "A woman goes out in what she goes out in. A man goes out in what he's got on."

Women have different outfits for everything. A woman will wear one outfit while making out a shopping list and then change into another outfit to go to the supermarket, then put on another outfit to go out to dinner—because she's too tired to cook dinner after all that shopping.

What man ever says, "Oh, we're going to the supermarket? Fine, let me change."

A man would happily never change clothes. Never.

He would wear the same pair of shorts until they shredded and fell off—and then he'd stay naked until his wife went out (in her "shopping for husband" outfit) and bought him a new pair.

And this is because American men have no shame, in great contrast to what we are seeing in Japan now, where the president of a major securities company wept in shame over the way his firm went straight down the toilet. By this time next week you'll be able to get a Lexus for eighty-five cents, and they'll throw in a Mitsubishi big-screen. Look for the ads in this very newspaper, which I'll be happy to pick up for you at 6:00 in the morning, in my underpants.

Mir Mortals

You wanna know what the Right Stuff is? It's twenty large, pal. You got to hand it to them Russkies. We're supposed to be the experienced capitalists, but they got this rich American pigeon Dennis Tito to fork over $20 million to hop on one of their rocket ships. It was a no-brainer. This starry-eyed dope came walking into the dacha packing a Salomon Smith Barney account with more zeros than a Siberian winter, and two suits from the Russian space program elbowed each other in the ribs and said, "Drop a net on this guy—it's Miller time!"

Nobody had ever made a donation of this magnitude to the Russians before; that Anastasia thing wasn't exactly voluntary. They love Tito. All over Red Square they have signs that say WEL-COME TITO. (The signs were left over from 1957. They crossed out "Marshal" and wrote in "Dennis.")

But let me ask you something: If you have that kind of money to blow on a rocket ride, why would you jump on something built by the people who gave us Mir?

The Mir. Now that was a great piece of work. It was the first space station to be covered in aluminum siding. Mir was cobbled together like something in a shantytown. Seriously, Tom Hanks did better work in *Cast Away*. The American space crew that spent time on Mir consisted of one astronaut and two guys from *This Old House*. You know how embarrassing it is for an astronaut to walk onto the launchpad wearing a tool belt? The Mir crew greeted them saying, "Are you happy to see us, comrades, or is that a lug wrench in your pocket?"

I wouldn't go into space on anything built in Russia. Years back, Laika the space dog did, and guess what happened to her.

Let's put it this way: The Soviet economy wasn't overburdened by Alpo expenses, if you catch my drift.

So now we've got the first Tourist in Space. (Tito's contract specified that the first thing the Russians have to do after he lands is drive him to a MotoPhoto.) But $20 million seems like an awful lot of money for a six-day vacation—considering how much of your time is taken up by *travel*. Okay, you've got a great view. But it's not like anybody's going to bring you a margarita as you sit and leisurely watch the sun set. (Which is probably a good thing, because in orbit the sun is setting every fifteen minutes; you'd be licking the tiles by Madagascar.)

Let's face it, you're living in a coat closet. And you're crammed in there cheek to jowl. I was in the company of Russian sportswriters at the 1994 Winter Olympics in Lillehammer. All they did was hoard oranges and smoke. After six days you could get cleaner air by inhaling bus exhaust.

I couldn't find much support for going into space. My friend Nancy said the only reason she'd go for six days was to "make it a diet issue." The stylish Michael Wilbon refused to even consider such a trip: "No outlet stores up there.")

Personally, I think Dennis Tito was way overcharged. The Russkies haven't got a dime. For $20 million he should have held out for the ride *and* a nuclear warhead.

Seriously, what's the upside for Tito? Please don't tell me the in-flight meals are good. With the Russian economy, Tito will be lucky if he gets potato-leek soup. Or even a leaky potato. And what good is getting frequent-flier miles on Aeroflot? He's going to cash them in on a free trip to Minsk for the Borscht Festival?

I'm sure Tito would rather have gone up on one of our spaceships. But noooooo. NASA isn't "selling tickets" yet. NASA says we're doing serious scientific research and experimentation in space, and a tourist would just get in the way.

Oh, please. We're trying to invent *more* Teflon?

What has NASA done for us lately? And by lately I mean in the post-Tang years. How about blowing a few billion bucks on that

Mars fiasco? Talk about sticking the landing! As I recall, after a thorough investigation, a blue-ribbon review panel recommended, and I quote, "Take your foot off the gas, stupid." I don't know who's having a worse run, NASA or Dick Ebersol.

And the restrictions NASA put on Tito are so petty. They actually made Tito agree that if he damaged anything inside the international space station (motto: "If You're Gonna Puke, Do It on Your Side, Okay?") he would pay for it. Like that's a problem for him. Still, it was probably a bit tacky for NASA to put up signs that said, YOU BREAK IT, YOU BOUGHT IT.

In another classic NASA hissy fit, Tito wasn't allowed to go into the American section of the station alone. He has to have an *escort* at all times. Like he's freakin' Donald Trump! What's NASA afraid of? That Tito's going to give all our secrets to the Russians? Hahaha. Robert Hanssen already did that!

I can't believe we're not selling rides to the public. We waste our time sending mummified politicians like John Glenn and Barfin' Jake Garn up in space, while the Russians understand that the next frontier is: Cash money! First class or coach?

Bird in the Wing

S panning the globe to bring you . . . birds in the news!
  I heard the following story the other day. I can't personally vouch for its authenticity. But, as an experienced journalist, I believe it to be fact because it was told to me by some guy I know who heard it from another guy, somebody's cousin, maybe.

Here's the tale exactly as it was presented to me:

"There's a company in Florida that makes cannons for its client, the U.S. Air Force. The cannon fires geese at jets."

Geese? Why are they shooting geese at jets?

"Because these planes cost fifty million dollars each, and they're designed to fly low, under the radar. But they don't work very well when a flock of twelve-pound geese gets sucked into a jet turbine intake. The Air Force needs to find a way to gooseproof the planes."

I get it. So these geese are flapping toward the planes, and the Air Force pilots practice taking evasive maneuvers?

(Silence.)

"They're not live geese flying at the plane, you imbecile. They shoot geese carcasses at the plane to simulate a high-velocity goose impact."

(Does Björk know about this? This would solve all her wardrobe problems. All she has to do is hang out at MacDill Air Force Base and wait for next year's Oscar dress to land at her feet.)

Gee, I'd think it would be tough to hit a plane going 800 miles an hour with a goose.

(Silence.)

"The planes are on the *ground*. If they were in the air and a goose hit them, they'd crash."

Oh. Right.

"Okay, so word of this cannon spreads. And in comes the British Air Force. Because England has a bird problem, too."

(Let me interject here to say what England has with birds is an "issue." What they have with *cows* is a "problem." And if they think those cows are mad now, wait until the RAF starts stuffing them into cannons and firing them at airplanes like Bessie the Bovine Cannonball. That would be udderly ridiculous. Sorry. Please, go on.)

"The Brits call the company in Florida. They acquire the cannon. They set it up. They fire a goose at a RAF jet. Bam! The goose goes right through the windshield and almost decapitates the pilot! It flies in like a freakin' cruise missile! So the Brits call the Florida company and raise hell. In their best British accents they say, 'What the ##%&@!!??'

"The Florida company is dumbstruck. Nothing like this ever happened before. They ask the Brits, 'Exactly what kind of geese do you people have over there?' Concerned representatives of the company and the RAF engage in a great technical discussion to get to the heart of the problem."

And? And? (Readers are waiting breathlessly for me to finish this lame story so they can go to Starbucks.)

"And the upshot is, the Florida company tells the Brits, 'Next time, *thaw* the goose out first.' "

We interrupt this column for an urgent disclaimer. Just minutes before press time, our source on this charming goose-and-cannon story called to say it's possible he might have been slightly off on a couple of minor facts. He said, and I quote, "It may have been chickens. And, um, it may have been Sweden. Is that a problem for you?"

You mean if the facts of this story are completely wrong, would that be troublesome for me? Hey, who died and made me Bob Woodward? I don't care if it's gerbils and Uruguay. I'm trying to fill twenty inches here.

That story, shall we say, dovetails nicely with this one, which was in the news last week: Famed baseball pitcher Randy "The Big

Unit" Johnson of the Arizona Diamondbacks was pitching in the seventh inning of a spring training game against the San Francisco Giants, when he cut loose with a 96-mph fastball. As the ball rocketed from the mound, a dove made the mistake of crowding the plate on Big Unit. About two feet in front of home, the fastball and the dove collided. Needless to say this chance meeting wasn't beneficial to either Big Unit's hope of catching the outside corner *or* the bird's hope of someday having chicks. Eyewitnesses said the dove exploded into a mass of feathers. (We are checking into a report that Björk was seen in the area with a dustpan and a seamstress.) Scott Ostler of the *San Francisco Chronicle* said he thought the bird's mistake was that it was guessing curveball.

What remained of the bird was in fowl territory. Fowl territory! God, I am funny. Oh, and I suppose none of you has thought to say: The umpire called the dove out because of the "infield *fly*" rule! (Stop, Tony, you're killing me.)

"I didn't think it was all that funny," Randy Johnson said of the incident.

Oh, please. That's because you've got no sense of humor. I mean, could the lesson be any more obvious? Next time, *thaw* the dove. Hahaha.

Note to animal rights activists: This column was written over the violent protests of Tony Kornheiser. He would never be so unfeeling about the horrible plight of these geese, chickens, or, you know, anything you might find in a sandwich. Also, he wants to assure you that no animals were hurt in the making of his upcoming TV special, "Benji on a Stick."

Tough Times for the Fat Cat

I was standing at the side of my house when—*whoosh!*—something furry and in a god-awful hurry crashed into my leg. I was terrified. My first thought was that it was Gary Condit running from the media. It turned out to be a large brown-and-white cat darting from under my front porch as if fired from some cat cannon.

I am a dog person, not a cat person. I don't want to go into a whole boring song and dance about the differences between cats and dogs. But I can assure you I would never put a *dog* in a blender, okay?

I bring this up because in the instant it took me to ascertain it was a cat—not a raccoon or a rat or Dick Cheney after a power surge—there came my faithful, loving dog Maggie, tearing after the hideous fur ball like Wile E. Coyote.

Between my yard and my neighbor's there's a chain-link fence, about four feet high, that the cat headed for. I've seen cats jump seven feet straight up, like Harrier jets, onto the limb of a tree. So a four-foot fence should have been an easy clear.

Except the cat was too fat. It smashed into the top of the fence and slid back down—like a bad sand shot.

In sports we call this "a momentum shift." It now looked like Maggie had won a free meal, including wine, tax, and tip. But Maggie, dripping adrenaline, leaped for the cat and soared a foot past her target. Maggie was so discombobulated that she slipped and rolled over on her back. That split second was all the cat needed. It took off like Marc Rich.

Now the chase was on, from backyard to front yard, through bushes, around trees. This is what a Brittany like Maggie was bred for: stalking and capturing another animal. Most of her life is spent padding around the block with a fat, bald, middle-aged man. Now she was in her element. She was going to catch this cat, shake it until dead, then roll around in its juices, perfuming herself in the glorious scent of the kill. (And let me suggest this is not exactly Chanel No. 5. Sometimes I've taken a big whiff of Maggie after she caught a bird, and my knees buckled. She smelled like a Dumpster after the Labor Day weekend. She always wants me to be part of her great triumphs: She brings in her gore-encrusted offerings and lays them on the porch. Like this was going to impress me, like now we should hang out and bond, have a couple of beers, chase some tail.)

So I watched in horror as Maggie sped around the yard, searching for the cat. I listened as Maggie howled. It was between a cry and a yodel—an eerily humanlike sound. It reminded me of Fran Drescher on *The Nanny.*

I wondered where the cat was; I hadn't seen it at all. Then I glanced up at the deck in the backyard, and the cat was there lying perfectly still—just like Mindy Krefsky (but that's another story)—on the top railing directly above the Weber gas grill in a spot that was impossible for Maggie to see.

The cat's scent was everywhere. Maggie flew around the yard, sniffing wildly. Once or twice she went up the deck steps and yodeled. But she never spied the cat. I looked away for fear Maggie would see me looking at the cat and follow my eyes. I didn't want to rat out the cat. I didn't want to be a stoolie. (Yeah, like Maggie is Lieutenant Columbo. I think I've seen too many dopey movies where the animals talk in the voices of Eddie Murphy and Jeff Goldblum.)

I knew I had to do something quickly. Only two things could happen, and both of them were bad. Either (1) Maggie would catch the cat and kill it; or (2) the cat would jump on Maggie's back and claw her eyes out like melon balls.

But what could I do? I certainly couldn't pick up the cat and carry it to safety. The cat would have clawed *my* eyes out. Besides,

I had on a new Polo shirt. You ever try getting blood stains out of pique cotton?

I tried coaxing Maggie over to me so I could grab her. But, hello, she's a dog. A dog in maximum overdrive. I have about as much chance catching a instinct-crazed Brittany as I have of winning the Olympic gold medal in the pole vault.

So thinking as fast as I could, I dashed into my house, opened the refrigerator, and pulled out a handful of sliced Virginia ham. (Oh, please don't tell my rabbi.)

Maggie fell for the old pork-and-switch. She smelled the ham and came bounding over. I grabbed her collar and took her inside. What an idiot she is. Hahaha. (I may be slower than Maggie, but I guess I showed her I'm still the Man in "It's Academic!")

She prowled around the house, yodeling for the cat for a while. But the scent was gone, and Maggie soon contented herself as she often does—by curling up on the couch and drooling.

Meanwhile, the cat was still up on the deck railing above the Weber grill. I watched quietly from the kitchen window. It was a full fifteen minutes before the cat felt safe enough to leave my deck and sprint toward the fence.

I'd been in on the whole horrifying drama. I was emotionally involved. But I also had an interest in this as a purely sporting proposition. This cat had disgraced itself on the first attempt to jump the fence. Now it had another crack. Clearly, if it couldn't clear the fence this time, it was that much closer to that great Chinese takeout in the sky. So I held my breath as it streaked toward the fence and . . . crawled under on its belly.

That cat really has to lose weight.

Bye-Bye, Baboo

Last week I took my sweet baboo Elizabeth up to college. Six hours on the road. Just me and her. Someone said I should "think of it as a great opportunity for the two of you to have a bonding experience."

I suppose—in the way that being trapped in an elevator with Chris Matthews might be a great opportunity to chew your own ears off.

Originally this was supposed to be a family trip. All of us would go together in the Jeep. But that was before Elizabeth began packing. When she finished packing, the seats had to be folded down and the wife and son had to be jettisoned. (What's the big deal? I slowed down first.)

She had a trunk, three large duffel bags, one enormous suitcase the size of a full-grown deer, enough clothing on hangers to stretch from my house to Mongolia, a computer, a printer, a boombox, linens, pillows, assorted other bedding, three backpacks, and 175 pounds of shoes. (All I can figure is, when she filled out her college application, in the box where they asked what she wanted to major in, she must have written "casual footwear.")

The highlight of our drive was going to be "the sex talk." I felt it was my obligation as a father to speak to my daughter about sex. I'd put it off for eighteen and a half years; the moment was at hand. I informed Elizabeth that I'd spent long, agonizing hours preparing my remarks and rehearsing to get the wording just right.

She was mortified.

"How long do you think this will take?" she asked fearfully.

"If you don't interrupt? About ninety seconds."

Years before, I had given her "the drugs and alcohol talk." It was brief and to the point. And I think quite masterful actually.

"There are drugs and alcohol out there," I said. "You're aware of that, right?"

"Yes, Dad."

"Don't take them."

It's not that I don't trust my daughter. In fact, I have great confidence in her. She is competent, levelheaded, and well grounded. I remember when her mother and I walked her to her first day of prekindergarten. She was four. She had never been out of our sight before. Other children were howling at the prospect of separating from their parents—literally clinging to their parents' legs and screaming! Not my kid.

Elizabeth got to the steps of the schoolyard—not the steps of the actual school, mind you, the steps of the schoolyard, fifty yards from the door. She dropped my hand, turned to me, and said, "It's okay. I can take it from here."

But it's every father's fear that his sweet baboo will get caught up in something she can't handle, like some smooth-talking, cool-walking, hot-to-trot, wrong-side-of-the-river boy. (The exact kind of lowlife her father was.)

Quick story: One distinguished graduate of the college my daughter attends is my friend Dick Schaap, the erudite sportscaster. The day I drove my daughter there, Dick had been asked by the football coach to say a few words to the team. I went with Dick, so the coach introduced me as well. On the slight chance I might be asked to speak, too, I prepared something from the heart: "My daughter is a freshman here. Keep your hands off her."

All things considered it wasn't a bad drive. The first two hours there couldn't have been more than five or six times that we got into shouting matches that caused me to threaten to stop the car, toss all her junk to the side of the road, and open up a Wal-Mart. One such blowup was about how many body piercings Elizabeth could get before I would refuse to let her back home during vacations. I said what any father would say: "Exactly one more than you have now. Or is it your goal in life to have more holes than Augusta National?"

After that the ride improved; Elizabeth slept much of the way. Halfway up I-81 in northern Pennsylvania, she was out cold. I felt that was the perfect time to have the sex talk. Let me recap the highlights. I said, "Sex. Don't have it." When she awoke, near Binghamton, I told her we'd already had the sex talk and it went great.

"I was asleep, Dad," she said.

"I thought that might be useful," I said. "Because after you get married, the only times you'll have sex, one or both partners will be asleep."

From there it was only thirty minutes to the college. When we got there, we drove to North Campus, where all the freshmen live. Moving in was a breeze; it took less than ten minutes to unload the car and bring everything to her room. (But then I had to settle accounts with the offensive line, which I'd dragged out of practice to lug all her stuff.)

For a while I stood outside her door wondering what I should do now, knowing soon I would have to say good-bye and make that long drive home by myself. She'd been in my house for eighteen and a half years, and except for summer camp she'd never been away for more than a few days. The next time I'd see her wouldn't be until Thanksgiving (unless there's a big shoe sale at Hecht's). As much as we'd scrapped over the years, I knew I'd miss her desperately, and at that moment our lives had changed forever.

She came outside, saw me moping there like a lost soul, and said, "Dad, I have to unpack and arrange my stuff. I can't keep coming down here to see if you're all right and keep you company."

"So should I go?" I asked.

"Yeah," she said. "I can take it from here."

The Long, Long, Long, Long Goodbye

This book contains a selection of Tony Kornheiser's Washington Post Sunday Style *columns that ran from 1997 to 2002. This is his final Sunday Style column, which was published September 30, 2002.*

Good-bye, my friends.

   Adiós. Auf Wiedersehen. Arrivederci. Shalom. Sayonara. Bonjour.

   Bonjour *means "Good day," you idiot.*

   This is a very sad time for me, saying good-bye to you, my loyal readers, after all these years. I don't know what I'll do without you. I'll miss you. I love you, I honestly love you.

   Oh, no, he's not actually going to do this, is he? He's not actually going to write one of those sappy good-bye columns?

   I remember the day the column started, November 12, 1989. I got up that morning, showered, ate breakfast, and went to the hardware store—the night before one of the porch bulbs had blown out, and I had to get a replacement; eighty watts. I prefer sixties on the porch because there's less glare. But they were out of sixties, so I got eighties. The next day, November 13, I had to go to the dentist. Did you ever get one of those pains in one of your molars, and it's so far back you can't reach it, even with a pencil? So I called my dentist. It was Dr. Shapiro then, before he found out his skin was allergic to the rubber gloves.

   Is he going to go through twelve years DAY BY FREAKIN' DAY? Isn't it enough we had to suffer through those endless columns about his dad who collected Styrofoam trays? I mean, he wrote three hundred columns about those Styrofoam trays. I wanted to call his dad and say, "Stop buying chicken, you old goat. Have a pizza delivered, why doncha?"

Of course, I want to thank my family.

Here it comes. His sweet baboo. Man, did he milk that kid for material. I hope her college tuition is so enormous it has to be sent up there in a Brink's truck. He owes her that much.

My sweet baboo. My son, Michael. My wonderful dog, Maggie. *Not the dog!*

They were all there for me. They stood by me when the night was cold and the land was dark and the moon was the only light I'd see. But I won't be afraid, no, I won't be afraid just as long as they stand, stand by me.

What about his wife? Why doesn't he ever mention his wife? I think his friend Nancy is his real wife, don't you? Either her or his smart friend Martha. Or maybe his friend Gino is his quote wife unquote— not that there's anything wrong with that.

As many of you know, I'm leaving this column to take on a new challenge. I have always been about challenges. This one is formidable. I'm going to do a daily television show on ESPN.

Television?! With that bald head and that puss? The man looks like one of those souvenir coconuts with a tiki face carved into it. This is a true story: Howard Cosell once looked at him on TV and said, "Doesn't he realize he's unsightly?" And Howard Cosell, you may recall, was not exactly Brad Pitt. That was ten years ago, when Tony was, um, less unsightly.

Some people, when they become big stars, forget the people who have helped them along the way. I can assure you that won't happen to me. My friend Nancy, my smart friend Martha, Man About Town Chip Muldoon, my editor of the last three years, Tim . . .

Tom.

. . . that other guy, the one with the dark hair and glasses— their faces are etched upon my mind. I'll never forget them. And if I do, I'll simply get my secretary to call them up on her computer list, and I'll have my driver deliver a box of candy or something.

Some of you have come up to me recently and said how sad you are that I won't be writing my column anymore, because it lights up your lives. Over the years we've become good friends, you and I, and you're devastated by this. You're wondering how you're going to cope with me not being in this space Sunday after Sunday after Sunday. . . .

Can you believe this egomaniac? What a blowhard. I get the Sunday paper for the Hecht's ads. The Post *will shove something else in this space, and in two weeks we won't even remember the bald guy's name. Hopefully, the next guy will be funny once in a while. That'll be new.*

Believe me, I understand. It's tough for me, too. It's an awesome responsibility being the funniest columnist in America.

Yes, and that's why Dave Barry is in 450 papers, and you're in the Savannah Shopper.

Of course, it's flattering knowing that you're going to be missed, and that no one can take your place. I guess I feel like Walter Lippmann.

Who? That must be some old guy. Tony is always referring to old dead guys. Like we have any idea who they are. One of the reasons this column bites is because it skews so old they use it to wrap mummies.

All I can say to you at this difficult time is that it has been an honor and a privilege to write this column for you. It was always about you.

Spare me. Anyone have a barf bag handy?

But all good things must come to an end. And so good-bye, farewell. If you see me on the street, please say hello. I'll be happy to autograph something for you. Bring a camera in case you want a souvenir photo with me. I miss you already.

Get out. And don't let the door hit you in the behind. TV! That's a joke. You'll be crawling back here for work in three weeks. Maybe we can find you something in the lunchroom.

$$
\begin{array}{r}
16 \\
16 \\
\hline
96 \\
16 \\
\hline
256
\end{array}
$$